The PRISON EXPERIENCE

Special Issues of Women in Prison

Merry Morash
Michigan State University

Pamela J. Schram
California State University San Bernardino

WAVELAND

PRESS, INC.

Long Grove, Illinois

For information about this book, contact:
 Waveland Press, Inc.
 4180 IL Route 83, Suite 101
 Long Grove, IL 60047-9580
 (847) 634-0081
 info@waveland.com
 www.waveland.com

Copyright © 2002 by Waveland Press, Inc.

10-digit ISBN 1-57766-202-4
13-digit ISBN 978-1-57766-202-0

Printed in the United States of America

8   7   6   5   4   3   2

Contents

To my children, SooJin and Valerie,
and my husband, Edward.
Merry Morash

To Larry K. Gaines.
Thank you for all your support and encouragement.
Life is Good!!!
Pamela J. Schram

Preface

In recent years, there has been a staggering increase in the number of women being sentenced to prison in the United States. Some have argued that this increase is due to a new, more violent, female offender emerging in our society. Others contend that this increase is essentially due to shifts in the criminal justice system's response to women offenders. For example the introduction of mandatory sentencing schemes and "three strikes" legislation has reduced judicial discretion; the war on drugs has sometimes been called the "war on women," because it has brought proportionately more women than men into prison settings. While the debate continues over why so many women are being incarcerated, one wonders "Who are these women?" "Why are they in prison?" "Where did they come from?" "Do they have families?" "What are their experiences while in prison?"

When we started thinking about writing this book, we wanted to learn more about women in prison and their experiences before, during, and after incarceration. Our major objective was to emphasize women's concerns by focusing on the issues that are salient in their lives. Some of these issues and experiences are also relevant to male prisoners. However, we took a feminist perspective with women prisoners as the center, rather than the periphery, of focus. We hope that we have been able to shed some new light on women in prison by considering a broad range of research and writing, and we hope that readers will share the excitement of discovery afforded by analysis and synthesis of the growing body of literature relevant to women in prison.

We are extremely grateful to a number of people who have helped us during this project. We wish to extend our deepest appreciation to our editor, Carol Rowe. Carol was extremely patient with us while writing this book. Throughout the process, she gave us words of encouragement as well as helpful ideas. We would also like to thank the following people who read portions of the book and provided us with insightful suggestions: Christopher Smith, Michigan State University; Barbara Koons-Witt, University of South Carolina; Larry K. Gaines, California State University, San Bernardino; Nancy Zang, Michigan Department of Corrections. As coauthors of this book we both want to express appreciation for what we gained from working collaboratively with each other; the struggles to meld and to elaborate on each other's ideas resulted in many new insights during the writing process.

We hope that in this book, the perspectives and voices of women in prison are revealed. The extent to which this is true is hampered by limitations in the research that has been done and the more general tendency to warehouse people in prison—and in so doing, limit the degree to which they can communicate with those of us outside. We hope revelations of some of the gaps in knowledge about women in prison will influence students, the public, and scholars to learn more about people who come to be incarcerated and the system that holds them in confinement.

1 ||||| **Introduction**

Much of social science research and theory reflects the values and interests of dominant groups in a society.[1] Criminal justice and criminology are informed by the theory and research of psychologists, sociologists, anthropologists, and other social scientists. In all of these fields, traditional depictions of the realities of social life have focused narrowly on the experiences of people privileged by their social location; that is, by their place in a society where gender, race, ethnicity, and social class influence access to power, resources, and opportunities. The emphasis has been on describing and explaining the experiences of white, European, middle-class men. What is referred to as "mainstream" research and theory has often ignored, marginalized, and distorted the experiences of individuals who were not privileged by their social location—specifically, of women, often of color and/or of lower social classes, who are overrepresented in correctional programs and institutions. Breaking with tradition and examining the experiences of people who are disadvantaged by their social location opens the door to a more complete understanding of social life, and in this book leads to an understanding of how gender in combination with race, class, and ethnicity affects the lives of women offenders. Alternatives to mainstream perspectives have critical implications for policy and for the design and implementation of correctional programs; alternative perspectives also focus attention on the way the world looks to and is experienced by women offenders who often have been misunderstood or ignored.

The study of women offenders—whether from a sociological, psychological, or anthropological perspective—typically has either ignored or trivialized the importance of gender as an organizing feature of society and thus has neglected gender's impact on resources,

1

opportunities, and barriers that people confront. Apart from mainstream research and theory, however, there has been a rapid increase
of knowledge about the standpoint of people whose social location does
not afford them access to privilege. There is a growing body of research
on how women of different races, classes and ethnic backgrounds perceive, experience and understand life—that is, on how things look and
feel from where they stand. We know more than ever about women
who are offenders, victims, and survivors. New knowledge extends
from women's own accounts and interpretations of life events and
experiences to observations from the standpoint of people with unique
understandings, including the information and analysis provided by
women's advocates and others privy to information about women and
the men with whom they interact. Yet, despite new and renewed
understanding of women's lives, there remain important gaps in this
knowledge, and throughout this book, we will point to these gaps.

Given the increasing growth of knowledge outside of the mainstream, it is essential to re-think how gender and race/ethnicity have
been incorporated into curricula and into research across various dis-
ciplines.[2] Depending on the instructor's background, the textbook or
other readings that are assigned, and the academic environment,
criminal justice and criminology curriculum varies considerably in its
treatment of gender. Similarly, research also considers gender in different ways. A well known feminist theorist, Kathleen Daly, identified
five stages of curricular change in criminal justice (see table 1-1).

At Stage 1, there is a total exclusion of women in the discipline. At
this stage, the focus is on "majority" men and their experiences. Even
the study of lower class men uses the experiences of well-to-do men as
the standard for what is "normal" and "acceptable."

Stage 2 is sometimes referred to as the "add women and stir" or
"add race and stir" approach. At this stage, marginalized groups are
not necessarily invisible. However, traditional perspectives are used to
interpret and to understand the effects of gender. Much of what is
written about the criminal justice system and crime causation is at
this stage. A textbook on corrections might take the mainstream perspective but include some sections or even a chapter on "women in
prison." Or, a theory developed to explain empirical observations of
men might be "tested" to see if it applies to women, but no attention
would be paid to whether unique gender-related experiences or opportunities influence a person's criminality.

Stage 3 is the first step in transforming the field of criminal justice
and criminology. Issues are raised concerning the exclusion of certain
groups from social science inquiry. For instance, why is there no research
on whether women charged with a crime see the process of working with
a lawyer and going to court as just? Why is there only very limited
research on correctional programs designed specifically for women?

Table 1-1 Stages of Curricular Change and Modes of Feminist Production of Knowledge

Stages of curricular change	Modes of feminist production of knowledge
Stage 1: Womanless.	Does not exist
Stage 2: Add women and stir; add race and stir.	Pre- or nonfeminist stage. Focus on experiences of women or on gender difference, but feminist theory or research is not used to interpret findings.
Stage 3: All women and men members of racial/ethnic minority groups "a problem or anomaly."	A. Early feminist critiques of criminology. Research challenges common-sense ideas about women's crime and liberation, raises questions about sources of data on crime, and brings formerly unrecognized victimization to light. B. Critique of feminist inability to deal with "problem or anomaly" of women of color. Critique of inability of criminology to deal with race and ethnic relations. Racial and ethnic differences among women raised as theoretical, research, and political problems.
Stages of curricular change	**Modes of feminist production of knowledge**
Stage 4: All women and men members of racial or ethnic groups are the focus.	Feminist questions and debates are central to the research enterprise. May begin outside criminology in raising questions or forming alliances and partnerships with other disciplines or organizations. Theoretical and methodological diversity. Stance of multiple and crosscutting social relations of class-race-gender-age-sexuality.
Stage 5: Fully transformed and inclusive knowledge.	The norm is feminist and inclusive.

Source: Kathleen Daly, "Looking Back, Looking Forward: The Promise of Feminist Transformation," in Barbara Raffel Price and Natalie J. Sokoloff, eds., *The Criminal Justice System and Women: Offenders, Victims, and Workers*, (2nd Ed.) (New York: McGraw-Hill, 1995), p. 445.

Stages 4 and 5 are more visionary. At Stage 4, marginalized groups are at the center, rather than the periphery, of study. By stage 5, transformed knowledge incorporates the interrelationships between gender, race, ethnicity, and social class.[3] How do these aspects of social identity and social status work together to make the experiences of particular offenders unique? Do they influence the paths that people take through the justice system? Do they influence the behavior and life experiences that bring people into contact with the justice system?

A number of concepts and definitions are useful in looking at women in prison and the impact of gender on their lives before and during their involvement with the correctional system. Below we briefly introduce some key concepts and recurring themes that will be considered at various points throughout this text. This list is not intended to be exhaustive. Rather, it is intended to acquaint readers with key themes and concepts relevant to women-centered frameworks.

KEY CONCEPTS AND THEMES FOR UNDERSTANDING WOMEN OFFENDERS

Sex and Gender

Few people would argue that there are no differences between females and males, though people vary considerably on what these differences are and why they exist. Some people stress differences in reproduction or hormones, and others stress differences like mathematical ability and parental responsibilities. There is also disagreement about the extent to which differences depend on biology, psychology, or social context.

The assignment of the labels "male" and "female" is pervasive in the social world. At the moment of birth, the sex assignment for a newborn is made by parents, doctors, midwives, and others surrounding the infant. An early step in the process is giving the infant a "female" or a "male" name, though a small number of people do give their children names that do not signify sex, or that actually contradict the child's biological sex.

Differences between women and men have been designated as either *sex* or *gender* differences. Sex differences typically include biological variations such as reproductive organs and hormones. Gender differences include social definitions of being a "woman" or "man," and extend to characteristics such as appearance and occupation. It is confusing when people use the terms sex and gender imprecisely and interchangeably, or assume that everyone understands their definition of sex and gender, and agrees on the significance of these characteristics.[4]

Some scholars also challenge the traditional view that sex is a fixed, biological condition. Sex is not necessarily seen as a binary category, an either/or status. The alternative view is that a person's sex varies on a continuum, and location on the continuum depends on differences in chromosomal, gonadal, and hormonal sex. Thus, the assignment of a person's sex is not invariate. This is most clearly seen when individuals elect to undergo "sex change" medical interventions, but there are less dramatic cases in which individuals' external sex organs do not match their hormones and/or their internal sex organs.

West and Zimmerman have tried to capture the complexity of the concepts sex and gender by distinguishing between *sex, sex category,* and *gender.*[5] *Sex* is determined through the use of socially agreed-upon biological criteria. The criterion for determining an individual's sex is primarily through identifying genitalia at birth or chromosomal typing prior to birth. There are instances when these two criteria do not agree—so there are no two clear-cut sex groups. An individual is located in a *sex category* by applying socially determined criteria of sex. By applying these criteria, society has defined sex as a binary category through sex categorization. However, the construction of sex as a binary category does not necessarily support its existence as such.

West and Zimmerman argue that *gender* is not a set of characteristics, nor a variable, nor a role. Rather, gender is a product of social "doings." *Gender* is activity considered appropriate for a person's sex category. These activities are determined through social constructions of sex and sex category. "Doing gender" is a continuous activity that is embedded in everyday interactions. That is, through their words and actions, people communicate and shape notions of being female and male. West and Zimmerman emphasize the importance of recognizing the independence of *sex, sex category*, and *gender* constructs. By understanding the independence of these constructs, people can question whether differences between women and men are due to sex or to social constructions of gender. For example, female inmates usually experience prison life differently than male inmates. How can this be explained? Are these experiences based on sex differences between women and men? Are these differences based on women and men involved in "doing gender?"

Chivalry and Paternalism

To understand the present implications of *chivalry*, it is essential to appreciate its historical context. The notion of chivalry emerged in Europe during the Middle Ages. Chivalry was an institution of service, and "ladies" were the distinctive recipients of this practice. Knights were sworn to protect "their" females against dangers such as dragons and devils. Although the practice of chivalry as a formal institution ceased centuries ago, many chivalrous practices toward women remain and are reflected in social interactions. These include men holding the door open for a woman, walking on the street side of sidewalks to protect women from traffic, and standing up when a woman is seated. Chivalrous attitudes are related to perceiving and to treating individuals as if they are on a pedestal.[6] Chivalrous treatment is more than just preferential treatment. It usually entails a bartering system in which men hold a more powerful status than women. It is essential to emphasize that social class and race/ethnicity are also intertwined with such treatment. Women of a certain social class and color are perceived as more worthy of chivalrous treatment than other women.

Paternalism has been described as follows:

> The derivation of the term "paternalism" from a Latin-English kinship term suggests its root meaning: a type of behavior by a superior toward an inferior resembling that of a male parent to his child. . . . Within different types of paternalistic systems, the following three basic ideas . . . can be found. First, since a child is defenseless and lacks property, he [or she] requires assistance and support. Second, since a "child" is not fully aware of his [or her] role and therefore not fully responsible, he [or she] requires guidance. . . . The third idea holds that since a "child" is ignorant, he [or she] can be deceived, or treated in such a way as to serve the interests of the "adult," without becoming aware of this.[7]

The concept of paternalism denotes that females need to be protected for their own good. In a broader social context, paternalism is organized around independence for males and dependence for females.[8]

Both chivalry and paternalism suggest that certain individuals or groups need protection because they are weak and helpless. This protection, however, can result in various types of control.[9] In reference to women offenders, individuals with chivalrous or paternalistic attitudes perceive women offenders as being weak and child-like. Thus, controlling girls and women "for their own good" is justified and is implemented throughout the criminal justice process—from arrest to sentencing to incarceration.

Some criminologists maintain that the criminal justice system treats women more leniently than men. This is commonly referred to as the chivalry hypothesis. On the surface, it may seem that women inevitably benefit from chivalrous treatment. This type of human interaction, however, is more like "political paternalism." Specifically, being the beneficiary of such treatment usually involves some cost. In order for women to receive preferential treatment, they have to acknowledge their inferior position in society.[10] If women are perceived as being irresponsible or unaccountable for their actions due to their status as women, then they will not be afforded the privileges associated with responsibility (e.g., employment, financial independence). For instance, people who see women from a chivalrous or paternalistic viewpoint may assume that upon release women will be taken care of by some male protector (e.g., husband). The cost of such treatment would be neglecting the reality that many incarcerated women are the primary caretakers of themselves and of their children. Therefore, they need to be financially and emotionally independent.

Numerous studies have examined whether there actually are gender-related differences in sentencing. These studies support four general conclusions:

- According to the earliest studies, the system does use different processing standards; the relevant factors seem to be issues such as childcare and differential culpability between male and female defendants.
- Compared to early research, more recent studies use stronger research designs that control for such factors as prior record, injury, and other sentencing factors that may have influenced decision makers besides, or in addition to, sex. When these factors are controlled, the apparent preferential treatment for women is reduced, but does not disappear.
- Some prior research findings that women who deviate from traditional gender role expectations are treated more harshly than women who conform to these traditional roles have been contradicted by other research findings, leaving the question of whether this is true unanswered.
- There is overwhelming evidence that increased imprisonment rates for women are due to equalization efforts in the system, specifically efforts to make the system equally harsh for all offenders through policies like determinate sentencing and sentencing guidelines. Women who had previously been treated with a degree of leniency no longer are treated as such.[11]

The above conclusions illustrate the complexity of chivalry and paternalism. To understand the implications of chivalrous and paternalistic treatment toward women for delivering justice, it is important to recognize this complexity.

Stereotyping

From antiquity to the present, cultures have categorized women into "either or" roles.[12] One such pervasive conceptualization is the Madonna/whore duality. This duality is grounded on two contrasting perceptions of what is assumed to be normal female nature or sexuality. The Madonna image personifies women as faithful and submissive wives as well as nurturing mothers. The whore image portrays women as temptresses of men and as prone to unleashing their sexuality and self-control.[13] Consistent with the intertwining of gender, class, and color, the Madonna/whore dichotomy has been applied primarily to white middle- and upper-class women. Women of color are not as commonly placed into the two categories "good" and "bad," but rather there has been a tendency to portray all women of color in a negative light. For example, the African-American woman has been described at certain times and in certain places as an "Amazon," a "sinister Sapphire," a "mammy," and a "seductress." Unlike the good/bad characterizations of white females, all the categorizations of African-American women are bad.[14]

Several scholars contend that these cultural ideologies have been reflected in the criminal justice system.[15] Stereotypes of female offenders are not created within a vacuum. Rather, these stereotypes are perpetuated by widespread assumptions about who is a "truly" deviant woman, and who is not. The result is that the harshest judicial treatment is reserved for African-American men who sexually assault white women, and the most lenient for white men who sexually assault women of color. It appears that women of color are assumed to be somewhat deviant or responsible for putting themselves at risk—not as virtuous, thus less deserving of reparation as their majority racial and ethnic counterparts, even when they are victimized. Evidence of a complex interplay of gender and other social characteristics as influences in the justice system is not unexpected. As a conglomeration of different institutions in our society, the justice system often reflects and reproduces stereotypes and assumptions about gender, class, race, and ethnicity.

Biased ideologies, driven by gender stereotypes, can have a profound effect on how women in prison are seen and treated.[16] Cultural stereotypes can influence day-to-day interactions with women and can constrain the types of programs available for female inmates. Even in some contemporary prison systems, vocational programs for female inmates continue to focus on reinforcing traditional role expectations, and women are prepared primarily for work in fields like cosmetology and sewing.[17] Idealizations and stereotypes of motherhood can influence attitudes concerning mothers in prison.[18] In some institutions, it is assumed that due to their incarceration status, women in prison cannot be considered "adequate" mothers; therefore, the best policy is to separate them from their children and terminate custody. Correctional staff sometimes think that women inmates are uniformly childlike and should be treated in a protective, paternalistic manner.[19] In prisons, interactions and opportunities that are driven by stereotypes and biases perpetuate stereotypes and reproduce gender-related inequities, both inside and outside of prisons.

This text will explore the degree to which gender stereotypes and bias drive what happens in correctional facilities for women. It also will highlight some important innovations and exceptions that break the mold. Some facilities have emphasized apprenticeship opportunities for jobs that women do not traditionally hold, such as carpenter or electrician. New York State prisons have nurseries where mothers care for their infants, make childcare arrangements for coverage during their work assignments, and make arrangements for care when the children must move out of the institution. Increasingly, correctional staff are educated and trained to question stereotypical assumptions about women offenders. There is a growing body of information about program elements that are tailored to women's experiences and situations and that are therefore essential to ensure the success of correctional outcomes.

"We Are Not Who You Think We Are"

Several years ago, women incarcerated at Bedford Hills in New York, working in collaboration with a film artist, chose the title "We Are Not Who You Think We Are" for a videotape that communicates the realities of their lives and incarceration. The media are prone to stress women offenders' violence and increasing similarity to men in prison. However, there is quite a bit of information to challenge this depiction.

General Characteristics

In 1975, the Law Enforcement Assistance Administration (LEAA) established a Task Force on Women to provide program recommendations to meet the special needs of women offenders, victims, and professionals in the criminal justice system. Twenty years later, an updated version of the task force report summarized changes that occurred over the years. More women were arrested, convicted, and sent to prison than in prior years. Women offenders comprised 6.4 percent of the state and federal populations. This is a major increase from 3.8 percent in 1975. The updated report also noted that the types of conviction crimes also had changed. In 1975, women were more likely to be incarcerated for crimes such as larceny, forgery, embezzlement, and prostitution. Twenty years later and continuing through the present, women were more likely to be incarcerated for drug-related offenses and larceny. Table 1-2 illustrates these changes during the past twenty years.

Unique Characteristics and Program Needs

Women in prison are unique in several ways. First, more than four in ten women reported that they had been abused at least once prior to their present incarceration. Approximately thirty-four percent reported being physically abused and thirty-four percent reported

**Table 1-2 Adult Female Offender Profile Comparison
1975 and 1995**

	1975	1995
Types of offenses resulting in incarceration	Larceny, embezzlement, forgery, prostitution	Larceny, drug-related offenses
Percentage of women represented:		
Nationwide arrests	13%	19%
Violent crime arrests	10%	14%
Serving federal prison sentence	5%	7%
Serving state prison sentence	4%	6%
Has one or more dependent children	73%	61% (federal) 67% (state)

Note: The information presented in this exhibit represents a compilation of the best data available for this time period.

Source: Office of Justice Programs Coordination Group on Women, *Women in Criminal Justice: A Twenty Year Update: Special Report* (Washington, DC: U.S. Department of Justice, 1998), p. 1.

being sexually abused. Second, over three-quarters of all incarcerated women had children; two-thirds of these women had children under the age of eighteen. A majority of women with children were the primary caretakers before incarceration. Third, incarcerated women used more drugs and used those drugs more frequently than incarcerated men. Approximately fifty-four percent of the women, compared to fifty percent of the men, had used drugs in the month prior to their current offense. Women were also more likely to report having used a needle to inject drugs as well as having shared a needle at least once in the past. Fourth, almost six percent of women in prison had been pregnant upon incarceration. Most of the pregnant women had received both routine gynecological exams and prenatal care. Finally, approximately eleven percent of the women were admitted to a mental hospital or health treatment program overnight prior to admission. Almost one in every six women had received prescribed medication for an emotional or mental problem since admission to prison.[20] We will further explore the characteristics of women in prison in chapter 2.

While there has been an increase in the number of incarcerated women, this increase has not always been matched by the implementation of specialized programs specifically for women. Specialized programs would include medical care and counseling for those with a history of prior victimization from battering or sexual assault, health care services, substance abuse treatment, parenting skills training, and academic and vocational education. Prison and jail administrators across the country have noted that establishing and maintaining such programming is difficult due to lack of space, large populations, and limited meeting resources.[21] At the individual level, women's needs often are not met in the prison setting. At the societal level, the disadvantages associated with being a woman, minority racial and ethnic status, and the criminal label are addressed only sporadically in contemporary correctional programs. Rather, disadvantages are often produced or magnified through the interactions that women have while they are in punitive and isolating institutional settings.

Focus of This Book

The major objective of this book is to reveal and analyze controversial issues relevant to incarcerated women. Some of these issues also pertain to male inmates. This text, however, is intended to frame these issues with women as the center, rather than the periphery, of focus. Thus, although problems, needs, and concerns may be relevant for both women and men who are incarcerated, the same problems may be experienced differently, and solutions to problems can differ. Further, while we primarily focus on women in state prisons, we occasionally mention women incarcerated in jails and in federal prisons. In some instances, we point to differences or unique features of federal prisons or jails in an effort to highlight the characteristics of state prisons and the women in them.

The first step to framing issues within a women-centered perspective is to understand the women who break the law and go to prison. Chapter 2 opens with a description of the influx of women into prisons, the misleading media portrayal of women offenders, and the stereotypes that influence prison staff to respond to women in restricting and disempowering ways. African-American women have been affected most negatively by increases in incarceration and by erroneous imagery reflecting who they are. There is a general failure to recognize variations among women in prison and that women are sometimes victims of circumstance. Alternatively, women often act with agency in trying to change and improve their lives. We review historical explanations of women's criminality that have fueled some inaccurate imagery, and we present contemporary research and theory that develops a more accurate understanding of women in prison and their circumstances. Theories of criminality differentially influence policy and program implementation. In some prison settings, feminist theories have resulted in what are called gender-responsive programs, but in much of the day-to-day routine of prison, there are at least remnants of the influence of largely discredited theories that perpetuate stereotypes of incarcerated women. Chapter 2, therefore, provides a detailed description of women in prison, of how they came to break the law, and of trends in their numbers and characteristics.

Women are in prison not only because they were apprehended for breaking the law, but because judges, with input from a variety of other people and influenced by current policies, have decided that they should serve time. Chapter 3 begins with a discussion of the near-total lack of research on how court processing looks to the women impacted by it. The best we can do is try to understand how judges arrive at sentencing decisions and imagine how the process looks to women. The validity of research findings on even this small aspect of court processing is difficult to determine, because most research has not obtained evidence of how judges or other court personnel actually make their decisions. Instead, research has concentrated on the degree to which certain characteristics of the offender and the crime predict sentencing outcomes. It is an inferential jump to assume that variables that predict sentencing outcomes are equivalent to ideas considered by decision makers in arriving at their choices. All we can say with some certainty is that if women in courts compare themselves to men and other women, it would not be unexpected for them to feel poorly represented, differentially judged, and unjustly treated.

Chapter 3 also considers the effects of federal and state reform efforts to establish sentencing guidelines that restrict or eliminate judicial consideration of extra-legal considerations in arriving at a sentencing decision. In the federal sentencing guidelines, family responsibilities and pregnancy were specifically named as things that should not influence sentencing; yet judges still do take them into account. However, in some courts the benefit of leniency is less for African-American women than for white women. Sentencing guidelines account for a general increase in prison populations, which certainly has had a negative outcome for women. It is debatable that guidelines have fully eliminated bias based on demographic differences. To the extent that this makes it possible for judges to consider women's lesser roles in criminal activities and their greater responsibilities as parents as well as the types of programs that are most likely to reduce women's recidivism, this bias may have some benefits.

Chapter 4 covers a number of special issues that mothers face in prison, including their anguish over their children and their children's tribulations and stresses. Since most incarcerated mothers were the primary caretakers before going to prison or jail, and will resume this responsibility upon release, they suffer pains of separation and fears about resuming care of their children upon release. Often visitation is difficult due to financial and transportation limitations. Some women are fortunate to be in prisons with outstanding programs that facilitate mother-child visits or other contacts that give women the opportunity to love and care for their children. In a few states, such empowering programming extends to pregnant inmates, who have special medical and emotional needs. However, some are not so fortunate, and visits either do not happen or are in sterile and crowded waiting areas where both mothers and children feel uncomfortable. Also, many women in prison have little or no opportunity to carry out what they would like to do for their children—for example keeping in touch with schools or having input into living arrangements. The suppression of efforts to assume responsibilities for children is compounded by the generally dependent status of prisoners. The forced dependence coupled with limited or no presence in their children's lives is antithetical to active and effective parenting. An additional topic in Chapter 4 is women prisoners' litigation to obtain and maintain opportunities to visit their children and to secure custody of them. Countervailing forces include the ease with which staff might use suspension of mother-child visits to exert controls, without regard for the effects on children.

The topic of chapter 5 is sexual abuse of women in prison. The history of women's incarceration is replete with examples of their sexual abuse by staff; in some contemporary prisons, serious abuse continues. A large percentage of women in prison have suffered from sexual abuse; this history exponentially increases their vulnerability to the damaging effects of abuse during incarceration. Most abuse is perpetrated by male correctional personnel, making it especially likely when the ratio of male correctional officers greatly exceeds female correctional officers. Although watchdog groups, and to a lesser extent government investigations and reports, emphasize the inadequacies of the correctional system and rampant and pervasive abuse, research is less clear, and there are counterclaims by correctional staff. Some resources and many innovations in training and legislation have been aimed at containing if not eliminating sexual abuse of prisoners. Still, watchdog groups continue to play a critical role in forcing examination of the prison enterprise and fueling efforts to hear women who reveal their devastation in the face of abuse. These efforts to push the system and the larger society to respond to such negative aspects of confinement prompt consideration of whether the extensive use of confinement causes more damage than the display of punitiveness is worth.

Chapter 6 is about mental illness among incarcerated women and looks at two contradictory perspectives. Staff and advocates for women who take a *mental health treatment perspective* make efforts to develop programming that is responsive to the mental health needs of women offenders. Prisons house a disproportionate number of women who are "dually diagnosed"—that is they suffer from a combination of mental health problems from addiction to drugs or alcohol and/or various other mental illness. In addition to incarcerated women who have been diagnosed with a mental illness, the oppressive conditions of confinement

may well contribute to mental health problems. Overlaid on these realities are stereotypes that suggest all women offenders are mentally ill.
Critics who recognize the tensions between mental health treatment
and the realities of prison life, and who therefore take a *control perspective on mental illness*, have publicized and acted on their beliefs that
control of women is often delivered in the guise of mental health care.
Such control extends to coerced drug therapies and intrusive therapies
that try to change women rather than enabling them to change.

Chapter 7 examines the need for gender-specific correctional programs. It presents and discusses the current controversy over whether
gender, race, class, and ethnicity are at all relevant to "what works" in
correctional programming. Many prison and state correctional administrators believe that to be effective, correctional programs and management approaches must be quite different for incarcerated women
and men. By and large, jail administrators do not hold this view.
Scholars fall on both sides of the argument. The debate over the need
for gender-responsive correctional programming raises fundamental
questions about the degree to which it is possible for an empowering
program to operate in a prison. A program that prepares women to
improve their social location and resources is undermined by the facts
of life in even the most humane of prison settings—punitive philoso-
phies and the stripping away of self efficacy.

Prisoner litigation by or on behalf of female inmates is the focus of
chapter 8. Echoing concerns about justice at the point of sentencing
women to prison or other options (chapter 3), the chapter presents the
debate about the relative justness of equivalent versus gender-responsive conditions and practices in prisons. A body of literature that is
called *feminist jurisprudence* questions, "Should female inmates litigate
for services and programs equal to those of male inmates, or should they
litigate for programs and services unique to women?" Litigation of particular relevance to women has centered on their medical care during
pregnancy, their access to abortion, and programs and services equally
responsive to the needs of women and the needs of men. Although the
pattern may be changing, women were formerly less likely to litigate (in
comparison to men) and lacked resources to carry through on litigation;
they also filed different types of cases. Despite these differences, litigation has had a major impact on the conditions of confinement for both
women and men and it has had some unique effects in selected women's
institutions. In the future, the use of litigation as a vehicle for change in
prison conditions and practices will be constrained by legislation that
has increasingly limited prisoner's access to the courts.

Finally, chapter 9 opens with a summary of the realities of prison
life. These realities provide a basis for trying to realize reform with some
urgency. Chapter 9 presents hopes for the future, and describes how
incarcerated women manage and even produce positive changes within

present realities. Each of the sections of the final chapter considers the dynamics of gender-influenced interactions and related stereotyping, and the incongruities between empowerment and imprisonment. These broader themes help the reader to appreciate that the different pieces of information presented throughout the book are not just detached concerns. When we understand where we are and where we have been in responding to female inmates, we can use this understanding for future decision making pertaining to women in prison. Chapter 9 attempts to a) incorporate the special issues raised in the previous chapters and b) provide suggestions for future policy and programmatic decisions.

CONCLUSION

Insofar as is possible given some major gaps in research, we have tried to understand the forces that impact women prisoners and their experiences from their standpoint. By emphasizing a woman-centered approach, we also present the view of scholars whose work examines how gender concepts structure and influence U.S. society and how individual actions and broader practices maintain gender arrangements. This can help us understand that prisons are not separate, isolated entities outside of our society. Rather, gender in combination with race, ethnicity, and other markers of power shapes the objectives and operations of prisons, and prisons contribute to maintaining women's situations.

ENDNOTES

[1] Margrit Eichler, *The Double Standard: A Feminist Critique of Feminist Social Science* (New York: St. Martin's Press, 1979); Sandra Harding, ed., *Feminism and Methodology* (Bloomington: Indiana University Press, 1987); Evelyn F. Keller, "Gender and Science," *Psychoanalysis and Contemporary Thought: A Quarterly of Integrative and Interdisciplinary Studies,* 1:409–433 (1978); Maureen C. McHugh, Randi D. Koeske, and Irene H. Frieze, "Issues to Consider in Conducting Nonsexist Psychological Research," *American Psychologist,* 41:879–890 (1986); Joyce McCarl Nielsen, *Feminist Research Methods: Exemplary Readings in the Social Sciences* (Boulder, CO: Westview Press, 1990); Liz Stanley and Sue Wise, "Feminist Research, Feminist Consciousness, and Experiences of Sexism," *Women's Studies International Quarterly,* 2:359–374 (1979); Marcia Westkott, "Feminist Criticism of the Social Sciences," *Harvard Educational Review,* 49:422–430 (1979).

[2] Margaret L. Andersen, "Moving Our Minds: Studying Women of Color and Reconstructing Sociology," *Teaching Sociology,* 16:123–132 (1988); Lynne Goodstein, "Feminist Perspectives and the Criminal Justice Curriculum," *Journal of Criminal Justice Education,* 3:61–74 (1992); Peggy McIntosh, "Interactive Phases of Curricular Revision," in Barbara Spanier, A. Bloom, and D. Boroviak, eds., *Toward a Balanced Curriculum* (Cambridge, MA: Schenkman, 1984). 25–34.

[3] Kathleen Daly, "Looking Back, Looking Forward: The Promise of Feminist Transformation," in Barbara Raffel Price and Natalie J. Sokoloff, eds., *The Criminal Justice System and Women: Offenders, Victims, and Workers,* 2nd ed. (New York: McGraw-Hill, 1995), 444–449.

[4] Judith Lorber and Susan A. Farrell, "Principles of Gender Construction," in Joyce Lorber and Susan A. Farrell, eds., *The Social Construction of Gender* (Newbury Park, CA: Sage Publications, 1991), 7–8.

[5] Candace West and Don H. Zimmerman, "Doing Gender," in Joyce Lorber and Susan A. Farrell, eds., *The Social Construction of Gender* (Newbury Park, CA: Sage Publications, 1991), 24–27.

[6] Joanne Belknap, *The Invisible Woman: Gender, Crime, and Justice*, 2nd ed. (Belmont, CA: Wadsworth Publishing Company, 2001), 132–133; Elizabeth F. Moulds, "Chivalry and Paternalism: Disparities of Treatment in the Criminal Justice System," in Susan K. Datesman and Frank R. Scarpitti, eds., *Women, Crime, and Justice* (New York: Oxford University Press, 1980), 279.

[7] David L. Sills, ed., *International Encyclopedia of the Social Sciences, 11* (New York: Macmillan, 1968), 422.

[8] Frank P. Williams and Marilyn D. McShane, *Criminological Theory*, 3d. ed. (Upper Saddle River, NJ: Prentice Hall, 1999), 251.

[9] Joanne Belknap, *The Invisible Woman: Gender, Crime, and Justice*, 132.

[10] *Ibid.*, 133; Elizabeth F. Moulds, "Chivalry and Paternalism: Disparities of Treatment in the Criminal Justice System," 278.

[11] Joycelyn M. Pollock, *Criminal Women* (Cincinnati, OH: Anderson Publishing Company, 1999), 88.

[12] Sarah B. Pomeroy, *Goddesses, Whores, Wives, and Slaves* (New York: Schocken Books, 1975), 8.

[13] Clarice Feinman, *Women in the Criminal Justice System* (New York: Praeger Publishers, 1980); Nicole Rafter, *Partial Justice: Women, Prisons, and Social Control*, 2nd ed. (New Brunswick, NJ: Transaction Publishers, 1990).

[14] Vernetta D. Young, "Gender Expectation and Their Impact on Black Female Offenders and Victims," *Justice Quarterly*, 3:322–323 (1986).

[15] Joanne Belknap, *The Invisible Woman: Gender, Crime, and Justice*; Clarice Feinman, *Women in the Criminal Justice System*; Dorie Klein, "The Etiology of Female Crime: A Review of the Literature," in Barbara Raffel Price and Natalie J. Sokoloff, eds., *The Criminal Justice System and Women: Offenders, Victims, Workers*, 2nd ed. (New York: Clark Boardman Company, Ltd., 1995), 30–53; Nicole Rafter, *Partial Justice: Women, Prisons, and Social Control*.

[16] Clarice Feinman, "Sex Role Stereotypes and Justice for Women," *Crime and Delinquency*, 25:132 (1979).

[17] Pat Carlen, "Papa's Discipline: An Analysis of Disciplinary Modes in Scottish Women's Prisons," *Sociological Review* 30:97–124 (1982); S. V. Carp and L. S. Schade, "Tailoring Facility Programming to Suit Female Offenders' Needs," in *Female Offenders: Meeting Needs of a Neglected Population*, American Correctional Association (1993); J. Chapman, *Economic Realities and Female Crime* (Lexington, MA: Lexington Books, 1980); Merry Morash, Robin N. Haarr and Lila Rucker, "A Comparison of Programming for Women and Men in U.S. Prisons in the 1980s," *Crime and Delinquency*, 40:197–221 (1994); Imogene L. Moyer, "Deceptions and Realities of Life in Women's Prisons," *The Prison Journal*, 64:45–56 (1984); Rita J. Simon and Jean Landis, *The Crimes Women Commit, The Punishments They Receive* (Lexington, MA: Lexington Books, 1991); Ralph Weisheit, "Trends in Programs for Female Offenders: The Use of Private Agencies as Service Providers," *International Journal of Offender Therapy and Comparative Criminology*, 29:35–42 (1985).

[18] Adela Beckerman, "Women in Prison: The Conflict between Confinement and Parental Rights," *Social Justice*, 18:171–183 (1991); Susan Mahan, *Unfit Mothers* (Palo Alto, CA: R&E Research Associates, 1982); Corrimae Mann, *Female Crime and Delinquency* (The University of Alabama Press, 1984).

[19] Kathleen Burkhardt, *Women in Prison* (Garden City, NJ: Doubleday, 1973); James G. Fox, "Women's Prison Policy, Prisoner Activism, and the Impact of the Contemporary

Feminist Movement: A Case Study," *The Prison Journal,* 64:15–36 (1984); Estelle B. Freedman, *Their Sister's Keepers: Women Prison Reform in America, 1930–1930* (Ann Arbor: University of Michigan Press, 1981); Joycelyn M. Pollock-Byrne, *Women, Prison, & Crime,* 2nd ed. (Pacific Grove, CA: Brooks/Cole Publishing Company, 2001); Joycelyn M. Pollock, "Women Will Be Women: Correctional Officers' Perceptions of the Emotionality of Women Inmates, *The Prison Journal,* 64:84–91 (1984).

[20] Office of Justice Programs Coordination Group on Women, *Women in Criminal Justice: A Twenty Year Update: Special Report* (Washington, DC: U.S. Department of Justice, 1998).

[21] Merry Morash, Timothy Bynum and Barbara A. Koons, *Women Offenders: Programming Needs and Promising Approaches.* National Institute of Justice Research in Brief (Washington, DC: U.S. Department of Justice, 1998).

2 ||||| The Women in Prison

Since 1980, the number of women in prison has grown by 500%.[1] In the decade between 1990 and 2000, the number of women in prison grew by 110%.[2] By contrast, the total number of men in prison grew by 77% in the same decade. Despite the increasing proportion of women prisoners in the United States, women still account for only 6.7% of prisoners. By midyear 2000, a total of 92,688 women were in State or Federal prisons.[3]

For both women and men, there are important interstate differences in the number of people incarcerated and the rate of incarceration. (The rate of incarceration is the number of people incarcerated per 100,000 in the population.) Texas, California and the Federal Prisons hold the largest numbers of prisoners. For both women and men, the number of people incarcerated per 100,000 residents is highest for Louisiana, Texas, and Oklahoma.[4] Between 1988 and 1998, growth in number incarcerated was fastest in Texas (see table 2-1). Since crime rates do not vary greatly by state, these statistics reveal women are incarcerated in some states who would have been directed to community corrections programs in other states.

There are profound racial differences in the rate of women incarcerated. Between 1990 and 1998, the rate of white women incarcerated grew from 19 to 34 per 100,000 women, and the rate for black women grew from 117 to 212 per 100,000. Compared to white women, black women who are not Hispanic are 6 times more likely to be incarcerated in a prison or jail; they are 3 times more likely to be incarcerated than Hispanic women.[5]

Table 2-1: Number of Incarcerated Women by State

Jurisdictions	Year End 1998	Rate per 100,000 Women Residents
Alabama	1,525	64
Arizona	1,780	66
California	11,694	67
Colorado	1,070	53
Connecticut	1,357	43
Florida	3,526	45
Georgia	2,474	61
Illinois	2,646	43
Indiana	1,198	39
Kentucky	1,046	51
Louisiana	2,126	94
Maryland	1,140	39
Michigan	2,052	41
Mississippi	1,213	77
Missouri	1,880	67
New Jersey	1,653	39
New York	3,631	38
North Carolina	1,932	35
Ohio	2,912	50
Oklahoma	2,091	122
Pennsylvania	1,517	24
South Carolina	1,412	63
Texas	10,343	102
Virginia	1,806	47
Washington	1,018	35
Wisconsin	1,169	42

Source: Lawrence A. Greenfeld and Tracy L. Snell, *Women Offenders* (Washington, DC: National Institute of Justice, 1999).

Very different kinds of crimes contribute to the large incarceration increases in women and in men. Beginning in the late 1980s, scholars concerned about the plight of women in prison pointed out that the so-called War on Drugs was in fact a War on Women, because policies and legislation were resulting in rapid increases in the proportion of sentenced women charged with a drug offense.[6] From 1990 to 1999, 39 percent of the growth in the number of incarcerated women (but just

18 percent of the growth for men) was due to drug offenses.[7] In contrast, 27 percent of the growth for women and 53 percent for men was attributed to violent offenses. The proportion of women entering prison because of a drug offense has increased, and the number entering because of a violent offense is growing slightly. The women inmate population is dominated more than ever by drug offenders, and the male population is dominated more by violent offenders.

The vast majority of women involved in drug offenses have been arrested for possession or very minor involvement in drug sales and distribution. With few exceptions, women play "no substantial role in drug trafficking."[8] Mancuso and Miller's interviews with women who were repeatedly involved in both substance abuse and crimes unrelated to drugs provided further confirmation that men dominated the highest-level acquisitions in drug markets, and women typically were involved in "low-level market activities, such as engaging in prostitution for drug money, holding small amounts of drugs, and often caring for the male partner."[9]

Although the much larger and still increasing number of men in prison has been emphasized by scholars, the media, and the public, the greater proportion of women inmates has sparked interest in their qualities, motivations, and circumstances. In part because women have historically been less involved in crime than have men, people want to know who the incarcerated women are and why they are in prison. In some instances, this curiosity is fueled by the sense that women who commit crimes are especially deviant, since women are assumed to be passive and law abiding by nature. Movies, television shows, and a steady stream of news stories have set forth the image of the unnatural and freakish woman who becomes an offender—or even more startling, a violent offender. The media have reinforced old ideas from theories that assumed that only peculiar biology or psychology accounted for crime by women.[10] The media neglect the large number of women who break the law after substance abuse treatment programs fail to reach them; exhausting any meager personal resources to escape victimization, and failing to overcome their own inadequacies that often result from deprived childhood and adolescence experiences. These women often commit the mundane offenses of possession of drugs, selling small amounts of drugs, fraud, and prostitution.

IMAGES OF WOMEN IN PRISON

Media emphasis on women's increasing involvement in violent and other offenses typically associated with masculinity—and some theories about this violence—have reinforced public interest in women in prison. The resulting distorted picture that does not depict the typical woman offender or explain the usual route leading to her incarceration is somewhat counterbalanced by sporadic, in-depth reporting that focuses on "run of the mill" women in trouble with the law.

The influences of gender and race on how offenders are portrayed in the media cannot be separated because they are as closely inter-twined in media images as they are in our lives and identities. In recent years, the enemy in the War on Drugs—the official government campaign to stop drug abuse—has been described as young black men, and to a lesser extent black women, whose use of crack cocaine has resulted in the deterioration of inner city neighborhoods and has threatened the rest of society.[11] Movies have depicted female prisoners as most dangerous if they are dark and have overdrawn Negroid and masculine characteristics.[12] Zupan's creative analysis of second-rate but readily available-for-rent movies or late-night TV reruns showed that these portrayals feature incarcerated women as either heroines guilty of nothing more than violating traditional sex role stereotypes (e.g., logical, rational) or as lower-class, vulgar, amoral, mentally defi-cient, promiscuous, and sexually voracious.[13] In the movies, heroines in prison are usually white and innocent people who were framed, and less admirable inmates are often black and criminally motivated. The extent to which people in the general public accept such clearly inac-curate and racist portrayals is not known, but this imagery is com-monly presented.

Providing another twist on inaccurate, popular imagery of women in prison is the media coverage of white women who commit homi-cides.[14] The assumption is that most white women would not break the law, and therefore there must be some extraordinary explanation. In contrast, a Hispanic woman, Lisa Lopez, who was arrested for the homicide of her daughter, was briefly described in the newspaper as a "crack addict" who, at the time of her arrest, was "ranting" and "wild-haired." There was no assumption that this was unusual, and thus no lengthy attention to what might have caused her behavior, even though there was some history of serious spousal abuse. As Miller and Levin put it, "[t]he media's consistent attempts to answer the question of why a particular white criminal has committed his or her crimes illustrates the extent to which whites as a category are not perceived as capable of crime by nature."[15]

Later in this chapter, our review of summary statistics, in-depth studies, and theories that explain women's criminality will provide evidence of unique problems and stresses that are likely to dispropor-tionately affect women in prison. It is not surprising that women inmates need psychological and medical help, or that they would become emotional and stressed about the circumstances of their chil-dren. Women's concerns and problems may be further aggravated by a common stereotype that correctional officers hold of them, which is that they are unreasonably emotional and particularly difficult to work with. In a study of one prison, Schram found that the gender stereotypes of correctional officers act as a form of social control.[16] Extremely sexist stereotypes, which were more often held by officers than by either program staff or women offenders working as peer counselors, negatively affected behavior intentions. For example, correctional officers were least likely to recognize women's need for employment after release. The correctional officers also had the most negative attitudes toward women maintaining ties with their children, apparently because they felt the children would be better off without contact with their mothers. As a result, correctional officers expressed their intent to provide women prisoners with little or no support in the form of encouragement or information that would promote the women's involvement in job preparation programs or mother-child oriented programs.

To remedy correctional officers' negative stereotypes of women prisoners, the National Council on Crime and Delinquency developed a curriculum to train correctional officers at the Pocatello Women's Correctional Center in Pocatello, Idaho. The curriculum challenged stereotypes and emphasized that, compared with male offenders, women offenders are: substantially less likely to engage in violent behavior; less likely to become entrenched in the inmate subculture; less physically demanding to supervise and manage; and more likely than their male counterparts to actively pursue positive change given access to appropriate services and programs.[17] However, not all prisons provide training for correctional officers, and many corrections departments hire custodial staff who have limited education and who change jobs frequently. In Michigan, for example, a shortage of correctional staff prompted the Department of Corrections to set aside its requirement that new staff complete 15 credit hours of college-level course work relevant to corrections before being hired. Efforts to change attitudes often are not intense or frequent enough to have much effect, and minimal standards for education are sometimes further reduced to accommodate the increased need to recruit officers in response to dramatic growth in U.S. prison populations.

Theorists in some cases also portray partial or incorrect images of imprisoned women. Bosworth wrote that many contemporary studies, including those that we will review in this chapter, emphasize women offenders' history of abuse and depict them as a "community of victims rather than a collection of victimizers."[18] Her own research revealed considerable variation in incarcerated women's identities. Many described their assertiveness and their sense of self as a "good mother" (despite many other people's views that they had failed in this regard). In no way did they fit the negative mold of dependent women or perpetual victims. It is important to take a much closer look at the complexities of individuality rather than assuming that all women in prison are alike. Reducing women to a few summary statistics or applying gender or racial stereotypes to them does not contribute to accurate portrayals.

CHARACTERISTICS OF WOMEN IN PRISON

There are two very different approaches to understanding and describing women in prison, each of which provides a partial picture of who the women are. The *summary approach* surveys a large number of women in prison or in the larger offender population for the purpose of generating statistics on the prevalence and incidence of various types of problems, circumstances, and characteristics. The statistics present averages and modes (i.e., most typical characteristics). Some of these differentiating factors include a history of being battered and sexually abused; gynecological health problems; pregnancy; addiction to drugs; limited or no work experience. This approach helps us to understand the typical characteristics and circumstances of women offenders and to gain perspective on their incidence and prevalence in prison populations nationally, in states, or more limited locations.

The second approach, the *detailed, comprehensive case approach,* involves interviewing or observing relatively few women to learn the details of each person's background, current problems, strengths, circumstances, and motivations. This approach provides rich descriptive information about particular women, who may or may not be typical of the offender population. It demonstrates the complexity of influences on women and their responses to these influences before, during, and after incarceration. This approach focuses on women in a geographic area, in an institution, or who have committed a particular type of offense. Often the samples are not random and thus cannot be assumed to represent typical or even sizeable groups of incarcerated women.

It is important to distinguish between the "typical" or "average" woman offender, and the actual characteristics and circumstances of particular incarcerated women. Table 2-2 presents a summary of typical characteristics described by Wellisch, Prendergast, and Anglin.[19]

However, as Wellish and her coauthors note:

> Although these characteristics have been found to typify the population of drug-abusing women offenders, they have different implications for programs. Individual women will differ in the manifestations and severity of these characteristics and attendant problems.[20]

Women are not an abstract assemblage of their demographic characteristics and problematic backgrounds, and while summary statistics give us important clues about the nature of incarcerated women, it is very important to have detailed information about individual women.

Table 2-2: Characteristics of Drug-Abusing Women Offenders

Health Problems
Prevalence of mental and physical illness. Cocaine users in particular at risk for extreme weight loss, dehydration, digestive disorders, skin problems, dental problems, gynecological and venereal infections, tuberculosis, hepatitis B, hypertension, seizures, respiratory arrest, cardiac failure.

Educational/Vocational Background
Unemployment or low-paying jobs, no high-school degree, inadequate vocational skills, lack of life skills and knowledge needed to function productively in society.

Psychosocial Problems
Families with a high incidence of mental illness, suicidal tendencies, alcohol or drug dependence, violence. Frequently have been victims of incest, rape, and physical or sexual abuse.

Parenting Responsibilities
Child-bearing age, have children, single. Receive little or no help from children's father(s), lack supportive family and social networks, have limited or no financial resources. Children often abuse drugs.

Drug Abuse and Treatment
Started abusing drugs and alcohol at an early age, used drugs, especially cocaine, on a daily basis prior to incarceration. Some have been in a substance-abuse treatment program, usually of limited duration and intensity.

Criminal Justice and Child Protective Systems
Much overlap between people involved with criminal justice and child protective systems and needing drug treatment.

Source: Jean Wellisch, Michael L. Prendergast and M. Douglas Anglin, *Drug-Abusing Women Offenders: Results of a National Survey* (Washington, DC: U.S. Department of Justice, 1994).

OFFICIAL STATISTICS AND NATIONAL STUDIES

Official Statistics

Statistics produced by the Bureau of Justice Statistics in the U.S. Department of Justice are an important source of *summary* information on the incarcerated population. For the *Survey of State and Fed-*

eral Prisoners, every six years, random samples of male and female offenders are surveyed by the U.S. Census Bureau and asked a lengthy set of questions about their background and current situation. Compared to the proportion of men included in the sample, the proportion of women is higher, so that it is possible to have a large enough sample to draw conclusions about all of the women in prison and to compare them to men in prison.

Data collected as part of the *Survey of State and Federal Prisoners* reveal that almost two-thirds of women in prison are black, Hispanic, or other races besides white.[21] Because 26.1% of the U.S. population are non-white and non-Hispanic, it is clear that racial and ethnic minority women are greatly overrepresented in the population of incarcerated women.[22]

The demographic characteristics differ for women in state and federal prisons. About 1 in 7 women in state prisons are of Hispanic origin, but nearly 1 in 3 female prisoners in federal custody are Hispanic.[23] Women in federal prisons are on average older than women in state prisons.[24] Finally, women in federal facilities are most likely to have attended high school (73% vs. 56% in state prisons).[25]

Government reports also show that women in state prisons are quite disadvantaged in terms of job experience, though most have a high-school or better education.

- Only 4 in 10 women had been employed full-time prior to arrest, and 37% of women had monthly incomes of less than $600 before arrest
- Almost 3 in 10 women had received welfare assistance before arrest
- Most incarcerated women have some high-school education (37%) or have completed high school through graduation or a GED certificate program (39%). Just 7% have an eighth-grade or less education.

Additionally, female state prison inmates typically have a history of drug abuse. Approximately 50% say that they had been using drugs, alcohol, or both at the time of arrest, 60% report using illegal drugs in the month before incarceration, and 33% said they had committed the offense that resulted in their incarceration to obtain money to support their need for drugs.

Along with substance abuse and employment problems, many incarcerated women have major responsibility for children under age 18. Sixty-five percent have children who are under 18, and about 60% of that group cared for them before incarceration. In most cases, women are single parents. Just 17% of incarcerated women were married before going to prison, and 47% have never been married.

Another distinguishing background factor revealed by the survey of women in prison is women's history of physical and sexual abuse (see table 2-3). Over half of women in state prisons and nearly 40 percent in federal prisons said they had been sexually and/or physically abused, and in many cases the abuse began before they were 18 years old. These numbers are much higher than for men in prisons. Over half of physically abused women said they were hurt by spouses or boyfriends, and somewhat less than a third by parents or guardians.[26]

The Bureau of Justice Statistics collects National Prisoner Statistics on the number of inmates with HIV infection.[27] By 1996, 3.5% of women inmates (and 2.3% of men) were known to be infected; at that time, the rate for women was growing faster than for men. Women's involvement in prostitution and also in intimate relationships with husbands or other partners who were HIV positive accounts for their higher rate of increase in HIV infection. Women who abuse alcohol or other drugs are much more likely to engage in risky sex than are men who are substance abusers, and they are also more likely to contract sexually transmitted diseases.[28]

The percent of women inmates known to be infected with HIV differs greatly by area of the country. For example, the proportion of women known to be infected was 20.5 percent in New York and 11.7 percent in Rhode Island. In contrast, in Nebraska and West Virginia, no women were known to be infected. Rates of known infection are highest for women prisoners in the Northeast (13.0%), followed by the South (3.0%), where Florida and Maryland influence the high average. They are lowest in the West (.7%), and next to the lowest in the Midwest

Table 2-3: Percent Experiencing Abuse before Sentence

	Ever		Before 18	
	Female	Male	Female	Male
Ever Abused before Admission				
State prison inmates	57.2%	16.1%	36.7%	14.4%
Federal prison inmates	39.9%	7.2%	23.0%	5.8%
Physically Abused				
State prison inmates	46.5%	13.4%	25.4%	11.0%
Federal prison inmates	32.3%	6.0%	14.7%	5.0%
Sexually Abused				
State prison inmates	39.0%	5.8%	25.5%	5.9%
Federal prison inmates	22.8%	2.2%	14.5%	1.9%

Source: C. W. Harlow, *Prior Abuse Reported by Inmates and Probationers* (Washington DC: U.S. Department of Justice, 1999).

(1.3%). It is important to keep in mind that these rates are of known cases, and thus are underestimates.

Additional differences between women and men in prison are identified by the *Survey of Inmates*:

- 65 percent of women in state prisons had a history of prior conviction, but a higher proportion, 77 percent, of men in state prison had such a history.
- 19 percent of women, but 38 percent of men, had a juvenile history.
- Fewer women (1 in 6) had a prior criminal record spanning both juvenile and adult years, and more men (1 in 3) had such a history.
- Approximately 20 percent of women in prison, but 8 percent of men, were serving time for their first sentence after conviction for a nonviolent crime.[29]

Before incarceration, women are less likely to have been working full time, and they are more likely than men to have been dependent on welfare and to have children under aged 18 living with them. Five percent of women admitted to state prisons are pregnant at the time of admission. On every measure of drug abuse, women reported greater use than men, but men were more likely to abuse alcohol.

Institutional or State Samples

Bedford Hills, NY Correctional Facility Inmates. Angela Browne interviewed 150 women and found that 70 percent had experienced severe violence from their parents or other caretakers and that 59 percent had been sexually molested as children. Later in life, 75 percent were sexually or physically assaulted by an intimate partner, and 77 percent had been subjected to severe physical or sexual violence by people other than their parents or partners. Of the 150 women, only 6% had not experienced an incident of serious physical or sexual assault in their lifetime.[30]

California Inmates. In 1993, Barbara Owen and Barbara Bloom developed a profile of women in the four California prisons for women.[31] Five hundred of the 7,043 women prisoners were sampled, and 294 agreed to and completed a face-to-face interview. Only 6 percent refused to be in the study, but several were released before the interview could be scheduled or were transferred from the prison to another facility. Owen and Bloom compared the women who did and did not complete the interview, and they were not different in any major ways.

Women in the California sample were very similar to national samples of women in race and ethnicity, marital status, number of children and responsibility for them before arrest, and pre-arrest employment. Like national samples, a large proportion of the women said that they had been physically or sexually abused prior to incarceration. The California women were less often older than 55 and more often had completed some high school or graduated from high school.

The California interviews revealed important details about the women. About half had never worked, and the most common explanation that they gave was that they had substance abuse problems. The second most common explanation was that they made more from "crime and hustling." For the 50% of women who had been working before being incarcerated, 31% said they supplemented their income with drug dealing or sales, and 15% said that illegitimate income, like prostitution or shoplifting, was their only source of income. In giving a reason for committing the offense that resulted in incarceration, over one third said the crime was motivated by drugs. Substance abuse provided a reason for not working at a legitimate job and for committing the offense that led to incarceration, and drug markets provided an important source of illegitimate income.

Many women had family members who had been arrested. Just less than half of the women currently had a partner or spouse, but half of those indicated that the spouse or partner had been incarcerated. Even more commonly, women had other family members who had been arrested, for example a sibling or a parent.

As a group, the California prisoners had surprisingly little prior contact with the justice system. More than half of the women were serving their first term in prison, over one third had not been on probation or parole at the time of the offense, about one quarter had never been on probation before, and the average age at first arrest was 21. Based on their examination of prior justice system contact and types of offenses, Owen and Bloom concluded that "much of the increase in the female prison population is fueled by less serious offenders," at least insofar as women are concerned.[32]

Because California has a very large number of incarcerated women, it is instructive to examine its female prison population as an example of a population in a large state that incarcerates at a high per capita rate. In California, 71.9% of women had been convicted on a drug or property charge, once again providing evidence that the type and number of women who end up in the prison population is driven largely by involvement in drug and other non-violent criminal activities.[33]

Women Felons in Minnesota and Oregon. A survey supported by a grant from the National Institute of Justice provides more detailed information about the characteristics and circumstances of women convicted of felonies in the 1990s.[34] The women lived in two counties of Oregon or the Minneapolis-St. Paul area, and many of them had been just released from prison or jail or had been diverted from prison terms. Although they are not a prison population, their backgrounds and characteristics, as well as their current circumstances, shed light on the lives of women who are in prisons.

When the 280 women involved in an intimate relationship with a man were asked, "In the last six months, did a date, partner, or husband physically hurt you?" about 1 in 4 answered "yes." The frequency of physical harm ranged from daily to once during the prior six months, and 1 of every 3 abused women indicated she was hurt at least once a week. All but a few had received some physical injury, and many of these were quite serious. Many (32.2%) of the women who said they were hurt reported bruises, cuts, or sprains. Additionally, 20.3% (12 of 59) described being slapped, hit or punched. Several women suffered a black eye, broken or fractured bones, or multiple injuries. Descriptions of specific incidents convey the brutality for some of the women:

- "Twisted my arm and dragged me from room to room"
- "Ripped hair out"
- "Busted my head

Another aspect of women's intimate relationships with men was the connection of their relationship to crime. In response to a question, "Did your partner get you in trouble with the law?" one fourth of the women indicated "yes." The outcomes were serious, usually a sentence to prison or jail or a conviction for a new offense, with some other sentence.

All people need support from others. This support can be emotional (for example listening to problems) or practical (involving such things as loans of money or assistance with childcare). Support also comes in the form of having people with whom to spend leisure time. Nearly all women felt they had emotional support—someone to talk with and understand their problems—from at least one adult. In most cases, the women reported two or more supporting adults. More women (16%) said they could not get either practical support or did not have an adult to share leisure time with, but this is still a minority. However, most women's support networks were populated by people who had been "in trouble with the law." Specifically, less than one-third of the women (31.1% of 402) said that no adults in their support network had been arrested, and the others said that one (33.8%), two (21.1%) or 3 or more (13.9%) had been arrested.

The Oregon and Minnesota women also had considerable involvement with the mental health system.

- Just about half indicated that they had been at some time evaluated by a psychologist or a psychiatrist.
- 14% had spent time in a mental health hospital or program overnight.

- The average number of stays in a mental health facility was 3 (n=41), and the average length of stay was 58.3 days (n=55).
- Almost one third of the women in the study sample had taken drugs prescribed for mental health problems.

Some, but not the majority of women, had only had mental health treatment or hospitalization while they were incarcerated; most had received mental health interventions in the community.

THE TYPICAL WOMAN IN PRISON

According to government statistics, in 1997 the typical female inmate was: over age 30, a member of a racial or ethnic minority, had abused drugs, had experienced physical or sexual abuse, and was unmarried; almost two-thirds had at least one minor child.[35] Owen and Bloom similarly concluded from a review of studies using the *summarizing approach* to understanding the characteristics of women in prison:

> Female prisoners are very low income, disproportionately African American and Hispanic, undereducated, unskilled with sporadic employment histories. They are mostly young, single and heads of households, with the majority of those imprisoned (80%) having at least two children. At least two-thirds of incarcerated women have children under the age of eighteen. Women prisoners have a host of medical, psychological and financial problems and needs. Substance abuse, compounded by poverty, unemployment, physical and mental illness, physical and sexual abuse and homelessness often propel women through the revolving door of the criminal justice system. Nationwide, women are more likely than men to be serving sentences for drug offenses and other non-violent property crimes.[36]

Descriptive information on multiple characteristics of imprisoned women gives us ideas about their typical background, needs, and circumstances.

In the next section, we will report on studies of how these factors come together in the lives of particular subgroups of women. The research that describes individual women, as opposed to summarizing the range and the averages in their characteristics, provides insight not only to them as people, but also the causation of their criminality. Who are the women in prison, and why did they break the law?

Unique Groups of Women Offenders

An accurate picture of the characteristics, circumstances and histories of imprisoned women must include an understanding of both those who are and who are not typical. The *summary approach* provides "average" characteristics of the group, assuming that offenders are all "typical." To avoid this, we will supplement the *summary approach* statistics that we have presented with the results of several *comprehensive case approach* studies.

Information from lengthy and sometimes repeated interviews with a small number of women can reveal both their characteristics and the circumstances and events that contributed to their criminality. The *detailed, comprehensive case approach* is particularly well suited to discovering complex cause-and-effect relationships, identifying previously unknown individual and structural influences on crime, and studying people with unusual circumstances and crimes. It also increases understanding of women offenders as people, since it allows for description of their unique attributes and the unique combination of these attributes. Purposive or snowball sampling is often used for these types of studies. An example of purposive sampling would be to select all women living in a particular prison and incarcerated for a particular crime, for example, homicide. An example of snowball sampling is to interview a small number of known prostitutes in a community, and to then ask each of them to provide introductions or names to facilitate interviewing other women involved in prostitution. The point is to understand the lives and circumstances of individuals.

Street Women in Milwaukee, 1979. In her book, *Street Woman*, Eleanor Miller used the *detailed, comprehensive case approach* to counteract stereotypes of women offenders that stressed that they were becoming more criminal and more like men (that is, less bound by gender stereotypes).[37] She did not limit her research to women in prison, but there is considerable overlap between the women she included in her study and prison populations. The women she initially interviewed were residents of one of several places:

1. two halfway houses for female offenders,
2. a correctional facility for individuals who had their probation revoked, were awaiting trial, were serving sentences of two years or less, or were awaiting transportation to prison,
3. women serving prison time, but with a work release provision.

Women in these three groups suggested other women who might participate in the study. Many of the women had been in or were likely to be in prison.

Miller wrote *Street Woman* to describe the actual experiences of women in contrast to theoretical generalizations about groups of unidentifiable individuals. As she stated, "[I]deally we should be able at least to recognize the individual in the picture painted of the group."[38] In fact, the subjects in her study, though they were interviewed in 1979, very much fit the typical women descriptions that are based on more recent *summary approach* research. The women were disproportionately minority in relation to the Milwaukee population, had children, were in their twenties, and had limited education and little legitimate work experience.

Miller's data reveal much more than similarity with *summary approach* findings. Very different life circumstances, ranging from extreme poverty to economic stability, shaped similar patterns of involvement in illegal work. Family relations and neighborhood conditions, as well as women's own desire for excitement and money, came into play. However, the influences of a deviant street network, which sometimes overlapped or at least coexisted with family networks, was essential to recruiting women into prostitution, selling drugs, stealing, and other "street hustles." The deviant street network also was important in maintaining and supporting women's involvement in crime.

For about half of the women whom Miller interviewed, running away from home during adolescence influenced their eventual involvement in deviant networks and illegal behavior. Most of the women were either from households in which they were abused (including through incest), severely neglected, or "pushed out" of the house as unwanted. Some women left families that were not involved in criminality because their families were strict and/or abusive. Others had families with members who pooled their resources (including earnings or goods obtained through crime) and had access to deviant networks that made it possible to earn an income. For example, it would not be uncommon for a cousin, a sister, or brother to introduce women to the possibilities for illegal earnings and to link women to networks that facilitated obtaining and selling drugs or linking up with "a man" to protect a prostituting woman.

Once women were involved in illegal activity, relationships with men provided affection, support and protection. One woman interviewed by Miller highlighted the importance of protection:

> The first couple of months I was down there [prostituting] I was dealing all by myself, you know. . . . And then, after a while, I started going with a guy, and he was nothin' but a pimp, you know, a player, or whatever. It was the first time I ever really paid, but at this time I felt that I needed to 'cause I needed him for protection more than anything else, you know, on the strip down there. . . . from the other pimps. 'Cause they were killin' girls down there, you know, at a steady rate.[39]

In addition to providing some benefits, relationships with "a man" exposed women to physical abuse, expanded deviant street networks, the need to obtain financial support for the man and others attached to him, and drugs.

Miller's documentation of the influence of incest, current or prior abuse by an intimate partner, various types of family problems during adolescence, and limited education and work experience on criminality confirms findings from studies using the *summary approach* to research. However, she also reveals that the mechanisms combine to influence involvement in crime through individual characteristics, proclivities, and exposure to poverty.

African-American Women Engaged in Violence, New York. Recognizing that they make up a small but important group of female offenders, Baskin and Sommers examined the life histories of African-American women who commit violent offenses. The New York City women were teenagers and young adults (and in a few cases, older adults) during the "crack cocaine" epidemic. They lived in communities composed of families that were often unable to provide financial or supervisory stability. Schools and leisure-time activities were inadequate, and attractive job opportunities were not available. Their neighborhoods, however, did have drug markets, particularly for crack cocaine: "The increased involvement of women in drug markets as sellers, manufacturers, crew bosses, and so on is clearly a phenomenon of the crack market."[40] One woman described the ease of entry into selling cocaine,

> I had lots of little jobs, but selling cocaine was always how I really made my living. My last job was, I was 18, I was a receptionist at a showroom. I was there maybe 1 year. It was okay. But I was already into selling cocaine. I started that much earlier when my father went to jail. I knew my father was selling coke . . . And I felt that as my duty as taking care of my family I started selling coke. Now, I'd be selling for about 7 years. I went up and down. I could make $500. I could make $3000 a week. . . . I never stood on the corner and sold bags or anything like that . . . I was selling ounces with some Colombians. They became like my suppliers and stuff. I started like with myself; when my father came out I started like working with him. Then I stopped working in offices altogether. [41]

After the emergence of crack cocaine markets in many different settings within the United States, there were not the barriers to entry that women found for previous drug markets, since crack cocaine is relatively easy and inexpensive to manufacture and distribute.

Brownstein and coauthors also reported on New York State women who were violent.[42] They interviewed women convicted of homicide, and in the study we will describe, they focused attention on 19 women who killed another person as a part of their involvement in drug markets, frequently for crack cocaine. In several of the situations that their study participants described, men were involved in the homicide in some way, either as the abusive partner who was killed or as a conspirator or participant in the murder. In a sense, as the authors conclude, most of the homicides were "gender related" insofar as they involved men with whom the women had some connection. In some cases described by Brownstein and his colleagues it is unclear whether there is any difference in women's and men's situations. For instance, the men who collaborated with women in killing someone could be said to have committed a "gender-related" offense just as easily as the women who collaborated with a man.[43] What is clear, however, is that in a study of over 200 women serving time for homicide, very few had drug-related, economic motivations. Of those, some committed murder at least in part because of a relationship with a man. Very few women committed the crime on their own and solely for economic gain.

Women Who Kill an Abusive Partner or Husband. Women who kill an abusive partner or husband stand out as being different from other women in prison. They often have limited or no record of prior criminality.[44] They usually are not the "typical" woman that Miller described from her research on women who are regularly involved in illegal work, and they usually do not have the circumstances or characteristics described in Baskin and Sommer's research on violent black women in New York City.[45] Of course, some women who make a living through hustling and some violent women from marginalized communities no doubt do kill an abusive partner; still, many women in prison who have killed an intimate partner have not been involved in any other crime.

Media Accounts, Summary Statistics and Case Studies

Do case studies of women who are violent offenders demonstrate that women offenders are often, or increasingly, violent? Do statistics on the small proportion of women who are in prison as a result of conviction for a violent offense indicate that violent women offenders are an unimportant group? The answer is "no" to both of these questions. As Baskin and Sommers pointed out, official statistics demonstrate that "black women are more likely to be arrested for robbery and aggravated assault than are white males."[46] Clearly, violent women offenders are a group that we need to understand. However, it is critical that we recognize that they do not constitute a large proportion of the women in prison and that specific social and individual factors explain their behavior.

THEORIES OF WOMEN'S CRIMINALITY

Two questions are important to understanding the causes of the illegal behavior that result in women's incarceration. One of these, which is beyond the scope of this book, is "Why are women so much less likely to break the law than men?" The other, which has a direct bearing on women in prison (because it explains how they started and why they persisted in breaking the law) is "Why did incarcerated women break the law?" Although we focus on this second question, it is important to keep in mind that some combination of biology, socialization, circumstances, and social location mitigates against women breaking the law in the higher proportions and with the extent of violence characteristic of men.

The complexion of women in prison raises another question: Why are women of color (African Americans and Hispanics, and in some places Native Americans) overrepresented in prison in relation to their proportion in the general population? Part of the answer to this question may lie in profiling practices of law enforcement and in sentencing disparities related to race (see chapter 3). However, there also is no doubt that women from disorganized and poorly resourced neighborhoods (like men from similar communities) are at greatest risk for victimization experiences that can contribute to criminality. They are also at risk for viewing participation in illegal activities as the most viable and/or exciting option for obtaining money.

Early Theories

Steffensmeier and Haynie identified several stages in the early development of theory to explain women's criminality.[47] During the late eighteenth and early nineteenth centuries, the emphasis was initially on biological and later on the psychological explanations of women's criminality. At the same time, men's criminality was at least partly explained as a result of environmental factors. Foreshadowing stereotypic assumptions that some people still hold, women who broke the law were seen as abnormal, but men who broke the law were viewed as normal people responding to negative economic conditions.

One theorist writing in mid-century, Pollak, did recognize that structural factors, especially poverty, had a similar effect on women and men.[48] He reasoned that the disadvantaged economic and occupational position of women, the influence of modern advertising, and a double standard about sexual morality contribute to female crime. Put in today's terms, women's *social location*, their place in society, could result in frustration, resentment and criminal desires. Results were women's perjury or false accusations against men, aggressive behavior toward partners or others, and temptation to steal. Pollak's theory is seriously flawed by his stereotype of women as inherently deceitful, which is his explanation for why women are more biologically and individually pathological than men. He erroneously assumed that women are equally as criminal as men, but due to their inherent biological and psychological makeup, they were motivated to and capable of hiding their criminality.

A 1973 article by Dorie Klein provided an expansive review of theories (like Pollak's) to explain women's criminality. She highlighted the tendency to locate causality in women's individual characteristics, in particular their sexuality.[49] Her seminal article demonstrated how theories perpetuated assumptions that the inherent sexuality of women (along with other individual, personal characteristics) accounted for girls instigating boys' gang delinquency, mothers promoting their daughters' delinquency, girls' promiscuity (driven by their need for people), and feelings of frustration rooted in a woman's inability to succeed as a mother and homemaker. The common thread through these and similar explanations is that girls' and women's own inadequacies account for their illegal behavior. The related strategy for rehabilitating women offenders, or preventing their criminality, has been to help them adjust to their circumstances by changing themselves. In practice, the emphasis in these theories results in helping a young woman adjust to recent experiences of incest as opposed to urging advocacy and support so that she can utilize the courts and welfare assistance to live apart from an abusive parent.

Two recent theoretical positions that seek to avoid the sexist assumptions of much prior theory are: (1) the same factors explain the criminality of women and men, but men are more criminal because they are exposed to more negative influences; and (2) qualitatively different explanations are needed, for women become offenders because of different circumstances than men and through different processes. Certainly some of the influences are the same. For instance, shifts in the contemporary illicit drug economy have placed more women on the streets in situations conducive to violent crime, and the same context explains both men's and women's criminality as influenced by the illicit drug industry.[50]

An exclusive focus on similar influences on the criminality of women and men does avoid the use of gender stereotypes to explain women's crime, but it ignores gender-related experiences of women in families, peer groups, intimate relationships, educational systems, and the workplace. The limited theories fall short in explanatory power. Differences in power, resources, and experiences result in women's and girls' greater abuse in their families and in dating and marriage partnerships, fewer opportunities for education and work, and other important outcomes. The current theoretical perspectives that we describe below place the force of gender, combined with other stratifying influences, at the center of explaining women's criminality.

Current Theoretical Perspectives

There is substantial documentation of women's patterns of criminality and involvement in the criminal justice system and both statistical and ethnomethodological information on the characteristics of women who are in prison. In contrast, theory that recognizes the influence of women's social location and situations to explain how women came to break the law is much more limited.

Kathleen Daly, by analyzing presentence investigations for a federal court, identified five distinct pathways that women follow to criminal involvement.[51] *Streetwomen* had been severely abused in childhood, lived on the streets, and were in court for crimes related to supporting their drug habit (for instance selling drugs, prostitution, and stealing). *Harmed and harming women* also were abused as children, and they responded with anger and acting out; for some, the use of alcohol or drugs contributed to their violence. *Battered women* typically had little or no criminal record, and they had harmed or killed men who had violently attacked them or threatened to do so. *Drug-connected women* used or sold drugs as a result of relationships with a male intimate, children, or their mother and also had a limited criminal record. *Economically motivated women* committed crimes to cope with poverty or out of greed. Although she focused more narrowly on circumstances leading up to women's abuse of crack cocaine, Sterk similarly documented different causes: a desire to experiment with drug effects, socialization by parents or others close to them to think marijuana and thus other drugs were acceptable, and a perception that their parents "disrespected" and therefore rejected them.[52] In recognition of the diversity of women offenders' histories, we will use Daly's categories to organize our discussion of why women break the law and how gender arrangements in our society have their impact.

Streetwomen. In her numerous writings on the topic, Chesney-Lind highlighted the significance of the high proportion of women and girls involved as offenders in the justice system who are also victims of abuse, including sexual abuse, for explaining their illegal behavior.[53] Young women who had been abused or raped ran away from home, and then, often when the courts failed to provide assistance or even punished her for running away, became involved in prostitution or petty property crimes in order to survive. With no marketable skills and little education, many women continued to support themselves with illegal activities when they became adults. Criminality is a reflection of the situations of women's and girls' lives, the failure of the juvenile courts to help them, and their attempts to survive.[54]

Based on interviews with women imprisoned in California, Owen extended the idea that victimization influences illegal behavior. She emphasizes that the majority of crimes committed by women are motivated by their efforts to survive within the constraints experienced by women, minorities, and lower classes.[55] This motivation includes emotional and psychological survival mechanisms as well as economic survival in a context where many women and girls are denied economic opportunities and/or are physically or emotionally abused. She described the interplay between social structure and immediate circumstances:

> The personal domains of drug and substance use, physical and sexual abuse, oppressive relationships with men, and the lack of economic skills shape . . . [women offenders'] immediate experience. The structural domains of racism, sexism, decreased economic

opportunity, and the devalued status of women, particularly marginalized women, limit their access to conventional roles.[56]

Research evidence supports a connection of childhood abuse, including sexual abuse, with girls' running away from home and working as prostitutes and women's drug abuse.[57] Yet, it is important to recognize that a pattern of criminality is just one possible outcome of childhood abuse; in fact, many girls who have been abused do not become adult offenders.

Harmed and harming women. A piece of research that was unique in its focus on women who had killed their infants revealed the extreme psychological harm that can result from childhood abuse of girls. The researchers interviewed 42 women incarcerated in New York State.[58] They had all been neglected or abused during childhood, but not all had followed the path of running away, prostitution, substance abuse, or other criminality. Their childhoods were marked by unavailability of predictable adults to meet their needs and keep them safe coupled with the lack of other supports. They grew up to have very poor self-esteem and also a limited capacity to gauge interpersonal relationships. Some women, for example, accepted being in an abusive relationship with a spouse because they did not see it as abnormal within a family setting. Many of the women had been sexually abused and/or neglected. Substance abuse often became a way to numb the pain resulting from childhood experiences. Labeling the women as "bad" or "mad" tended to mask the dynamic that characterized the homicide, specifically killing their children because of their inability to understand the child's motives, or in an attempt to maintain what few relationships they did have with other people when those people threatened to leave if the child remained. While homicide of a child is a relatively rare outcome of women's prior histories of abuse and neglect, it is an extreme case of the damage that can result from such a history.

Battered and entrapped women. Angela Browne interviewed 42 women charged with a crime in the death or serious injury of their partners and 205 women who had been in abusive relationships but who didn't take lethal action against the abuser.[59] All of the women were currently with their partners, had been with him at the time of his death, or had been out of the relationship for less than one year.

Several circumstances of the relationship culminated in the homicide. When homicides occurred, women were committed to "working things out." Women were in despair and terrified because violence had become more frequent and more severe, and because repeated physical and emotional attacks and injuries made them feel trapped and desperate. They might still be very concerned about maintaining the relationship and taking care of children, but their focus on survival and escape became proportionally greater.

Browne identified seven dynamics that best differentiated women who did and did not kill their abusers:

- the frequency with which abusive incidents occurred
- the severity of women's injuries
- the frequency of forced or threatened sexual acts by the man
- the man's drug use
- the frequency of his intoxication
- the man's threats to kill
- and the woman's threats to commit suicide.[60]

In the eventual homicide incidents, many of the men actually dared their partners to kill them, or ran against the gun as the women were firing. It is noteworthy that the circumstances surrounding the homicide explained the incident, rather than any unique or unusual characteristics of the women who killed their partners.

Browne explained why women "often spend years trying to understand what went wrong, hoping that if they can once comprehend it, they can then fix it."[61] Drawing on the theories of Chodorow[62] and Gilligan,[63] who proposed that women reason about right and wrong differently than do men, she reasoned that women have been oriented toward empathizing with others, building dependencies and close connections, and valuing relationships. Thus, when faced with beatings that seem "random, non-contingent in nature,"[64] many women responded by attempting to understand the abuse and look for solutions, rather than leave. There is strong cultural support for women to hold a family together, even when the husband is abusive. In Browne's theoretical framework, the battering incident continues to evoke the responses to trauma: a focus on "self protection and survival" along with "shock, denial, disbelief, and fear"; however, these responses occur in the larger context, in which gender organization results in women's strong investment in understanding others and maintaining relationships. Some of the precursors of battering—a man's possessiveness, jealousy, and related controlling behavior—are not considered unusual by people who assume that it is natural for men to dominate women. In general, the interactions leading up to battering and homicide "are extensions of our cultural expectations for romance and husband-wife relating."[65]

Browne shows how "[t]he decisions a woman makes in an abusive relationship are based on her perceptions of patterns and alternatives."[66] This applies to the critical decision to kill the batterer. Women adjusted to living conditions and attacks that became increasingly severe and injurious and that involved increasing isolation from other people. However, when they felt there was an unprecedented threat to themselves, physical or sexual abuse of a child, or that "he had never done that before," they did take lethal action.[67] Descriptions of specific cases of homicide illustrate that the women felt they could no longer adapt, for they would be killed or a child would be gravely harmed.

Beth Richie's work on gender entrapment of incarcerated women further explains why only some battered women kill their abuser and how abusive relationships can result in other patterns of women's criminology.[68] She reveals the interplay of social structure (especially race and gender), a woman's victimization, and criminality in her study of the circumstances and effects of battering for three groups of women incarcerated at New York City's Rikers Island jail. The thirty-seven women whom she interviewed were in one of three situations: non-battered and African-American, battered and African-American, or battered and white. The battered African-American women had been seen as talented or capable children within their families, and they were brought up to expect a man to sustain a positive marriage with them. In contrast, women offenders who were not battered were brought up without significant men in their lives and did not expect to depend on or be involved with men as they grew older. Compared to the mothers of battered women, the mothers of this second group were less tolerant of being abused themselves. The situation of African-American battered offenders was tied to their efforts to maintain a "typical" household regardless of the abuse meted out by a partner.

The women who were battered had married early and perceived a need to avoid getting their abusive partners involved with the justice system, in part because the system was unjust for black men. Jailed African-American women who were not in battering relationships had experienced victimization by abusive men, but their goals and circumstances were not characterized by this sort of gender entrapment. As a result, they did not remain in continuing abusive relationships. Factors that kept some women in ongoing abusive relationships included: "1) gender-identity development; 2) early relational circumstances; 3) cultural loyalty to men; 4) women's response to male violence; and 5) social conditions."[69]

What Richie refers to as *entrapment* in an abusive relationship is linked to women's criminality in several different ways. For some women, the abusive relationship resulted in the death of a child, and women were charged as accessories or perpetrators. For others, constant beatings by one man resulted in a woman's murdering another man when she felt threatened. Some men forced women into prostitution and beat them if they would not bring in adequate income; some would beat women unless they brought home illegal income, such as that obtained by stealing from their employer. In particular, black women, who tended not to use social services to get help, killed their abuser in retaliation. Battered women also took drugs in an attempt to share an activity and intimacy with their abusers, or to numb the pain caused by abuse; resulting dependency on drugs fueled criminal activities.

In our previous examination of summary statistics on women felons, it was clear that many women who have been convicted of a felony have also been abused by a male partner in a recent relationship. It is unclear whether battering is typically or even frequently a factor leading to women's criminality, but Richie's work clarifies several ways that it can be. Her book, *Compelled to Crime*, shows how the connection works, and the effect of racial differences on that connection. White battered women were more likely to try to leave, although circumstances often prevented their leaving; black battered women primarily persisted in trying to maintain a relationship with their abuser as well as a nuclear family. One woman explained the importance of keeping the family together,

> What happened was my co-defendant wanted me to stop caring for my boy, who was only four years old. He was jealous of him and tried to take over from me and be his father. At first I was glad because it made us seem more like a real family, but my son was very close to me.[70]

Another woman explained how she tried to present her marriage as successful, which resulted in her being cut off from her family and contributed to her entrapment in an abusive relationship,

> My family respected me because I got a "good man" . . . little did they know! I was getting really scared. The beatings were getting really rough, and he was getting us into illegal stuff, but since I'd lost contact [with my family], they was no one to tell. Besides, who'd believe he *made* me rip people off? Not me, no never. He had the phone taken out, and cut my contact with my folks. He went everywhere with me, which they thought was cool—like he was being a good man. I didn't have a single chance to run from him; he watched my every step.[71]

Women's entrapment resulted from their strong belief in maintaining the domicile; their childhood role models themselves often remained in abusive relationships.

Drug-connected women. Richard Mancuso and Brenda Miller described women who break the law and whose lives are marked by the use of alcohol or other drugs involved in *the lifestyle*.[72] These women share many similarities with the women Miller described in *Street Woman*.[73] The *lifestyle* promotes continued criminality. For instance, "[p]rostitution may promote further drug taking simply as a way of handling the stress and negative, pejorative view of their lives, held by the women themselves as well as others. Thus, there becomes a vicious cycle of prostitution to support drug use, and drug use to cope with prostitution."[74] In turn, drug dependency can create the motivation for illegal activity that involves a woman in the underworld and criminal subcultures, as illustrated in one woman's statement:

> I went out and shot around. I needed so much more to overcome the methadone habit that I sold it. I used to deal an ounce or two ounces a day. . . . I didn't look for business. Okay? I know, being an opiate user for many years, many other opiate users, you know,

and being with my man, so I didn't need to find people to sell to.
They were always there and they weren't there for just five or ten
dollars' worth; they were there for large amount.[75]

As this woman's statement illustrates, exposure to the deviant street
network facilitates continued illegal activity. Women's criminality may
be further supported by broader social forces and conditions such as
community tolerance of alcohol use, the limited availability of treatment for substance abuse, and community drug market activity.[76]

Economically-motivated women. A number of theorists have
integrated individual and circumstantially based explanations of crime
with an emphasis on women's economic marginalization and the related
lack of employment opportunities as root causes of their criminality.
From this perspective, petty property crime is a rational response to
poverty and economic insecurity.[77] Rising divorce rates, female-headed
households, fathers' failure to support their children, the segregation of
women in low-paying and traditionally female occupations, and women's
feeling the primary responsibility for childcare all work together to
increase economic pressure on women.[78] For some women, a trend
toward what is called the "feminization of poverty" results in increased
consumer-based crimes, such as shoplifting and welfare fraud. Economic
marginalization can also contribute to battered and stalked women's
desperation, keeping them at risk for abuse and increasing the odds
that they will take fatal action to end the abuse.

Barbara Owen explained how economic marginalization inter-
twined with women's individual propensities and their circumstances
to move them toward increased criminality.[79] Based on interviews
with women imprisoned in California, she concluded that most held
quite traditional views of gender roles. Contradicting some media stereotypes, the women identified themselves as wives and mothers, not
as aggressive criminals acting outside the boundaries set for the traditional woman. For many, the initial step in becoming a mother was an
early pregnancy that had the eventual effect of interrupting their
schooling and their residing in parental homes, both of which create
barriers to participating in the labor market. Once they were economically marginalized, women had few resources and used sexual activities as "bargaining chips" for obtaining food, shelter, drugs, etc. For
most women in prison, "roles that model non-motherhood, roles that
encourage educational and vocational preparation outside the traditional middle-class role of wife and mother are absent . . ."[80]

Daly's study of white-collar defendants provided support for the
economic marginalization explanation.[81] Among white-collar defendants, most of the men but only a few of the women held high-level
positions. The majority of women were clerical workers; they were
more likely to be nonwhite, to have less than a college education, and
to have fewer economic assets.

Judith and Michael Collins studied women confined to federal prison after conviction for a white-collar offense of fraud or embezzlement.[82] Unlike male offenders, the incarcerated women did not have particularly low levels of self control. The women were, however, "other- rather than self-motivated."

> During the interviews, a common theme for the commission of the crimes was that husbands, parents, or children were in financial trouble. Several females said they committed the fraud because of health care and other related problems of either parents or family and for which there were no financial resources.[83]

Additionally,

> Every woman in this sample expressed remorse for her crime—a finding that is in sharp contrast with interview reports of male inmates, many who claimed their white collar crimes were business necessities.[84]

Women serving time for fraud or embezzlement were not lower in empathy than non-offending women in similar managerial positions.[85] In fact, their concern for others seemed to be implicated in their motivations to break the law. They were, however, characterized by a combination of extroversion and assertiveness with a tendency not to comply with society's norms (socialization trait).

In contrast to Collins and Collins' findings, a study by Miller described women and men who committed robberies as similar in motivation, though gender shaped the way that they carried out their offenses.[86] Males tended to rob other men and to use direct confrontation, physical violence, and guns. Women were more likely to rob other women and either use a knife or no weapon; they also often used sex to make the men vulnerable, for instance by enticing them to employ them as prostitutes, and then stealing from them.

CONCLUSION

Incarcerated women vary considerably from each other in personal motivations, needs that are or are not related to their criminality, and the degree to which they can achieve their goals and live their lives as they want. What they share is a common place in society for women and the disproportionate experience of circumstances related to this place. Ethnic group disadvantages, such as growing up in a neighborhood that is marginalized from all but illegal economies, are compounded by stereotypes that all women face regarding capabilities to do certain types of work or to achieve certain levels of education.

Viewing women in prison as a collection of needs and deficits invites programming that will act on them rather than programming that will enable them to act for themselves. Government statistics, particularly those generated by the Bureau of Justice Statistics on a regular basis, provide very useful information. But beyond official statistics, there is an unfilled need for more theoretical research that identifies the different pathways to criminality and the possible points when women can be empowered to escape dangerous or oppressive situations. Daly's study of pathways to crime provided an excellent model.[87] It should be repeated to provide information about women in state prisons today and the economic and personal conditions that affected their behavior.

It is important to consider the information presented in subsequent chapters in light of the complexities of particular women's characteristics and circumstances emphasized in this chapter. Successful programs and policies must consider the totality of a woman's characteristics and circumstances within the broader structural context, including factors related to the structural contexts of gender, social class, race and ethnicity.

ENDNOTES

[1] General Accounting Office, *Women in Prison: Issues and Challenges Confronting U.S. Correctional Systems* (Washington, DC: General Accounting Office, 1999).

[2] Allen J. Beck and Jennifer Karberg, *Prison and Jail Inmates at Midyear 2000* (Washington, DC: Bureau of Justice Statistics, 2001).

[3] *Ibid.*

[4] Lawrence A. Greenfeld and Tracy L. Snell, *Women Offenders* (Washington DC: National Institute of Justice, 1999); T. M. Hammett, P. Harmon, and L. M. Maruschak, *1996-1997 Update: HIV/AIDS, STDs, and TB in Correctional Facilities* (Washington DC: U.S. Department of Justice, 1999).

[5] Allen J. Beck and Jennifer Karberg, *Prison and Jail Inmates at Midyear 2000*.

[6] Kathleen Daly, *Survey Results of the Niantic Interviews: December 1983 and May 1986* (Unpublished manuscript, 1987); Tracy Huling, *Breaking the Silence* (Vol. March 4) (New York: Correctional Association of New York, 1991); Daniel D. LeClair, *The Incarcerated Female Offender: Victim or Villain?* (Boston: Research Division, Massachusetts Division of Correction, 1990); Rhode Island Justice Alliance, *Female Offender Survey* (Rhode Island Adult Correctional Institution, Women's Division, 1990).

[7] Bureau of Justice Statistics, *Bureau of Justice Statistics 2000: At a Glance* (Washington, DC: U.S. Department of Justice, 2000).

[8] Susan D. Phillips and Nancy Harm, "Women Prisoners: A Contextual Framework," in Judy Harden and Marcia Hill, eds., *Breaking the Rules: Women in Prison and Feminist Therapy* (New York: Harwood Press, 1998), 1–9.

[9] Richard F. Mancuso and Brenda Miller, "Crime and Punishment in the Lives of Women Alcohol and Other Drug (AOD) Users: Exploring the Gender, Lifestyle, and Legal Issues," in Clair M. Renzetti and Lynne Goodstein, eds., *Women, Crime, and Criminal Justice* (Los Angeles: Roxbury Publishing Company, 2000), 95.

[10] Dorie Klein, "The Etiology of Female Crime: A Review of the Literature," *Crime and Social Justice: Issues in Criminology* 8:13–30 (1973).

[11] Laura T. Fishman, "Images of Crime and Punishment: The Black Bogyman and White Self-Righteousness," in Coramae R. Mann and Marjorie Zatz, eds., *Images of Color, Images of Crime* (Los Angeles: Roxbury Publishing Company, 1998), 109–126.

[12] *Ibid.*

[13] Linda L. Zupan, "Reel Women behind Bars?" *American Jails, Sept/Oct*:22–24 (1996).

[14] Jody Miller and P. Levin, "The Caucasian Evasion: Victims, Exceptions, and Defenders of the Faith," in Coramae R. Mann and Marjorie S. Zatz, eds., *Images of Color, Images of Crime* (Los Angeles: Roxbury Publishing Company, 1998), 217–233.

[15] *Ibid.*

[16] Pamela J. Schram, *The Link between Stereotype Attitudes and Behavioral Intentions among Female Inmates, Correctional Officers, and Program Staff. A Dissertation* (Michigan State University, East Lansing, 1996).

[17] Bona Miller, "Different Not More Difficult: Gender-Specific Training Helps Bridge the Gap," *Corrections Today* 60:142–144 (1998).

[18] Mary Bosworth, *Confining Femininity: A History of Gender, Power and Imprisonment* (New York: Fordham University, 1999).

[19] Jean Wellisch, Michael L. Prendergast and M. Douglas Anglin, *Drug-Abusing Women Offenders: Results of a National Survey* (Washington, DC: U.S. Department of Justice, 1994).

[20] *Ibid.*, 2.

[21] Lawrence A. Greenfeld and Tracy L. Snell, *Women Offenders*.

[22] *Ibid.*

[23] *Ibid.*

[24] *Ibid.*

[25] *Ibid.*

[26] C. W. Harlow, *Prior Abuse Reported by Inmates and Probationers* (Washington DC: U.S. Department of Justice, 1999).

[27] T. M. Hammett, P. Harmon, and L. M. Maruschak, *1996–1997 Update: HIV/AIDS, STDs, and TB in Correctional Facilities* (Washington DC: U.S. Department of Justice, 1999).

[28] National Center on Addiction and Substance Abuse, *Behind Bars: Substance Abuse in America's Prison Population* (New York: Columbia University, 1998).

[29] Lawrence A. Greenfeld and Tracy L. Snell, *Women Offenders*.

[30] Office of Justice Programs, *Conference Proceedings: National Symposium on Women Offenders* (Washington, DC: Office of Justice Programs, 1999).

[31] Barbara Owen and Barbara Bloom, "Profiling Women Prisoners: Findings from National Surveys and a California Sample," *The Prison Journal* 75:165–185. (1995).

[32] *Ibid.*

[33] Barbara Bloom, Meda Chesney-Lind, and Barbara Owen, *Women in California Prisons: Hidden Victims of the War on Drugs* (San Francisco: Center on Juvenile and Criminal Justice, 1994).

[34] Merry Morash and Timothy Bynum, *Findings from the National Study of Innovative and Promising Programs for Women Offenders* (Washington, DC: National Institute of Justice, 1995).

[35] General Accounting Office, *Women in Prison*.

[36] Barbara Owen and Barbara Bloom, "Profiling Women Prisoners."

[37] Eleanor M. Miller, *Street Woman* (Philadelphia: Temple University Press, 1986).

[38] *Ibid.*, 7.

[39] *Ibid.*, 47.

[40] Deborah R. Baskin and Ira B. Sommers, *Casualties of Community Disorder: Women's Careers in Violent Crime* (Boulder, CO: Westview Press, 1998).

[41] *Ibid.*, 89.

[42] Henry H. Brownstein, Barry J. Spunt, Susan Crimmins, and Sandra Langley, "Women Who Kill in Drug Market Situations, *Justice Quarterly* 12:473–498 (1995).

[43] *Ibid.*

[44] Angela Browne, *When Battered Women Kill* (Simon and Schuster: The Free Press, 1987).

[45] Deborah R. Baskin and Ira B. Sommers, *Casualties of Community Disorder*.

[46] *Ibid.*

46   Chapter Two

[47] Darrell Steffensmeier and Dana L. Haynie, "Structural Sources of Urban Female Violence in the United States: A Macrosocial Gender-Disaggregated Analysis of Adult and Juvenile Homicide Offending Rates," *Homicide Studies*, 4:107–134 (2000).

[48] Otto Pollak, *The Criminality of Women* (Philadelphia: University of Pennsylvania Press, 1950).

[49] Dorie Klein, "The Etiology of Female Crime."

[50] Jeffrey Fagan, "Women and Drugs Revisited: Female Participation in the Cocaine Economy," *Journal of Drug Issues* 24:179–225 (1994); James A. Inciardi and Anne Pottieger, "Crack Cocaine Use and Street Crime," *Journal of Drug Issues* 24:273–292 (1994); Candace Kruttschnitt, "Gender and Violence, in Clair M. Renzetti and Lynne Goodstein, eds., *Women, Crime and Criminal Justice* (Los Angeles: Roxbury Publishing Company, 2001), 77–92.

[51] Kathleen Daly, "Women's Pathways to Felony Court: Feminist Theories of Lawbreaking and Problems of Representation," *Southern California Review of Law and Women's Studies* 2:11–52 (1992).

[52] Clair E. Sterk, *Fast Lives: Women Who Use Crack Cocaine* (Philadelphia: Temple University Press, 1999).

[53] Meda Chesney-Lind, "Girls' Crime and Woman's Place: Toward a Feminist Model of Female Delinquency," *Crime and Delinquency* 35:5 (1987); Meda Chesney-Lind and Noelie Rodriguez, "Women Under Lock and Key: A View from the Inside, *The Prison Journal* 63:47–65 (1983).

[54] Regina Arnold, "Women of Color: Processes of Victimization and Criminalization of Black Women," *Social Justice* 17:153–156 (1990); Meda Chesney-Lind, *The Female Offender: Girls, Women and Crime* (Thousand Oaks, CA: Sage, 1997); Meda Chesney-Lind and Noelie Rodriguez, "Women Under Lock and Key."

[55] Kathleen Daly and Meda Chesney-Lind, "Feminism and Criminology," *Justice Quarterly* 5:497–535 (1988); Barbara Owen, *"In the Mix": Struggle and Survival in a Women's Prison* (Albany: State University of New York Press, 1998).

[56] Barbara Owen, *"In the Mix."*

[57] Cathy S. Widom, "Childhood Sexual Abuse and Its Criminal Consequences," *Society* 33:47–53 (1996).

[58] Susan M. Crimmins, Sandra C. Langley, Henry B. Brownstein, and Barry J. Spunt, "Convicted Women Who Have Killed Children: A Self-Psychological Perspective," *Journal of Interpersonal Violence* 12:49–69 (1997).

[59] Angela Browne, *When Battered Women Kill.*

[60] *Ibid.*

[61] *Ibid.*

[62] Nancy Chodorow, *The Reproduction of Mothering* (Berkeley: University of California Press, 1978).

[63] Carol Gilligan, *In a Different Voice: Psychological Theory and Women's Development* (Cambridge, MA: Harvard University Press, 1982).

[64] Angela Browne, *When Battered Women Kill.*

[65] *Ibid.*

[66] *Ibid.*

[67] *Ibid.*

[68] Beth E. Richie, *Compelled to Crime: The Gender Entrapment of Battered Black Women* (New York: Routledge, 1996).

[69] *Ibid.*

[70] *Ibid.*, 107.

[71] *Ibid.*, 110.

[72] Richard F. Mancuso and Brenda Miller, "Crime and Punishment in the Lives of Women Alcohol and Other Drug (AOD) Users."

[73] Eleanor M. Miller, *Street Woman.*

[74] Richard F. Mancuso and Brenda Miller, "Crime and Punishment in the Lives of Women Alcohol and Other Drug (AOD) Users."

[75] Eleanor M. Miller, *Street Woman*, 137.

[76] Richard F. Mancuso and Brenda Miller, "Crime and Punishment in the Lives of Women Alcohol and Other Drug (AOD) Users."

[77] Ngaire Naffine, *Female Crime: The Construction of Women in Criminology* (Winchester, MA: Allen & Unwin, 1987).

[78] Darrell Steffensmeier and Cathy Streifel, "Time Series Analysis of the Female Percentage of Arrests for Property Crimes, 1960–1985: A Test of Alternative Explanations," *Justice Quarterly* 9:77–104 (1992).

[79] Barbara Owen, *"In the Mix."*

[80] *Ibid.*

[81] Kathleen Daly, "Gender and Varieties of White-Collar Crime," *Criminology* 27:769–797 (1989).

[82] Judith M. Collins and Michael D. Collins, *Female Frauds in the Corporate Suite: Biodata and Personality Predictors.* Paper presented at the Annual Conference of the American Psychological, Boston, 1999.

[83] *Ibid.*

[84] *Ibid.*; Judith M. Collins, *Integrity in the Executive Suite: Leaders Who Lie, Cheat and Steal.* Paper presented at the Academy of Management Annual Conference, 1999.

[85] *Ibid.*

[86] Jody Miller, "Up It Up: Gender and the Accomplishment of Street Robbery," *Criminology* 36:37–66 (1998).

[87] Kathleen Daly, "Women's Pathways to Felony Court."

3 |||||

Sentencing Women to Prison

Despite the large number of women who are brought before the court for breaking the law, there has been no research on their view of plea bargaining or trial, conviction, and sentencing. The published literature is largely silent on how women see and experience going to court, whether they think it is fair, or how court processing affects them. Our knowledge of gender and sentencing is limited to theory and research focused on decision making about the type and severity of sanction. We have models and descriptions to explain the behavior of judges and others who are actors in the justice system, but we can only imagine how the process looks and feels to the women who go through it.

The narrow literature that we do have on women in criminal court is dominated by reports on tests of statistical models of the variables related to sentencing outcomes. There is a smaller literature on predictors of the outcome of charge (plea) bargaining and on the recommendations and content of presentencing reports. Contrary to the common problem of decontextualized research subjects, the literature on the court experience of women offenders is characterized by a focus on the context around women offenders in court. What is missing is attention to the perceptions and feelings and experiences of those offenders as they pass through the court system when bail is set, during preliminary hearings, during presentence investigations, and in their interaction with attorneys. The apparatus and machinations of

48

the court context are described, but the offenders themselves are essentially absent. Prediction models of decision outcomes present a very limited number of characteristics (such as race, class, and type of offense); the quantitative analysis focuses on whether these variables predict if the women will be sentenced to prison and if they are, the length of the sentence. This information reveals little about the women's social location. Rather, it is linked with the responses of people working in the justice system. The actions of women offenders in trying to influence decisions made about them and/or their reactions to what happens to them during court processing have been ignored.

The lack of research on women during the sentencing process is consistent with the silencing effect that the legal process often has on defendants. Several people, including lawyers and experts, present offenders to the judge and sometimes to a jury. They often repackage a woman's experiences to make them the basis for a legal defense or a justification for arguments for or against leniency. The result can be a contribution to "the muting, distortion or elimination of a particular woman's story."[1]

Beaman analyzed how discourses in the courtroom—for example, stereotypic portrayals of postpartum depression as a defense for harming a child, premenstrual syndrome as a defense for violence, and battered women's syndrome as a defense for harming the batterer—can work against the interests of some women. The first two of these defenses, which emphasize biological predispositions, can negatively label women as inferior and as driven by their biology. These defenses can perpetuate an erroneous assumption that if some women are negatively affected by gender-linked hormones, all women are so affected. The defense of battered women's syndrome can work against women who fail to act consistently with its predictors. Thus, women often find themselves presented to court officials and the jury as members of a gender group with uniform experiences; this denies their unique situations and can result in negative decisions about them in the end.

In the absence of research or theory relevant to the standpoint of women in criminal court, this chapter will focus on the complexities of how decisions are made and the reasons for these complexities. We also will provide some discussion of probable and potential meaning and effects of going to court on women offenders.

LEGAL DEFENSE

If women are unable to afford an attorney, they are represented by either court-appointed or public defenders; if they have financial means, they hire private defense attorneys. Not unexpectedly in light of women's limited financial resources, most of the women who are in prison have been represented by court-appointed or public defenders. There are great disparities in the quality of representation for indigent women and men before the criminal courts, with poor quality representation especially characteristic of areas that use a non-competitive bid process to select defenders for indigent offenders. In courts with such a process, judges essentially contract with attorneys for the indigent, and there may be no effective procedure for guaranteeing quality defense. Aside from the general sense that legal defense will vary dramatically in quality depending on the location of the court, there is almost no information on how women offenders navigate and manage (or fail to manage) in the defense system, or on how attorneys understand and react to the women they defend. Given women offenders' myriad gender-related circumstances and characteristics (chapter 2), how do their legal defenders go about providing them adequate defense and, if they are found guilty, adequate counsel and advocacy during the sentencing process? Do restorative justice processes or drug courts take into account unique circumstances and characteristics of women offenders?

Despite the lack of information on the process of obtaining and interacting with defense attorneys, there is some research evidence of the outcomes of the legal defense that women receive. A study published in 1985 revealed that men and women had similar rates of innocent pleas, but men pleaded guilty to a reduced charge nearly twice as often as women.[2] Both women and men bargained more when their charges were serious; however, women's less serious crimes resulted in less bargaining, and their attorneys presented weaker defenses. Additionally, men (but not women) who pleaded guilty were rewarded with more lenient sentences. In a sense, the system was set up so that people with the most serious offenses benefitted the most from plea bargaining. This disadvantaged women, whose offenses were usually less serious. A lack of legal resources for women compared to men placed them at even more of a disadvantage. At least in some locations, women have gender-specific experiences with legal defense and with the courts during the charge and sentence bargaining processes, and those experiences increase their chances of incarceration.

THE PRESENTENCE REPORT

The presentence report is typically prepared by probation or other specialized staff at the court, and sometimes includes a psychiatric, psychological, or other evaluation. Its primary purpose is to provide information and a recommendation that a judge can use in arriving at a sentencing decision. The influence of presentence reports on the sentencing of women has been studied primarily outside of the United States. In Australia, presentence reports presented women who committed violent or drug offenses as more pathological than similar men, but also as more readily rehabilitated; as a result, judges sentenced the women more leniently.[3] Research in New Zealand showed that women's criminality was seen mainly as a result of psychological disturbance, but the evidence of psychological dysfunction was weak or questionable.[4] A study in Great Britain similarly found that presentence reports did not appear to discriminate based on race or ethnicity, but there was quite a bit of difference in how women and men were described.[5] Explanations for the offending of women more often relied on emotional stress and depression. Just one study has considered the influence of presentence reports on sentencing outcomes for women offenders. That study concluded that the presentence reports could have a biasing effect against racial groups and for aboriginal women in Australia.

THE LEGACY OF SEX-BASED DISCRIMINATION IN SENTENCING

Prior to the 1970s, the courts considered it acceptable that judges would sentence women differently than men. In 1963, the President's Commission on the Status of Women issued the following statement:

> Since the Commission is convinced that the U.S. Constitution now embodies equality of rights for men and women, we conclude that a constitutional amendment need not now be sought in order to establish this principle. But judicial clarification is imperative in order that remaining ambiguities with respect to constitutional protection of women's rights be eliminated.[6]

This statement provided the motivation for those who were actively seeking to challenge legally sanctioned sex-based discrimination.[7]

As will be discussed in chapter 6, although the first all-women prisons emphasized reform rather than punishment, many of the efforts to improve conditions backfired and resulted in women receiving harsher treatment or being subjected to more severe prison regimes in comparison to men. For instance, despite campus and cottage style architecture that seemed less oppressive than the fortress-like buildings in prisons for men, women's reformatories continued to produce oppressive environments in the name of instituting treatment.[8] As Rafter noted,

> . . . women's reformatories ignored a fundamental principle of justice, according to which the punishment should fit the crime. Those who lobbied for reformatories maintained that it was quite proper to ignore the rule of proportionality because their aim was not to punish but to treat—to retrain and reform, processes that required time. But in light of the concept of proportionality, up-to-three (or however many) years was a high price to pay for minor offenses. Second, women's reformatories were harsher because

they punished women more severely than men who had committed
the same offenses. Custodial prisons were more evenhanded: they
held men and women convicted of similar crimes.[9]

The establishment of sex-segregated prisons has been associated with
discriminatory, sex-specific sentencing laws; sentencing laws reflected
this "reforming" ideology by emphasizing the differences between
women and men offenders.

The belief was that women were more responsive to rehabilitation
and would, therefore, benefit from an indeterminate sentencing
approach that allowed them to be treated until they were deemed
rehabilitated. Consistent with this view, the courts upheld different
sentencing practices based on the rationale that there were sex differences.[10] For instance, in *The State of Kansas v. Heitman* (105 Kan.
139; 181 P. 630, 1919), the Kansas Supreme Court, arguing that there
were gender-related physical and psychological differences, upheld a
statute that allowed the courts to sentence women to indeterminate
sentences (see illustration 3-1).

**Illustration 3-1 Rationale for Differential Sentencing
for Women Offenders**

The following is taken from *State of Kansas v. Heitman* case,
which illustrates the rationale for different sentencing practices
between male and female offenders:

It required no anatomist, or physiologist, or psychologist, or psychiatrist, to tell the legislature that women are different from
men. In structure and function, human beings are still as they
were in the beginning—"Male and female created He them." It is
a patent and deep-lying fact that these fundamental anatomical
and physiological differences affect the whole psychic organization. They create the differences in personality between men and
women, and personality is the predominating factor in delinquent
careers. It was inevitable that, in the ages during which woman
has been bearer of the race, her unique and absolutely personal
experiences, from the time of conception to the time when developed to be embraced by the term womanhood. Woman enters
spheres of sensation, perception, emotion, desire, knowledge, and
experience, of an intensity and of a kind which man cannot know.
Her individualities and peculiarities are fostered by education
and by social custom—whether false and artificial or not is of no
consequence here—and the result is a feminine type radically different from the masculine type, which demands special consideration in the study and treatment of nonconformity to law.

Source: *The State of Kansas v. Heitman*, 105 Kan. 139; 181 P. 630 (1919).

Another well-known example of discriminatory sentencing practices that were sanctioned by the courts was the Pennsylvania Act of July 25, 1913, P.L. 1311, known as the "Muncy Act."[11] Under the Muncy Act, Pennsylvania established the State Industrial Home for Women. The sentencing judge was required to appropriate a general sentence to women convicted of offenses punishable by more than one year of imprisonment, to appropriate a three-year sentence if the maximum allowed by law was three years or less, or to fix the term at the maximum allowable where the permissible term was longer than three years. One untenable effect of the Muncy Act was that for women, but not for men, the sentencing judge had no discretion to give a sentence less than the maximum or to give a minimum sentence with parole eligibility. Another untenable effect was that most women were sent to the penitentiary at Muncy for offenses which, if committed by men, would result in a short jail term.[12]

The Muncy Act and similar statutes in other states were based on equal protection grounds.[13] On May 3, 1966, Jane Daniel was convicted of simple robbery. The trial judge sentenced her to serve one to four years in the county prison. Approximately one month later, her sentenced was vacated on the basis that it was illegal; rather, she was to be sentenced under the Muncy Act, which would require her to serve a ten-year sentence. The trial court maintained there was no reason to change the sentence; thus, the case was appealed to the Supreme Court of Pennsylvania.[14] In *Commonwealth v. Daniel* (430 Pa. 642; 243 A.2d 400, 1968) the court overturned the Muncy Act, noting that

> ... the considerations and factors which would justify a difference between men and women in matters of employment, as well as in a number of other matters, *do not govern* or justify the imposition of a longer or greater sentence of women than is imposed upon men for the commission of the same crime. In particular, we fail to discern any reasonable and justifiable difference or deterrents between men and women which would justify a man being *eligible* for a shorter maximum prison sentence than a woman for the commission of the same crime, especially if there is no material difference in their records and the relevant circumstances.

In *State of New Jersey v. Chambers* (63 N.J. 287; 307 A.3d 78, 1973), the State Supreme Court rejected the rationale that women were more amenable to rehabilitation and, therefore, required longer periods of incarceration. It was not until 1979, however, that the State of New Jersey established a new code which eliminated sex discrimination in sentencing in the criminal statutes.[15]

In *United States ex rel. Robinson v. York* (1 F.Supp 8, 1968), the federal court ruled that the Connecticut indeterminate sentencing statute was unconstitutional. As with *Chambers*, the court rejected the state argument that women's institutions were rehabilitative and, thus, required longer sentences. Specifically, the court noted that "[t]his purports to be a way of concealing the abrasive nature of imprisonment under the charming image of an educational institution. But this should not blind one to the fact that the institution is still a place of imprisonment."

During the civil rights and feminist movements in the 1960s and 1970s, state and federal task forces as well as new legislation were created to eliminate sex-based discrimination.[16] Despite resistance, most discriminatory sentencing practices were overturned in favor of sex-neutral sentencing laws.[17] Subsequently, beginning in the 1970s, many criminologists have examined whether gender-based discrimination has been eliminated in crime case processing.

EARLY EVIDENCE OF DISPARATE SENTENCING OF WOMEN AND MEN

As we noted above, research on the effect of gender in the sentencing process has generally conceptualized gender as a characteristic of the offender and viewed it as having its effect either singly or in interaction with one or a few other variables. Notions of gender as a sociological concept—that is, of gender arrangements at the societal level and of one's location within those arrangements—are largely absent. We cannot overemphasize that the available research captures only a snapshot of a particular part of women's processing through court and omits the effects of this processing on women or their view of it.

The research on sentencing outcomes has emphasized legal and extra-legal variables. Legal variables include influences that according to a just deserts framework should be taken into consideration in making the sentencing decision—notably the nature and seriousness of the crime and prior criminal history. Extra-legal factors include such things as the race and sex of the offender and victim, and a host of other social and individual characteristics, which increasingly are viewed as irrelevant to the sentencing decision now that legislation has restricted judicial discretion and emphasized punishment.

Kathleen Daly and Rebecca Bordt conducted an extensive analysis of studies that analyzed data collected in the 1970s.[18] They addressed the key questions: "What are we to make of statistical studies of gender and sentencing" and "What does this body of research show, and what can we learn from it?"[19] Of the fifty studies they examined, approximately 50 percent of the cases revealed sex effects favoring women (n=26), 25 percent demonstrated mixed effects (n=12), and the remaining 25 percent revealed no effects (n=12). Early studies of gender and sentencing explained different sanctioning outcomes as the result of extra-legal variables, but they often neglected to consider the legal factors, criminal history, and seriousness of the current offense.[20] When later research took into account the connection of criminal history and seriousness of the current offense, these legal factors explained much of the variation in sentencing outcome that had been attributed to gender differences.

Crew summarized several different hypotheses that have been used to identify the independent variables that might predict differing sentencing outcomes for women and men (see table 3-1).

The hypotheses identified by Crew provide a useful scheme for categorizing existing research, but it should be noted that they are largely detached from any broader theory of how individuals think about or interact with women offenders or others in the court setting, or subsequently how people arrive at their judgments about women and the sentences they should receive. Rather, the hypotheses do little more than specify one or a few variables that are expected to be statistically related to sentence outcome.

Table 3-1   Summary of Hypotheses Concerning Gender and Criminal Sanctions

Hypothesis	Predicting Sentencing of Female Offenders Compared to Males	Intervening or Conditional Factors
Chivalry/paternalism	Less severe	(Male) legal officials label women as less dangerous and culpable than men.
Evil woman	More severe	(Male) legal officials label women as more dangerous than men.
Combined	Varies with crime	Women receive leniency unless their crimes violate sex role expectations.
Dependency	Varies by status	Women who are economically dependent on a man are treated more leniently, especially if they have dependent children.
Legal model	Similar (after offense type is controlled)	Women committing less serious crimes have less serious criminal records than men.

Source: B. Keith Crew, "Sex Differences in Criminal Sentencing: Chivalry or Patriarchy?" *Justice Quarterly* 8:62 (1991).

In chapter 1, we discussed the difference between "chivalry" and "paternalism." Generally, chivalrous treatment involves placing a person on a pedestal and treating that person in a gallant manner; paternalistic treatment involves treating a person in a childlike and protective manner.[21] The propensity for female offenders to receive less severe criminal sanctions was traditionally explained as a demonstration of one of these predispositions on the part of the judge. Past and contemporary research on the influence of judicial paternalism and chivalry has generally assumed these predispositions from findings of more lenient treatment of women than of men, though there is a growing recognition that the process of judicial decision making may be more complex than such an assumption suggests.[22] There has been very little attention to what judges or other people who influence judicial decision making actually think; that is, whether they actually have paternalistic or chivalrous views toward women offenders. Thus, the inference that any leniency in their decisions can be attributed to their chivalry or paternalism is a quite a stretch from the available data.

According to what is called the evil woman hypothesis, illegal behavior that violates traditional gender roles results in the most severe sentencing for women. Nagel and Hagan argued that the "evil" woman and chivalry/paternalism hypotheses are complementary.[23]

> When a woman's illegal behavior is within the realm of socially acceptable sex role expectations, consistent with the chivalry/paternalism hypothesis, she will receive more lenient sentences. The potential for a more lenient sentence is even greater if the women fulfill traditional roles, like wife and mother. However, if a woman commits a crime that is outside the realm of acceptable sex role behavior, she will receive an equal or more severe sanction compared to a man committing a similar offense.[24] In this view, the courts engage not so much in chivalry as in the judicial enforcement of female sex-role expectations more harshly to female than to male behavior.[25]

Consistent with the dependency hypothesis, Kruttschnitt found that Minnesota women who fit stereotypes about being economically dependent were sentenced more leniently than others.[26] Further analysis of the same data revealed a number of other predictors of women's sentence severity. Economically disadvantaged women and women previously subject to legal control, black women convicted of either disturbing the peace or of drug law violations, and women supported by welfare were sentenced particularly severely.[27]

Decision-model testing research has continued to examine the effect of legal and other factors on sentencing. Table 3-2 presents a listing of studies that have found that the legal factors are predictive of sentence severity. In general, women before the court can expect to be treated more severely at sentencing if they have a history of delinquency and adult criminality, multiple prior arrests and convictions,

Table 3-2   Research on Legal Factors Predicting Sentencing Outcomes for Women

Criminal History	Study
Prior convictions	Bickle and Peterson (1991); Chevalier-Barrow (1992); Spohn and Spears (1997); Steffensmeier, Ulmer, and Kramer (1998); Flavin (1995); Ghali and Chesney-Lind (1986); Zingraff and Thomson (1984); Kruttschnitt (1982)
Prior arrests	Kruttschnitt (1985); Spohn and Spears (1997); Kruttschnitt and Green(1984); Ghali and Chesney-Lind (1986)
Prior drug convictions	Spohn and Spears (1997)
Juvenile record	Kruttschnitt and Green (1984)
Most serious or type of prior conviction	Bickle and Peterson (1991); Chevalier-Barrow (1992); Steffensmeier, Ulmer, and Kramer (1998); Kaukinen (1995); Flavin (1995)[28]

Source: Barbara Koons-Witt, "Gender and Justice: The Role of Gender in Sentencing Decisions in the State of Minnesota, Pre- and Post-Sentencing Guidelines." Paper presented at the annual meetings of the American Society of Criminology, San Francisco, (2000), p. 6.

and prior convictions for drug or particularly serious offenses. However, there will also be considerable difference in how they are treated related to extra-legal factors.

A great deal of research has documented that female offenders who are married or who have children receive more lenient sentences compared to males or unmarried and childless females. Some people have attributed the statistical connection of marriage and children with sentencing to the impracticality of taking women out of their families and the importance placed on maintaining the family for the welfare of the children.[29] As with many other explanations of sentencing outcomes, researchers' conclusions that the judge decided to keep a woman with her spouse and children exemplifies questionable ex post facto reasoning, without any information on the judge's actual reasoning process.

There was a tremendous advance in theory development when Daly broke with statistical model testing research and actually interviewed court officials (prosecutors, defense attorneys, probation officers, and judges).[30] Based on her interviews, she discarded chivalry and paternalism as explanations of sentencing outcomes. She discovered the importance of what she called familial paternalism (rather the female paternalism). Familial paternalism is the interest of court officials in protecting family life, keeping women involved as nurturing mothers to their children, maintaining fathers in the breadwinning role, and generally supporting people who are dependent on the offender. Her interviews revealed that court officials' family-based conception of justice was an overriding theme when considering various sanctions. Furthermore, gender-based disparities in sentencing may occur in the following manner:

> If familied men or women are jailed, social disorder may increase, bonds of economic and affective responsibilities to others may be severed, and victims, particularly children, may be punished. Differences in the treatment of familied men and women arise because familied women are thought to be "more responsible" than familied men and child care is considered more important than economic support to maintain family life.[31]

Daly corrected the failure of prior research on gender and sentencing to demonstrate the way in which the various court officials construct justice as well as rationalize their decisions.

In a study of women and men who were sentenced after forgery convictions in eight federal courts, Bickle and Peterson focused on women's place and roles in families.[32] There were variations for women in different family situations and the sentencing outcomes were not the same for black and white women. First, there were differences in women's treatment related to their marital status and living arrangements. Sentencing advantages (more lenient treatment) of being married were greater for black than for white women. White women received more severe sentences if they lived alone. Second, women with and without children were sentenced differently depending on their race. White women with dependents were treated more leniently than white women without dependents. Yet, not all black women with dependents were treated harshly. Black women who were described in presentence reports as providing higher levels of emotional support to their children also received more lenient sentences. Bickle and Peterson concluded that whereas white women are sentenced more leniently when they have dependents, "black women do not benefit from simply occupying this central family role [of having dependents]; they must perform this role well."[33]

A final example of research that supports the importance of judges' considerations of children when they make sentencing decisions is a study of men and women convicted of cocaine offenses.[34] Aside from the commonly documented strong association of severe sentences with prior convictions and drug use (and for men with seriousness of offense) judges sentenced women more leniently if they were single mothers with custody of their children or if they were women without children who lived with adult family members.

As in Bickle and Peterson's research, lenient sentencing of black women who were mothers was restricted to those who were labeled as "good mothers"—that is, those who had maintained custody of their children.

The restriction of lenient treatment to certain, but not all, women is not always connected to parental responsibilities and situations.[35] Overall, regardless of the issue of motherhood, women with minority status, especially African-American women, are not treated as leniently as are white women.[36] In light of some research that shows that race and gender influence judges to sentence at least some women particularly harshly, it is difficult to make sense of the myriad of studies that conclude that women overall are treated more leniently than men before the court. We have already pointed to the need to consider the combination, or the interaction, of race and gender of the offender in making sense of the effects of these statuses on sentencing severity.

Kathleen Daly and Michael Tonry identified problems in interpreting the literature on sentencing and gender.[37] First, if less serious white offenders are not arrested or prosecuted as frequently as their black counterparts, equal treatment of white and black defendants at sentencing is not an accurate indicator of race effects. The white offenders who appear in court may have committed qualitatively more serious offenses. Therefore, if these two already differentiated groups receive similar sentences, there has been a cumulative disadvantage for the minority offenders. Second, racial disadvantage can be incorporated into policy. For instance, possession of crack cocaine (the drug of choice of many minority offenders) results in far harsher penalties than possession of powder cocaine, which is more often sold and used by whites. Finally, quantitative research often does not capture critical differences:

> For example, suppose that male crack dealers typically dealt in larger quantities than female dealers. This might occur if men typically held higher positions in distribution networks or if more women sold small quantities to support a habit. Even a statistical analysis that controlled for many variables, including the statutory code of the conviction offense, might show that men were sentenced more harshly than women. Unless data were also available on drug quantities and on individuals' drug trafficking roles, the analysis might well (but wrongly) conclude that women were sentenced more leniently than men for these drug charges.[38]

Throughout chapter 2, we emphasized both subtle and major gender differences in the reasons people break the law. Unless these differences, which often vary by type of offense, are considered in quantitative research on gender and sentencing outcomes, and unless prior decisions about offenders and bias built into policy are considered, conclusions from research on the relationship of gender or race to sentencing outcomes can be quite misleading.

Women before the courts will be asked questions about their personal characteristics, family circumstances, responsibilities, and how well they fulfill these responsibilities during presentence investigation; the answers to these questions (and the information on these matters that is gathered from other places) will be related to sentencing outcomes. No doubt some women who go to prison are aware that they are treated differently than other women, and some (especially those with partners or friends who break the law) would know whether they are treated more or less leniently than men. It would seem that how they are treated might have some effect on how they see themselves in general and as mothers, as adult children, and as spouses or other partners in relationships, and how they think others see them in these roles. Also, their experiences of differential sentencing would contribute to their sense of justice (or injustice), and their understanding of whether they are considered valuable members of social groups (i.e., families and society in general) or as expendable.

SENTENCING REFORMS

During the 1980s and 1990s, women offenders in U.S. criminal court have been affected by dramatic changes in sentencing laws. Sentencing guidelines, mandatory sentences, and "three-strikes" laws were enacted in an effort to provide rigorous, consistent, fair, and economically efficient punishment for offenders regardless of race, ethnicity, class, or gender.[39] In 1984 the United States Sentencing Commission was created to draft Federal Sentencing Guidelines. These guidelines provided sentencing ranges determined by the current offense and associated criminal conduct of the offender as well as his or her criminal history. The guidelines also included criteria that allow the sentencing range to be increased or reduced based on certain circumstances.[40] At the state level, many states have also enacted sentencing reforms including sentencing guidelines (see table 3-3).

Acknowledging a problem of race, class, and gender discrimination in the sentencing process, both liberals and conservatives supported more uniformity in sentencing structure. Liberals contended that sentencing changes were necessary because discrimination in the criminal justice system was epidemic. Conservatives argued that changes would provide more certainty in sentencing decisions and less coddling of offenders. The coalition of liberals and conservatives resulted in the widespread adoption of reforms of different types in many states. These reforms are now criticized by some people on the grounds that discrepancies in sentencing outcomes continue for certain offenders, and that reforms have disproportionately brought women drug users into the prisons, despite their involvement in relatively minor offenses.[41]

Table 3-3   Summary of State Sentencing Guideline Systems

Jurisdiction	Effective Date	Scope and Distinctive Features
Utah	1979	voluntary; retains parole board; no permanent commission until 1983; linked to correctional resources since 1993
Alaska	01/01/80	no permanent sentencing commission; statutory guidelines' scope expanded by case law
Minnesota	05/01/80	designed not to exceed 95 percent of prison capacity; extensive data base and research
Pennsylvania	07/22/82	covers misdemeanors; retains parole board, encourages nonprison sanctions since 1994; substantially revised effective 1995
Florida	10/01/83	formerly voluntary; overhauled in 1994 and 1995
Michigan	01/17/84	voluntary; retains parole board; commission to submit guidelines to legislature in July 1996
Washington	07/01/84	includes upper limits on nonprison sanctions, some defined exchange rates, and vague, voluntary charging standards; resource-impact assessment required
Wisconsin	11/01/85	voluntary; descriptive (modeled on existing practices); retained parole board (abandoned 1995)
Delaware	10/10/87	voluntary; narrative (not grid) format; also covers misdemeanors and some nonprison sanctions; linked to resources
Oregon	11/01/89	grid includes upper limits on custodial nonprison sanctions, with some defined exchange rates; linked to resources; many new mandatory minimums added in 1994; commission abolished 1995 (but guidelines kept)
Tennessee	11/01/89	also covered misdemeanors; retains parole board; sentences linked to resources (abandoned 1995)
Virginia	1/01/91	voluntary; judicially controlled, and parole board retained, until 1995; resource-impact assessment required since 1995
Louisiana	01/01/92	includes intermediate sanction guidelines and exchange rates; linked to resources (abandoned 1995)
Kansas	07/01/93	sentences linked to resources
Arkansas	01/01/94	voluntary; detained enabling statute; resource-impact assessments required
Massachusetts	1994	commission established 1994; interim reports submitted to legislature in 1995; draft guidelines include intermediate sanctions and linked to resources

Effective Jurisdiction	Date	Scope and Distinctive Features
North Carolina	01/01/95	covers misdemeanors; sentences linked to resources; includes intermediate sanctions
Missouri	07/01/95	voluntary guidelines took effect in July 1995
Montana	1996	commission to report legislature on advisability of guidelines in May 1996
Ohio	1996	presumptive guidelines take effect July 1996; include intermediate sanctions; linked to resources; parole abolished
Oklahoma and South Carolina	(in process)	enabling statutes encourage resource matching

Source: Michael Tonry and Kathleen Hatlestad, "Sentencing Reform in the United States," in Michael Tonry and Kathleen Hatlestad, eds., *Sentencing Reform in Overcrowded Times: A Comparative Perspective* (New York: Oxford University Press, 1997), p. 14.

Criticisms of Drug Control Policies and Sentencing Reform

Criticisms of sentencing reforms extend beyond claims of gender bias to inequities based on race, especially for African Americans:[42]

> Reforms that were supposed to lead to uniform punishment instead continue to permit discretion and subsequent discrimination. Unfortunately, the current sentencing laws have not eliminated or eased problems faced by this minority group. The failure to eliminate discretion and bias, increased sentences and the criminalization of certain activities have a particularly adverse effect on African-Americans. The changes in sentencing laws have adversely affected both the African-American male and female populations, albeit in different ways.[43]

Specifically, the "war on drugs" has greatly increased an African-American woman's likelihood of incarceration. There has been increased emphasis on street-level drugs (cocaine, crack, heroin) and the use of the same punishments for people involved in conspiracy to distribute drugs as for those who control the criminal enterprise. The result of these policies is that the majority of women incarcerated for drug offenses have used drugs in places that are heavily policed and public, and that are associated with men who are involved in the drug market.[44] This places African-American women, and to a lesser extent Hispanic women, at increased risk for incarceration.

Sentencing reform on the federal level sought to eliminate consideration of children at the point of sentencing.[45] As we discussed in chapter

2, an overwhelming number of female offenders are the primary care-takers of their children. A policy statement, issued in conjunction with the Federal Sentencing Guidelines, noted that family responsibilities are not "ordinarily relevant" when deciding to reduce mandatory sentences. An incarcerated woman is more likely to lose custody of her children if she is the primary caretaker; an incarcerated man will most likely have the mother of his children retain custody. Thus, sentencing reforms have not only affected female offenders, but they can also have a negative influence on their dependents.[46]

Pregnancy is also covered in the reformed Federal Sentencing Guidelines, which include the statement that an individual's physical condition is not ordinarily reason for a more lenient sentence than the guidelines specify. While some states have made provisions for the special needs and situation of pregnant offenders, the federal guidelines do not encourage this. Thus, the Federal Sentencing Guidelines lessen the opportunity for judges to impose probation, residence in a half-way house, or other alternative forms of incarceration that might allow the pregnant mother to establish and maintain a bond with her child.[47]

Despite official guidelines, some judges do consider differences between female and male offenders. The Advisory Committee of the Ninth Circuit Gender Bias Task Force reported that out of the 1,541 departures for a downward sentence, 4.3 percent (n=66) were for family responsibilities.[48] When comparing departures for female and male offenders during another time period, the Committee's report revealed that out of 378 departures women received, 17 percent (n=63) were for family responsibilities; out of the 1,443 departures men received, 3 percent (n=49) were for family responsibilities. Specifically,

> . . . women offenders were 30% more likely to have custody of their children than male offenders before incarceration, and . . . children are more likely to go without either parent if the mother is incarcerated. These statistics show that few departures are granted for family reasons, that women are more adversely impacted by the current FSG [Federal Sentencing Guidelines] by nature of their being primary caretakers.[49]

White female offenders received 45 percent of these departures; however, as mentioned in chapter 2, women of color make up approximately two-thirds of the prison population.[50] Thus, white women received almost half of the departures for family responsibilities but make up just one-third of the female prison population. The pattern is similar to the harsher treatment of women of color compared to other women with children.[51] Although the sentencing guidelines were intended to eliminate sentencing disparity, women of color continue to experience the more punitive aspects of these sentencing reform efforts.

A study of sentencing in Chicago, Miami and Kansas City also showed that in certain court jurisdictions gender, particularly in combination with other things, was connected to leniency after the institution of sentencing reforms.[52] Offense type and seriousness are most strongly related to sentencing outcomes for men, though they also are related for women. In Kansas City, women with dependent children were less likely than others, all other things being similar, to be sent to prison.

Overall, studies of both state and federal systems affected by guidelines have revealed that even after the implementation of various sentencing reform policies, an offender's gender continues to influence his or her sentencing outcome in some court jurisdictions.[53] For instance, in an evaluation of the Federal Sentencing Guidelines, Celesta Albonetti's study revealed that among drug offenders, sentencing disparity was associated not only to offense-related factors but also with legally irrelevant factors such as race/ethnicity, gender, and noncitizenship.[54] Darrell Steffensmeier and his colleagues examined sentencing guideline data from Pennsylvania.[55] Their study showed that women were favored in the context of judges' decisions to depart from the guidelines; the primary justifications for these departures included a nonviolent prior record, a mental or health problem, parental responsibilities, a minor role in the current offense, and a demonstration of remorse. Barbara Koons-Witt compared the sentencing outcomes for drug offenders in the state of Minnesota before and after the implementation of sentencing guidelines in 1980. Even after the implementation of these guidelines, gender continued to be a significant predictor of sentencing decisions.[56]

Equal *versus* Special Treatment at Sentencing

There are distinctions between equality for women and men who have broken the law and justice for women. Chesney-Lind and Pollock highlighted the differences in a description of three positions on whether equality under the law necessarily benefits women, and thereby promotes justice.[57] The first position is that women are best protected by efforts to ensure that they are treated in the same way as are men, for even differential treatment based on concern for women's special needs would set a precedent for inequalities that in the long run harm women as a whole. An opposing argument is that since women do have special needs and characteristics, they should be treated differently than men, with the stipulation that the differential treatment does not disadvantage them. A more radical alternative to either of these positions is to recognize that the law is itself unjust if men are always the standard.

Some advocates for women offenders have argued for equal treatment of women and men at the point of sentencing. They believe that although women and men do differ, special treatment is problematic because the laws that were intended to protect women have usually oppressed them.[58] The argument for equal treatment is that

[s]pecial treatment of women in sentencing potentially undermines the strong principles of justice and equity that animate contemporary notions of blameworthiness and proportionality.
Moreover, a special treatment approach to criminal sentencing
should trouble feminists, because it perpetuates damaging stereotypes of female weakness, implying a moral inferiority that undermines claims to full citizenship and even personhood. The
blameworthiness that supports notions of proportional punishment implies a recognition of the full moral agency of the offender.
Society believes that it is inappropriate to punish the very young
or the insane, because, unlike responsible adults, they cannot be
expected to conform their behavior to the norms of the law. Only
those fully capable of understanding criminal norms and conforming their behavior to those norms are fit subjects for punishment.
Thus, when women are granted special treatment, they are
reduced to the moral status of infants. [59]

Nagel and Johnson, who take the equal treatment position, maintain
that a gender specific or responsive approach to sentencing in a criminal justice context raises fundamental ideas of moral autonomy that
are not at issue when discussing such issues as equal treatment in
employment rules or insurance benefits.

Advocates for special treatment at sentencing maintain that the
differences between women and men can only be adequately
addressed within a special needs and circumstances—not an equality—framework. The gender-responsive approach is that while the
justice system should be fair and not sentence people based on gender
stereotypes, it does need to consider particular circumstances.[60]

It is not clear why taking the offender's situation into account will
necessarily result in her being treated as a child. It is not a weakness
or evidence of childlikeness to be supported in efforts to care for dependent children, for example. The larger question, though, is whether the
justice system is equipped or able to take gender-related considerations into account during the sentencing process. Sentencing guidelines in some states allow for greater consideration of rehabilitation,
which gives judges more discretion.[61] At least in some states, legislation allows consideration of women's needs and circumstances in sentencing. Sentences that provide women with opportunities to
participate in programs that empower them, build their resources, or
allow them to continue roles as parents or in other positive relationships would not be infantilizing.

Advocates of the position that the law itself is unjust if men are
the standard argue for a radical change in the existing legal system.
Justice requires that the norm for a legal individual (that is, a person
to whom the law is applicable) is a woman in a typical situation, for
example, a pregnant woman or a mother, and the law and court decisions would be formed so as to be just for such a person, but not unjust

for others.[62] This last approach certainly provokes considerations of how law would develop differently if women were equivalently or more advantaged than men.

CONCLUSION

The very limited focus of available research narrows any examination of women's experience in court to a primary emphasis on predictors of sentencing outcomes. Historically, gender was considered to be a legally relevant factor when deciding criminal sanctions. When this sentencing strategy was in effect, women usually had harsher sentences compared to men who had broken the law. Subsequently, legislatures enacted statutory changes that resulted in gender being deemed a legally irrelevant factor. Even with these legislative changes, gender continued to be a predictor of sentencing outcomes.

Various hypotheses have been tested in order to build some understanding of gender-based differences in sentencing outcomes. Most recently, it has become clear that women with particular combinations of family characteristics (e.g., primary caretaker, marital status, pregnancy) and racial status will have different outcomes when they are sentenced, even if their offenses and criminal histories are similar. In part to address the issue of sentencing disparity due to these extralegal variables, and also to promote a "just deserts" approach to judicial decision making, national and state policymakers have enacted sentencing reforms. Yet, gender continues to be a predictor of departures from legally mandated sentencing length.

The last section of this chapter considered alternative feminist perspectives on ideal decision-making approaches for deciding on a punishment and/or rehabilitation for women before the court. Alternative conclusions by people who start with the premise that oppression and the resulting unequal status of women that permeates U.S. society may seem paradoxical at first glance. Some feminists argue that gender oppression is reduced by treating women in the same way as men are treated; others argue that it is reduced by paying attention to women's special needs. It is important to recognize, however, that treating men and women as equals does not necessarily mean treating them in the exact same way. There are both blatant and subtle differences in the crimes that women and men typically commit. As we will explain in chapter 8, some types of programs in some types of settings (prison, detention other than prison, or community corrections) are particularly promising for women offenders, and different than programs designed for men. Taking gender differences relevant to criminal involvement and motivation as well as rehabilitation potential into account can make sentencing more just for women and can result in sentences that are more likely to empower them and offer opportunities for taking responsibility for themselves and for others than if they were treated just like men.

What seems to be missing most in our understanding of women in court and the process that brings them from court into prison is any sense of the women themselves. Do they feel that they are being treated chivalrously, paternalistically, or as children? How do they see efforts to detect and respond to mental health concerns during the pre-sentencing investigation? Are they satisfied with their legal representation, and do they think that they are treated fairly by the courts, or do they feel that they are being stereotyped based on gender, race, ethnicity, or other characteristics? How do women of different races, ethnic groups, ages, and social classes see and experience court involvement differently? It would seem that the answers to these questions would be necessary to draw sound conclusions about whether sentencing is just.

ENDNOTES

[1] Lori G. Beaman, "Women's Defences: Contextualizing Dilemmas of Difference and Power," *Women and Criminal Justice* 9:87–115 (1998).

[2] Josefina Figueira-McDonough, "Gender Differences in Informal Processing: A Look at Charge Bargaining and Sentence Reduction in Washington, DC," *Journal of Research in Crime and Delinquency* 22:101–133 (1985).

[3] M. Wilkie, *Sentencing Women: Pre-Sentence Reports and Constructions of Female Offenders* (Nedland, WA, Australia: University of Western Australia Crime Research Center, 1993).

[4] Deane Heather, "The Influence of Presentence Reports on Sentencing in a District Court in New Zealand," *Australian and New Zealand Journal of Criminology* 33:91–106 (2000).

[5] Loraine Gelsthorpe, "Social Inquiry Reports: Race and Gender Considerations" *Research Bulletin* 32:17–22 (1992).

[6] President's Commission on the Status of Women, American Women Executive Order No. 10,980, 3 C.F.R. 138 (Washington, DC: U.S. Government Printing Office, 1963).

[7] Carolyn Engel Temin, "Discriminatory Sentencing of Women Offenders: The Argument for ERA in a Nutshell," in Susan K. Datesman and Frank R. Scarpitti, eds., Women, Crime, and Justice (New York: Oxford University Press, 1980), 255.

[8] Joanne Belknap, *The Invisible Woman: Gender, Crime, and Justice*, 2nd ed., (Belmont, CA: Wadsworth Publishing, 2001).

[9] Nicole Hahn Rafter, *Partial Justice: Women, Prisons, and Social Control*, 2nd ed. (New Brunswick, NJ: Transaction Publishers, 1990), 41.

[10] Joycelyn M. Pollock-Byrne, *Women, Prison, & Crime*, 2nd ed. (Pacific Grove, CA: Brooks/Cole Publishing Company, 2002), 154.

[11] Carolyn Engel Temin, "Discriminatory Sentencing of Women Offenders," 258–261.

[12] Lawrence Bershad, "Discriminatory Treatment of the Female Offender in the Criminal Justice System," *Boston College Law Review* 26:399 (1985).

[13] *Ibid.*

[14] Carolyn Engel Temin, "Discriminatory Sentencing of Women Offenders," 261.

[15] Clarice Feinman, "Criminal Codes, Criminal Justice and Female Offenders: New Jersey as a Case Study" in Imogene L. Moyer, ed., *The Changing Roles of Women in the Criminal Justice System: Offenders, Victims, and Professionals*, 2nd ed., (Prospect Heights, IL: Waveland Press, 1992), 61.

[16] *Ibid.*

[17] Joanne Belknap, *The Invisible Woman*, 131.

[18] Kathleen Daly and Rebecca L. Bordt, "Sex Effects and Sentencing: An Analysis of the Statistical Literature," *Justice Quarterly* 12:141–175 (1995).

[19] *Ibid.*, 142.

[20] Barbara Koons-Witt, "Gender and Justice: The Role of Gender in Sentencing Decisions in the State of Minnesota, Pre- and Post-Sentencing Guidelines." Paper presented at the annual meetings of the American Society of Criminology, San Francisco, 2000.

[21] Joanne Belknap, *The Invisible Woman*, 131–132.

[22] Barbara Koons-Witt, "Gender and Justice."

[23] Ilene H. Nagel and John Hagan, "Gender and Crime: Offense Patterns and Criminal Court Sanctions," in Norval Morris and Michael Tonry, eds., *Crime and Justice*, vol. 4 (Chicago: University of Chicago Press, 1983), 91–144.

[24] B. Keith Crew, "Sex Differences in Criminal Sentencing: Chivalry or Patriarchy?" *Justice Quarterly* 8:60 (1991).

[25] Lee H. Bowker, *Women, Crime, and the Criminal Justice System* (Lexington, MA: Lexington Books, 1978), 216–217.

[26] Candace Kruttschnitt, "Women, Crime and Dependency—An Application of the Theory of Law" *Criminology* 19:495–513 (1982), 221.

[27] Candace Kruttschnitt, "Social Status and the Sentences of Female Offenders," *Law and Society Review* 15:247–265.

[28] Gayle S. Bickle and Ruth D. Peterson, "The Impact of Gender-Based Family Roles on Criminal Sentencing," *Social Problems* 38:372–394 (1991); M. Chevalier-Barrow, "Gender and Sentencing: An Investigation of Prior Record, Current Offense, Family Status and Sociodemographic Characteristics," Unpublished doctoral dissertation, Fordham University (1992); Cassia Spohn and Jeffrey Spears, "Gender and Sentencing of Drug Offenders," paper presented at the 1997 Annual Meetings of the American Society of Criminology, San Diego, CA (1997); Darrell Steffensmeier, Jeffrey Ulmer, and John Kramer, "The Interaction of Race, Gender, and Age in Criminal Sanctioning: The Punishment Cost of Being Young, Black, and Male," *Criminology* 36:763–793 (1998); Jeanne M. Flavin, "Of Punishment and Parenthood: The Relationship Between Family-Based Social Control and Sentencing," unpublished doctoral dissertation, American University (1995); Moheb Ghali and Meda Chesney-Lind, "Gender Bias and the Criminal Justice System: An Empirical Investigation," *Sociology and Social Research* 70:164–171 (1986); Matthew Zingraff and Randall Thomson, "Differential Sentencing of Women and Men in the U.S.A."; Candace Kruttschnitt, "Respectable Women and the Law," *The Sociological Quarterly* 23:221–234; Candace Kruttschnitt, "Legal Outcomes and Legal Agents: Adding Another Dimension to the Sex-Sentencing Controversy," *Law and Human Behavior* 9:287–303; Candace Kruttschnitt and Donald E. Green, "The Sex-Sanctioning Issue: Is it History?" *American Sociological Review* 49:541–551 (1984); C. E. Kaukinen, "Women Lawbreakers Constructed in Terms of Traditional Definitions of Feminism: The Sentencing of Women in Conflict with the Law," unpublished master's thesis, University of Windsor, Ontario, Canada (1995).

[29] Gayle S. Bickle and Ruth D. Peterson, "The Impact of Gender-Based Family Roles on Criminal Sentencing," 373.

[30] Kathleen Daly, "Structure and Practice of Familial-Based Justice in a Criminal Court," *Law and Society Review* 21:267–290 (1987).

[31] *Ibid.*, 286–287.

[32] Gayle S. Bickle and Ruth D. Peterson, "The Impact of Gender-Based Family Roles on Criminal Sentencing," 372–373.

[33] *Ibid.*, 388.

[34] Jeanne Flavin, "Of Punishment and Parenthood: Family-based Social Control and the Sentencing of Black Drug Offenders" *Gender and Society*: 15:611–633 (2001).

[35] Joanne Belknap, *The Invisible Woman*, 135.

[36] Biko Agozino, *Black Women and the Criminal Justice System* (Aldershot, England: Ashgate Publishing Company, 1997); Gayle S. Bickle and Ruth D. Peterson, "The Impact of Gender-Based Family Roles on Criminal Sentencing"; Marvin Krohn, James P. Curry, and Shirley Nelson-Kilger, "Is Chivalry Dead? An Analysis of Changes in Police Dispositions of Males and Females," *Criminology* 21:417–437; Candace Kruttschnitt, "Social Status and Sentences of Female Offenders"; Darrell Steffensmeier, John Kramer, and Cathy Streifel, "Gender and Imprisonment Decisions," *Criminology* 31:411–443.

[37] Kathleen Daly and Michael Tonry, "Gender, Race, and Sentencing," *Crime and Justice* 22:233–235 (1997).

[38] *Ibid.*, 231.

[39] Christopher M. Alexander, "Crushing Equality: Gender Equal Sentencing in America," *Gender & Law* 6:200 (1997); Richard S. Frase, "Sentencing Guidelines are 'Alive and Well' in the United States," in Michael Tonry and Kathleen Hatlestad, eds., *Sentencing Reform in Overcrowded Times: A Comparative Perspective* (New York: Oxford University Press, 1997), 12–17; P.M. Ditton and D.J. Wilson, *Truth in Sentencing in State Prisons* (Washington DC: Bureau of Justice Statistics, 1999).

[40] Christopher M. Alexander, "Crushing Equality: Gender Equal Sentencing in America," 201–202.

[41] *Ibid.*, 205.

[42] David B. Mustard, "Racial, Ethnic, and Gender Disparities in Sentencing: Evidence from the U.S. Federal Courts," *Law and Economics* 44:285–312 (2001).

[43] Christopher M. Alexander, "Crushing Equality: Gender Equal Sentencing in America," 214.

[44] Katherine Van Wormer and Clemens Bartollas. *Women and the Criminal Justice System* (Boston: Allyn & Bacon, 2000).

[45] Havey Wallace and Shanda Wedlock, "Federal Sentencing Guidelines and Gender Issues: Parental Responsibilities, Pregnancy, and Domestic Violence," *San Diego Justice Journal* 2:395–427 (1994).

[46] *Ibid.*; see also Leslie Acoca and Myrna S. Raeder, "Severing Family Ties: The Plight of Nonviolent Female Offenders and Their Children," *Stanford Law and Policy Review* 11:133–144 (1999).

[47] *Ibid.*, 408.

[48] *The Preliminary Report of the Ninth Circuit Gender Bias Task Force: Discussion Draft* (1992), 165.

[49] Havey Wallace and Shanda Wedlock, "Federal Sentencing Guidelines and Gender Issues," 412.

[50] *Ibid.*

[51] Gayle S. Bickle and Ruth D. Peterson, "The Impact of Gender-Based Family Roles on Criminal Sentencing."

[52] Cassia Spohn and Dawn Beichner, "Is Preferential Treatment of Female Offenders a Thing of the Past? A Multisite Study of Gender, Race, and Imprisonment," *Criminal Justice Policy Review* 11:149–184 (2000).

[53] Barbara Koons-Witt, "Gender and Justice," 12.

[54] Celesta A. Albonetti, "Sentencing Under the Federal Sentencing Guidelines: Effects of Defendant Characteristics, Guilty Please, and Departures on Sentence Outcomes for Drug Offenses, 1991–1992," *Law & Society Review* 31:789–819 (1997).

[55] Darrell Steffensmeier, John Kramer, and Cathy Streifel, "Gender and Imprisonment Decisions"; see also John H. Kramer and Jeffery T. Ulmer, "Sentencing Disparity and Departures from Guidelines," *Justice Quarterly* 13:81–105 (1996); Darrell Steffensmeier, Jeffrey Ulmer, and John Kramer, "The Interaction of Race, Gender, and Age in Criminal Sanctioning."

[56] Barbara Koons-Witt, "Gender and Justice," 7.

[57] Meda Chesney-Lind and Joycelyn Pollock, "Women's prisons: Equality with a vengeance," In M. V. Merlo and Joycelyn M. Pollock, eds., *Women, Law & Social Control.* (Boston: Allyn & Bacon, 1995), 156–157.

[58] Ilene H. Nagel and Barry L. Johnson, "Gender Issues and the Criminal Law: The Role of Gender in a Structured Sentencing System," *Journal of Crime and Criminology* 85:194 (1994).

[59] *Ibid.*, 197.

[60] Myrna S. Raeder, "Gender and Sentencing: Single Moms, Battered Women, and Other Sex-Based Anomalies in the Gender-Free World of Sentencing Guidelines," *Pepperdine Law Review* 20:905–909 (1993); Meda Chesney-Lind and Joycelyn Pollack, "Women's Prisons: Equality with a Vengeance," in M. V. Merlo and J. M. Pollack (Eds.), *Women, Law, & Social Control.* Boston: Allyn & Bacon, 1995. 155–175.

[61] Darrell Steffensmeier, Jeffery Ulmer and John Kramer, "The Interaction of Race, Gender, and Age in Criminal Sanctioning: The Punishment Cost of Being Young, Black, and Male," *Criminology 36*, 763–793 (1998).

[62] Zillah R. Eisenstein. *The Female Body and the Law.* (Berkeley: University of California Press, 1988), 213.

4 ||||| Mothers in Prison

As mentioned in chapter 2, many incarcerated women are the primary caretakers of their children. In 1999, the Bureau of Justice Statistics reported that women under the supervision of criminal justice agencies were mothers of approximately 1.3 million children under the age of 18 years.[1] Approximately 64 percent of mothers in state prison and 84 percent in federal prison were living with their minor children prior to incarceration; about 44 percent of fathers in state prison and 55 percent in federal prison were living with their minor children prior to incarceration. There were also dramatic differences between mothers and fathers in prison concerning their children's current caregivers. About 28 percent of the mothers in prison reported that the father was the child's caregiver, while 90 percent of the fathers said that at least one of their children was living with his or her mother.[2]

Aside from incarceration, hospitalization, school, military service, or other circumstances can result in the separation of mothers and their children. Separation due to incarceration, however, acquires an additional stigma.[3] Not only is a mother separated from her child, but that separation is due to her criminal activity. Ironically, attitudes toward a mother's separation due to her incarceration may be more negative than attitudes toward fathers similarly separated, partly because many fathers did not have their children living with them prior to incarceration[4] and partly because mothers are seen as the primary nurturer for children.

In this chapter, we present information relevant to understanding the experiences of mothers in prison and the impact of a mother's incarcera-

71

tion on her children. First, we examine the general concept of motherhood and explore how it can influence attitudes toward women in prison. Contrary to the stereotype that only an irresponsible person would commit a crime that would separate her from her child, many mothers in prison are deeply committed to staying or becoming involved with their children, and they often feel that they are good mothers. Second, we examine the notion that children with mothers in prison are unintended and often hidden victims of incarceration. The negative results of separation are compounded by the many ways that the prison environment strains and breaks ties between mother and child. Finally, we will present various policies and programs that have some bearing on mother-child relationships within a prison setting; some of these have positive outcomes for mothers and their children, while others have negative outcomes.

Our exploration of ideals about motherhood, the thoughts and experiences of incarcerated mothers and their children, and the response of correctional institutions and programs demonstrates the ways that incarceration can compound the negative effects of mother-child separation. It also highlights the importance and the difficulty of empowering mothers in prison so that they can help their children, and in some instances maintain their own motivation to overcome substance abuse, avoid illegal activity after release, and obtain education or job training that improve the chances of employment. Idealized and rigid views about motherhood, which we discuss below, are not useful as a part of the foundation for programs, and they fail to incorporate an understanding of the ethnic group, class, and other differences in approach to how one can be a successful and effective mother.

THE IDEALIZED
CONCEPT OF MOTHERHOOD

Mothers do not experience prison in a vacuum, devoid of societal influences. They are affected by the broader context of cultural and societal constructions of motherhood.

An ideology of perfect motherhood in the United States is that:
- Motherhood and womanhood are intermeshed; to be considered a mature, balanced, fulfilled adult, a woman should be a mother.
- A "good" mother is always available to her children; she spends time with them, guides, supports, encourages, and corrects as well as loves and cares for them physically. She is also responsible for the cleanliness of their home environment.
- A "good" mother is unselfish; she puts the needs of her children before her own needs.

- The individual mother should have total responsibility for her children at all times.
- Mothering is a low-status but important, worthwhile, and intrinsically rewarding job in our society. The non-material rewards outweigh the lack of financial and status rewards.[5]

This Western version of motherhood is so pervasive in some groups within our culture that it is usually assumed without question by those groups.

Questioning the reified and idealized view of motherhood, Shari Thurer wrote that motherhood—the way we perform mothering—is culturally derived.

> Each society has its own mythology, complete with rituals, beliefs, expectations, norms, and symbols. Our received models of mother-hood are not necessarily better or worse than many others. The way to mother is not writ in the stars, the primordial soup, the collective unconscious, nor in our genes. Our predecessors followed a pattern very different from our own, and our descendants may hew to one that is no less different. Our particular idea of what constitutes a good mother is only that—an idea, not an eternal verity. The good mother is reinvented as each age or society defines her anew, in its own terms, according to its own mythology.[6]

During the beginning of the 1900s, the concept of the ideal mother evolved due to cultural and scientific changes.[7] As a result of this transformation, mothers were held responsible and accountable for child-rearing as well as child-bearing. Barbara Ehrenreich and Deirdre English illustrated this conceptual transformation by citing President Roosevelt's address to a group of women:

> The good mother, the wise mother—you cannot really be a good mother if you are not a wise mother—is more important to the community than even the ablest man; her career is more worthy of honor and is more useful to the community than the career of any man, no matter how successful, can be . . .

> But . . . the woman who, whether from cowardice, from selfishness, from having a false and vacuous ideal shirks her duty as wife and mother, earns the right to our contempt, just as does the man who, from any motive, fears to do his duty in battle when the country calls him.[8]

Thus, motherhood was more than just a biological condition or a part-time occupation; it was changing into a "noble calling."[9]

Understanding the construction of motherhood provides us with a greater appreciation of how female offenders are doomed to being designated by many people as unfit mothers, and therefore among the most despised of women. Societal attitudes toward female offenders are often more judgmental than those about male offenders because of stereotyped conceptions of motherhood:

the female felon offends society's idealized vision of women as all-caring, nurturing, and attentive to their children. She therefore poses a threat to the established social order unlike that presumably posed by male felons. The female felon's criminal activities raise concerns about her ability to be a "good" mother.[10]

Inherent in the stereotypic view of motherhood is the assumption that women have a natural, maternal instinct. It is "natural" for women to assume a caring role.[11] It follows from this stereotype that a man, as a parent, is replaceable; a mother, due to her maternal instinct, is not replaceable. Thus, a mother's incarceration can be viewed as a particularly egregious failure on her part.

Sue Mahan provided a critical examination of motherhood and incarceration by analyzing narratives from eleven women incarcerated in a New Mexico state correction facility. She found that motherhood was salient in the women prisoners' identities. However, she also pinpointed three sources of stress and disillusionment that incarcerated mothers felt when they thought about their children:

- Incarcerated mothers are separated from their children and are unable to nurture them. Due to their incarceration, they are designated unfit and may have been insulted and accused of mistreating their children.
- In many instances, the prisoner's extended families must take on the responsibility for the care of her children. This may cause the families a great deal of financial and emotional strain. Subsequently, the families may resent this burden, and the children may feel unwanted.
- The majority of incarcerated women may have endured great hardships, both financially and emotionally. When looking into the future, they may see problems associated with their roles as mothers, especially financial independence. This will be even more difficult given the stigma attached to an incarcerated felon on the "outside."[12]

The loss and failure that some mothers in prison feel is reflected by one woman's experiences:

> Separated from her child by time and space, Helen found her life farther and farther removed from the institution of motherhood. She described a painful conversation she once had with the prison supervisor about her child. He had asked her, "If you care about your kid so much, why are you a bad mother?" She could not answer. She saw the role of mother as lost to her. . . . In this way Helen remained outside the institution of motherhood but looked to her own behavior for the loss. She never questioned the institution itself.[13]

Even though some incarcerated mothers may endure feelings of failure and loss and have little or no contact with their children, their identification as mothers is central. However, they may hold themselves to the standard set by ideal constructions of motherhood and feel inadequate in comparison.

INCARCERATED MOTHERS

Based on interviews with women in prison, Baunach wrote

> Whatever else they had, imprisoned mothers had one thing to hang onto before their incarceration: their children. Whether the relationship was healthy or otherwise for mother and child, when a woman goes to prison she takes with her the good memories of that relationship and cherishes the times spent in sharing joy and love with her children. Perhaps she truly loved and cared for her children in a positive healthy relationship; perhaps she reversed roles with her children and they primarily nurtured her; perhaps she paid little or no attention to her children at all. In any case, imprisonment engenders the feelings of loss and failure. . . . Whatever else prison does to or for a woman, it enables her to reflect for hours on end about herself and the consequences of her behavior on both herself and her children.[14]

There are many other studies that support Baunach's findings. One researcher who interviewed 55 incarcerated mothers in Minnesota described incarcerated mothers' commitment to parenthood as deeply tenacious.[15] In interviews with incarcerated New York women, Fox found that they worried that their children were not receiving adequate care and that the children would forget who their mothers were.[16] Women in prison fear that they are inadequate as mothers and that they will not be able to readjust to living with their children upon release. They are troubled by practical matters that include regaining custody, relocating children, and locating suitable family housing.[17] From interviews in a progressive prison, Henriques found that the mothers all tried to maintain contact with children through visits, letters, and phone calls but worried about the children's physical care and emotional development.[18] A nurse who conducted research on women who had a child while incarcerated, and then experienced separation from that child, identified grief at separation along with a sense of relatedness to the child as recurring themes in the women's experiences.[19] Finally, women who had killed their infants (those women described in chapter 2 whose actions were motivated by their fear that they would lose other important relationships because of the infant or by their inability to understand the infant's behavior) hoped for a program that would help them deal with the trauma of their loss.[20] There is no doubt that most if not all incarcerated mothers experience concern, worry, frustration, guilt, and anguish when they are separated from their children—and that the women want and attempt to maintain contact with and to ensure the safety of their children.

One of the most common types of programs for mothers in prison are parenting programs. Parenting programs, which may be attached to mother-child visitation programs or life-skills programs, are based on the assumption that mothers in prison lack basic knowledge about how to care for and discipline their children. The literature on substance-abusing mothers, a group that overlaps with women in prison, does lend some support to this assumption. Despite research findings about substance-abusing women, it would be misleading to conclude that all incarcerated mothers are deficient in parenting skills or are unaware of their responsibilities as mothers. In fact, women are typically aware of what they should be doing to support and nurture their children.[21] Compared with mothers of a similar socio-economic background, age and marital status who were not offenders, inmate mothers were the same in their perceptions that it was important for them to provide for the interpersonal, emotional, physical, and spiritual needs of their children.[22] Most mothers in prison believe they are good mothers and want to create supportive homes.[23] The realities of incarceration and (for many mothers) substance abuse, lack of financial means, and in some cases lack of knowledge about childrearing, however, does clash with the sense of being a good mother and wanting to fully care for children.

Whether or not they have strong parenting skills, incarcerated mothers do confront some special problems. A meta-analysis of 56 studies published between 1979 and 1993 revealed that the use of illicit substances and/or alcohol significantly affected the physical and motor development of neonates/infants exposed in utero.[24] Cocaine-using mothers have less positive and nurturing interactions with their newborns, in part because the newborns had been negatively affected by the cocaine (for example, being more distressed at novel situations and having lower weight at birth and for the months after birth).[25] Children exposed to alcohol before birth had higher levels of negative affect and insecure attachments—and at ages 5 and 6, more depression—regardless of the mother's current drinking.[26] In a group of low-income women, substance abuse was routinely associated with more severe disciplinary practices and a higher potential for inattentiveness.[27] Substance abuse has negative outcomes for the children, and substance-abusing mothers are more likely than others to parent in a style that has negative outcomes for the children. As we will discuss below, the mother-child separation negatively affects children. During separation due to incarceration, many children live in low-resource neighborhoods and in families with limited financial means.

Thus, even women with strong parenting skills will face special challenges as they begin to interact with infants exposed to drugs or children traumatized by separation, and they are likely to continue to experience difficulties as the children get older and exhibit learning or other problems.

HIDDEN VICTIMS—CHILDREN

Anybody who thinks they don't go through hell when we are in this place doesn't know children very well. They do your time. [from an incarcerated mother][28]

Incarceration not only affects the mothers but their children as well, thereby adding to the mothers' challenges in meeting their needs. Studies have revealed that children of incarcerated parents experience similar negative effects of separation as do children who were placed in foster care, whose parents were divorced, and who experienced the death of a parent.[29] The children of incarcerated mothers are often hidden victims of the sentencing policies that have resulted in the influx of women into prisons.

Although incarcerated women's relatives are typically willing to take the children during imprisonment, or have already been caring for them, the children often are a burden to the new caregivers. In interviews with 30 mothers and some of their children, the children's caregivers, or the children's foster parents, Henriques found that all of the parties caring for the children had financial difficulties because they were living on incomes limited to public assistance.[30]

It is a common perception that the state supports most children with incarcerated mothers. According to Peter Breen, in the state of California, the estimated amount of tax monies to provide Aid to Families with Dependent Children (AFDC) and foster care for children of incarcerated mothers was over $56 million a year. Nationally, excluding AFDC, the estimated annual costs to provide foster family or group care for children of incarcerated mothers was approximately $78 million. When including welfare costs, the estimated cost is closer to a half a billion dollars.[31] Breen further contends that this group of "at risk" children are often overlooked and there is a lack of state- or local-level coordination of services to address their needs.

Despite the costs documented by the California study, it is important to recognize that many children with incarcerated mothers do not receive state support. In a Michigan sample of 56 caregivers taking care of 95 children, the caregivers carried the burden of support.[32] Two-thirds of the children lived with a caregiver who had not been appointed as legal guardian, and thus the children were not eligible for any financial support from the state. Less than 1 in 5 of the children lived with a legal guardian other than a parent, and only 14 of the 95 lived with their father. A majority of caregivers were concerned about limited financial resources and the effects of this on the children; indeed, almost half of them had a monthly household income of less than $1,000. Of the caregivers for two or more children, over half were subsisting on less than $1000 a month.

In the Michigan sample, consistent with the caregivers' low incomes, many lived with the children in neighborhoods that were neither cohesive nor particularly safe. One third of the caregivers felt that the children were unsafe in their neighborhoods at least sometimes, and almost 10% (all in government-subsidized housing) felt that the children were usually not safe. Most of the caregivers stated that there were no people in the neighborhood to give them support, especially in areas such as childcare or shopping.

A barrier to delivering supportive services to children who are at risk for various negative outcomes at least in part because of their mothers' incarceration is that caregivers, many of whom are grandmothers or other relatives, are often fearful of revealing the children's circumstances.[33] They may think that the children will be placed in even more negative situations or that there will be unwanted interference in the household. There are few resources to develop advocacy and education services for the caregivers, and delivery of what services are available is difficult because the caregivers are scattered throughout the state.

Research conducted in the 1970s showed that a mother's incarceration results in stigmatization and traumatization of her children and related problems in school, such as declining grades and instances of aggression.[34] The more recent study by Morash and Bramlet-Hecker revealed that the caregivers of about half of the school-age children felt that the children were doing well or very well in school, but that the other half felt the children were doing poorly or just fairly well.[35] Many of the school-aged children had no leisure-time activities, and at least a third of the children, especially if they had witnessed their mother's arrest, frequently expressed confusion and stress about their mother's absence or the arrest incident.

Children separated from their mothers by incarceration also exhibit emotional and health problems such as nightmares, bedwetting, withdrawal, daydreaming, and fear of darkness.[36] Some children exhibit symptoms of post-traumatic stress disorder, and a mother's incarceration seems to precipitate some girls' pregnancy.[37] Other problems that incarcerated mothers report include learning and school-related difficulties, behavioral problems, mental health concerns, and alcohol and drug abuse.[38] Some of the difficulties that children experience stem from the distress that their mothers feel because they feel responsible for meeting the children's needs but are immobilized to do so.[39]

There is some concern that the children of incarcerated mothers will themselves become involved in the criminal justice system.[40]

I've been in corrections for 18 years and I've seen three genera-
tions of people in facilities—grandmother, mother, and daughter at
the same time. I've seen where the mother was here, gave birth to
a child, and the child is now here.[41]

At this time, we do not know the specific risk of children's involvement
in the justice system associated with separation from the mother due
to incarceration. Some degree of risk is likely due to the separation
and subsequent instability in the children's lives, living in poverty,
and a myriad of other factors.

The case example in illustration 4-1 reveals the trauma that children can experience when their mothers are incarcerated and the negative results that can follow.

Illustration 4-1   One Child's Experience of
Having a Mother in Prison

Beth, a twelve-year-old youngster, was placed in a foster home
one year ago, after her mother was convicted of possessing stolen
property. A week before sentencing, the mother took Beth to stay
with her grandmother, assuming that Beth would remain there.
About a week later, a worker from the welfare department
arrived at Beth's school and removed her to a foster home. Neither the mother nor the grandmother was consulted. The welfare
department's position was that since Beth had been in foster care
briefly some two years earlier, the department still had custody.
The welfare department did not believe that Beth's grandmother
could provide a suitable home.

In Beth's words, "When my mother was arrested . . . they just
came in and took her away. . . . I was at school, but my grandmother guessed what had happened. Then my mother called
after a few days. A week later the welfare worker just came to
school and told me I was going to the home."

Beth says that the home hasn't been as bad as she thought it
would be. However, her foster mother feels that the child has had
a very difficult time adjusting to the placement. When she first
arrived, she was very anxious to please, but she was frequently
moody and hurt herself in a temper by banging her head against
the wall. Midway through the school year, as she seemed to
become more comfortable in the home, she began to have difficulty in school, refusing to do her homework, acting up in class
with other students. The foster parents met with the school staff
but nobody seemed able to reach the child. Finally, in March, after
a fight with another student, Beth was suspended. At that point,
the agency supervising the placement decided Beth should be sent

to the girls' detention center for a week—the child was starting to behave like her mother and would have to learn some limits.

In discussing the suspension, however, Beth explains that the kids in school often teased her about her mother and that one girl, with whom she had all the fights, kept calling her mother a jailbird. Since she returned from the detention center, the kids have left her alone.

Beth says that she doesn't have anyone with whom she can discuss her worries. Her foster parents are all right, but they are very strict and don't talk too much. And although she now has a boy friend and a best friend in school, she isn't allowed to see them much and couldn't talk to them anyway. Therefore, she just keeps things to herself.

When asked what was going to happen after her mother was released from prison, Beth put her head down and said, "I don't know. It's kind of scary. I want us to live together, but . . . "

Source: Brenda G. McGowan and Karen L. Blumenthal, *Why Punish the Children? A Study of Children of Women Prisoners* (Hackensack, NJ: National Council on Crime and Delinquency, 1978), pp. 45–46.

THE PRISON ENVIRONMENT AND MOTHERHOOD

Numerous obstacles make it difficult for incarcerated mothers to maintain ties with their children. The location of many institutions in isolated areas, often due to placement of a prison because of that area's need for jobs, impedes families from finding reliable transportation for visits. Barbara Bloom and David Steinhart's study of incarcerated mothers revealed that over 60 percent of the children lived over 100 miles from their mother's place of incarceration.[42] Telephone communication can be problematic especially when many U.S. prisoners are allowed only one fifteen-minute (collect) phone call per month.[43] The type of contact permitted for child visitations varies from being quite limited (e.g., through partitions) to being relatively extensive (e.g., overnight stays) (see table 4-1).[44]

Barbara Bloom and David Steinhart's study also revealed that mother-child visits are rare. Over half of the children never visited their mothers while they were incarcerated; slightly less than 10 percent visited once or more per week; and just under 17 percent visited once per month.

In many instances there is limited emotional support within the prison environment for women trying to maintain ties with their children.[45] Women are sometimes criticized as being overly emotional or manipulative when they express their grief at the loss of contact with their children or even permanent loss of custody, and there are few professionals available to help them cope with separation.

Table 4-1   Types of Contact Allowed during Personal Visits between Children and Incarcerated Mothers

	Number (421 types)	Percent
Open area visiting	288	65.6
Visits through partition	39	8.9
Overnight family visits	51	11.6
Other	43	9.8

Source: Barbara Bloom and David Steinhart, *Why Punish the Children? A Reappraisal of the Children of Incarcerated Mothers in America*, (San Francisco: National Council on Crime and Delinquency, 1993), p. 27.

Judith Clark, a prisoner at Bedford Hills Correctional Facility in New York, observed that the prison environment encourages infantilization and dependency among mothers:

> Women are told when to get up, when to eat, where to go. They must ask for their cell room doors to be opened and shut by the correctional officer. They are limited to 15 phone numbers, which must be approved prior to calling family and friends. If a woman's child goes to the hospital or has to stay with a neighbor, it can take days to get to a prison counselor to make a call to find out whether everything is all right.[46]

Prisons create a forced dependency that is antithetical to caring for a child. Inmate-mothers become dependent upon the institution for survival and are unable to take responsibility for themselves or for their children. Therefore, it should not be surprising that some women find it hard to resume care of their children upon release.[47]

Public opinion does not seem to favor the bleak realities of prison for mothers, at least as shown by the limited research that is available. A public opinion survey of Michigan residents revealed that over 86 percent of a random sample of citizens supported the provision of parenting classes for incarcerated mothers; almost 80 percent supported planned activities during visits; and approximately 80 percent supported assistance to individuals taking care of the children during their parents' incarceration. There were some differences among respondents with respect to who was more likely to favor programming for incarcerated mothers and their children: compared to men, women were more likely to support some type of assistance, young adults were more likely to recognize the need for some type of programming, while senior citizens were more likely to recognize the need for assistance to caregivers; people with lower household incomes favored programming more than those with higher incomes.[48] Despite these differences, all groups seem willing to help children with incarcerated mothers.

The continuing emphasis on "get tough on crime" by legislators and politicians deprives women of programming and visiting privileges in the prison despite public opinion that supports such policies. When mothers are incarcerated, both they and their children endure the separation. Many women will eventually be released to reunite with their children. As Judith Clark stated, "just as women in prison need to accept emotional and intellectual complexity to wrestle with difficult and painful issues, so too must policy makers . . ." [49]

POLICIES AND PROGRAMS AFFECTING MOTHERS IN PRISON

Policies and programs that apply to mothers in prisons are controversial. Some people advocate relaxing the rules and ameliorating prisoners' deprivation so that women have more contact with their children and involvement in their lives. Others argue that trying to support relationships between incarcerated mothers and their children creates problems, including increasing the chances that contraband will be brought into the prison; requiring the allocation of new resources; and the negative effects of exposure to the prison environment and criminal mothers on children.[50]

Depending on location and leadership, state and institutional policies vary from reflecting a compromise between security concerns and interest in supporting mother-child relationships to reflecting an overarching philosophy that prisons should be punitive and not make any special provisions for mother-child contact. Will the mother be incarcerated near to the place where her children live? Are women who give birth while incarcerated allowed to keep their infants for a period of time, or are they allowed to move to an alternative setting designed for mothers and children to complete their sentence? What is the nature and the quality of permitted contacts with children? Do they include a setting where children can stay overnight for weekend visits or can visit for several hours a day while lodging with a local volunteer family? Do children and mothers visit in a sparsely furnished visiting room with many other prisoners and their visitors, or do they visit in a home-like setting, with children's furniture, toys and games? Can mothers visit with several children at once? Can they touch their children and pick them up during visits? Existing policies, the influence of prison leadership on how policies are implemented, and the physical and monetary resources of the institution are major influences on the contact and the relationship between imprisoned women and their children.

In 1995, in an effort to encourage strong ties between mothers and children, the Federal Bureau of Prisons issued a policy statement on parenting program standards. Since 1996, unlike many state prisons, there has been funding for parenting programs at all federal prisons. The current policy is to identify appropriate visiting-room space, separate from other visiting rooms if possible, and to establish parenting education, social service outreach, and community-based service providers. The overall policy objectives include the following:

- Positive relationships, family values, and mutual support and nurturing, which may be sustained after release, will be promoted and reinforced among prisoners and their spouses and children.
- Each prisoner will have opportunities to counteract negative family consequences resulting from his/her incarceration.
- The institutional social environment will be improved through opportunities for prisoners to maintain positive and sustaining contact with their families.
- Social service and community-based organizations will be included in parenting programs whenever possible.[51]

Although the policies provide for some support of parent-child relationships, they also reflect administrative concerns with equity for all prisoners, the routines of a prison, and security. Thus, they include stipulations that visiting hours be the same for mothers and children as they are for women and other people, and that staff at all times adhere to local visiting-room policies and procedures.

Advocacy efforts for children of incarcerated parents have stressed the importance of maintaining family ties. These efforts include recommending legal remedies in such areas as criminal sentencing, corrections, and child welfare law.[52] One controversy pertains to babies remaining with their incarcerated mothers:

> The fact that there is existing state legislation allowing mothers to retain infants or young children does not necessarily mean that programs for implementing the law are in place. States such as California, Minnesota, New Jersey, New York, and Wisconsin have statutory provisions for mothers' retention of their infants, but only New York has nurseries in correctional facilities that enable newborns to remain with their incarcerated mothers for a limited time .... Only a small number of the 50 states specifically address the issue of the birth of babies to incarcerated women, or the fact that incarcerated women are mothers of infants or young children. The vast majority of states make no mention in their legislative codes of either providing services to inmate mothers or securing the placement of children of women prisoners at the time of their incarceration.[53]

Centerforce, an organizational network of California state prison visitor hospitality centers, designed a legislative initiative in an effort to meet the following two goals:

- The children of incarcerated parents would be recognized as being "at risk" in order to enhance their eligibility for various programs and services.
- All state departments involved with children's issues would be required to recognize the unique needs of these "at risk" children.[54]

While the initiative was passed by both chambers of the California legislature, an amendment to the resolution (ACR38) was included to "conduct a comprehensive study of the problems faced by and associated with children of incarcerated parents." The study, conducted by the Assembly Office of Research, was quite disappointing for it did not provide any additional insight or information not previously known. In addition, the Assembly member who was strongly committed to moving this initiative to the national forum died during the congressional campaign in 1992. California's ACR38 has been redrafted and reviewed as a national model by various members of the U.S. Congress. Similar advocacy efforts for children of incarcerated parents have been initiated in Pennsylvania and Illinois.[55] Breen concludes that

> [T]he lives of many children have been clouded with self-doubt, despair, and great loss due to parental incarceration. Although progress seems slow, change is taking place on many levels throughout the country. Through these and other advocacy efforts, children of incarcerated parents may soon take a place on our national children's policy agenda.[56]

Unfortunately, little change has yet occurred.

In fact, in recent years incarcerated mothers are facing new obstacles to maintaining custody of their children.[57] A major reason is legislation that has enhanced linkages between federal and state criminal justice, welfare, and adoption systems. Specifically, in 1996 the United States Congress enacted the Personal Responsibility and Work Reconciliation Act (PRWRA), also known as "welfare reform." This Act places strict limits on the length of time children receive benefits. Additionally, it requires that the parents seek employment with the assumption that such employment is obtainable, pays a living wage, and child care is available. As discussed in chapter 2, many women offenders are living in poverty without benefit of education or employment skills. Given their felony conviction status, obtaining suitable employment becomes even more problematic. A rarely discussed aspect of this Act is a key provision that explicitly excludes individuals convicted of drug-related felonies from receiving welfare benefits for an extended period of time. Compared to men, more women offenders are sentenced for drug-related offenses. This provision disproportionately penalizes women as well as their children. Thus, "when a women drug offender is released from prison with a few dollars and a bus ticket, she will have fewer resources to reestablish a home for herself and her children."[58] Furthermore, the new legislation restricts her time frame to legally reunite with her children.

Another potential hindrance to women offenders reuniting with their children is the Adoption and Safe Families Act enacted in 1997. While the Act advocates the "safety and health of the child," it also limits the timelines on family court processes as well as on necessary support services to assist families. Specifically, parents (including those in treatment for substance abuse) whose children are placed in foster care have approximately one year to demonstrate their ability to adequately take care of their children. A family court judge subsequently must decide whether the dependent children will be reunited with their families or will be placed in an adoptive or other permanent placement. The long-term effects of this Act on women offenders has not been studied.

> The 1996 NCCD [National Council on Crime and Delinquency] study revealed that 54 percent of women prisoners interviewed were serving a sentence longer than one year and 15 percent reported that one or more children had become a ward of the court. Since incarcerated parenting women are not exempted from the provisions of the Adoption and Safe Families Act, and since those children in foster care generally will be unable to meet family court requirements within 12 months, it appears more likely that their parental rights will be terminated.[59]

Advocacy groups for women in prison, and the women themselves, are stretched thin as they try to respond to the new legislation that threatens family ties.

THE COURTS AND MOTHERS' CUSTODY OF THEIR CHILDREN

As mentioned previously, the experiences of parenthood are different for incarcerated women and men. Prior to incarceration, a large number of women were the primary caretakers of their children. Although incarcerated fathers also have needs related to separation from children, more men than women in prison had lost contact with their children before incarceration or have a situation in which the children's other parent is maintaining the family and bringing the children for visits. Many women move their families close to the prisons where their children's fathers are kept.[60] If incarcerated mothers do not have relatives to care for their children, they could lose their children through the termination of parental rights and adoption proceedings.

Even if they are eventually able to reunite, custody and visitation issues can temporarily but severely restrict their interactions with children.

At least 25 states have termination-of-parental-rights or adoption statutes that explicitly refer to incarcerated parents. In an additional four states lacking legislation that addresses incarcerated parents, termination of parental rights is allowed for those parents who are convicted of certain types of crimes against children.[61] Various factors that facilitate the termination of parental rights include correctional policies regarding parent-child contact; inadequate prison programs and services, inadequate counseling and advocacy for parents and children; inadequate screening, training and support for caregivers; inadequate legal services for incarcerated parents; and systematic failure to include parents in placement planning and decisions.[62] Illustration 4-2 presents case examples that show how these factors exacerbate the potential to terminate parental rights.

Illustration 4-2 Case Examples Describing the Factors that Promote the Termination of Parental Rights

Inadequate Screening, Training and Support for Caregivers

Yolanda had a 4-year sentence to serve. After an initial foster placement, her two sons, ages 2 and 5, were placed with a private guardian by the juvenile court. When Yolanda refused to consent to the adoption of the children, the guardian refused to care for them any longer and dropped them off at the state foster care agency. The children were placed in a state foster home that was licensed to care for children with special needs. The children soon reported that they had been physically and sexually abused in the home of the guardian; a medical report indicated evidence of severe sexual abuse. When the first mother-child visit was planned, the children reported that their mother also had sexually abused them. The next two visits were extremely tense; the children acted afraid to be near their mother, and she was baffled and hurt by their behavior as well as their false allegations against her. She chose not to pursue regular visits when the foster father convinced her that visits were only upsetting the children and that it was better for them to have time away from her to sort out their confusion. Two years passed. It was then discovered that the foster father had coached the children to make allegations against their mother, threatening them with extreme punishment if they said their lines wrong, and he was charged with forcing another foster child to make similar allegations against her mother to prevent her return home from foster care. The foster parents' license was investigated but not revoked. Six months later, the foster mother revealed that the foster father

---

had regularly battered her, left him, and filed for divorce. Yolanda's younger son then revealed that a broken leg he previously maintained was accidental actually was inflicted by the foster father. By then Yolanda's relationship with her sons was so attenuated that she decided to surrender parental rights to the foster mother. The foster mother continued to allow the abusive foster father to visit the children, and they were removed and placed in a series of foster placements. The children began taking out their anger on younger children, and understandably were unable to trust adults. A positive, permanent home for the two boys as they grow into adulthood would require a miracle.

Inadequate Legal Services for Incarcerated Parents
Juana's children were ages 7, 9, and 12 when she was arrested, and they had always been in her care. She had 2 years to serve on a drug-related charge. The paternal grandmother took custody of the children and became their official foster parent through the state child welfare agency. Juana had two visits with her children; then she was transferred to a facility hundreds of miles from her home, and the visits ended. Although she wrote to her children regularly, the foster care agency found the distance too great to bridge and did not provide visits or include Juana in the plans for her children. When Juana was brought to court for a routine hearing, the caseworker persuaded her to sign custody over to the grandmother "temporarily." In front of the judge, Juana was handed a piece of paper to sign but was not given time to read it. She signed the document. She later discovered that she had signed a permanent surrender of her children and that her parental rights had been terminated on the next court date on the basis of the surrender.

Systematic Neglect to Include Parents in
Decisions such as Placement and Planning
Martha was an accomplice to a robbery in which her codefendant was convicted of felony murder, and she was sentenced to 20 years. Her 5-year-old daughter was placed in foster care. Martha contacted her cousin in another county, who agreed that it would be best for her and her husband to raise Martha's daughter so that she would have a sense of family and would grow up knowing her mother. The cousin's home passed the state adoptive licensing process with flying colors. Martha did not have access to legal advice, and she signed a surrender of custody, intending that her cousin would adopt her daughter. However, a specific consent naming her cousin as the adoptive parent was needed to protect her plan. The agency caseworker opposed the cousin's petition, preferring nonrelative foster parents. The judge fol-

> lowed the caseworker's recommendation and allowed the unrelated foster parents to adopt the child.
>
> Source: Gail Smith, "Practical Considerations Regarding Termination of Incarcerated Parents' Rights," in Katherine Gabel and Denise Johnston, eds., *Children of Incarcerated Parents* (New York: Lexington, 1995), pp. 186–188.

State procedures to terminate parental rights of incarcerated parents fall into one of four categories.[63] Some states terminate parental rights based on the argument that offenders understand that their criminal activity can ultimately result in incarceration; therefore, by breaking the law they consciously abandon and neglect their children. This reasoning fosters the stigmatization of incarcerated mothers that we previously described. It also ignores the importance of the relationship to the child and the mother. The well documented concern, anguish, and guilt that incarcerated mothers express for their children contradicts the assumption of intent to abandon and neglect.

Second, some states consider the nature of the felony offense as well as the circumstances to determine unfitness and, subsequently, termination of parental rights (e.g., California Civil Code, 1994; California Welfare and Institutions Code, 1994; *Matter of Vernia,* 1989; *In re Terry E.,* 1986). While Fleischer contends this procedure is better than using only the fact of incarceration, it still has the potential to sever a positive parent-child relationship or a relationship that could become very positive. This approach, as with the previous one described, ignores the offender's ability to be a good parent, and too readily places the permanent label of *unfit mother*.

The third category takes into consideration whether parents are able to provide a safe and secure home for the child as well as whether the parent has maintained contact with the child while incarcerated (e.g., *In re Adoption of Herman,* 1980; *In re Dolores B.,* 1988; *In re H.G.B., M.A.B., & D.J.B.,* 1981; *Jordan v. Hancock,* 1974). This approach can still result in erroneous assumptions about what mothers intend to do and will do once released. The numerous obstacles that the prison itself creates to preserving and improving a mother-child relationship often provides a contradictory reality to tendencies to blame only the mother for lack of contact and concrete support of children.

The fourth category assesses the psychological effects of incarceration on the child, the parent-child relationships prior to incarceration, and the parent's potential ability to assume parental responsibilities. An essential feature of this approach is to implement an extensive analysis of the parent-child relationship based on individualized circumstances rather than on a general, comprehensive procedure. Fleischer incorporates various aspects of this category to outline his suggestions for terminating the parental rights of incarcerated parents.

An ideal approach to parental rights termination proceedings would be one that provides a full hearing at which the parent is present and represented by counsel. The court should look at several criteria to determine if a statutory basis exists to terminate parents rights as well as what is in the best interests of the child. These criteria should include: the nature of the parent-child relationship before and during the parent's incarceration; the parent's ability to maintain a relationship with the child and to fulfill his [or her] parental duties, focusing especially on the length of the incarceration; the psychological effects of incarceration and visitation in prison on the child; and the child's age and need for stability and permanency. Only after considering these factors can an accurate decision be made as to whether termination of parental rights is warranted. This procedure could be expensive and time consuming, but terminating a fundamental relationship with a lesser procedure is constitutionally unacceptable and fails to acknowledge the varied effects of parental incarceration on children. Because of the constitutional protection owed to parent-child relationships, the sanctity of those relationships, and the varied impact of parental incarceration and termination of parental rights, states should enact legislation that implements thorough procedures assuring a full and fair hearing of all relevant facts and circumstances before parental rights are terminated.[64]

One way to lessen the negative effects of parent-child separation is through positive experiences for a child during prison visitation. In addition to the barriers to visitation that we have already discussed, such as transportation, there are legal barriers.[65] For instance, in some states when a mother is arrested, if she had physical custody of a child, she needs to give temporary custody to another guardian. To obtain visitation rights while incarcerated, she must have the original custody order changed to reflect the temporary custody of the child. This legal process is difficult to achieve since prisoners have limited access to legal services pertaining to family law.

Some mothers have tried to use the courts to ensure that when their children do visit, the experience is positive. For example, in *Blackburn v. Snow* (1985) the plaintiff challenged the institutional practice of strip searching men, women, and children visitors in order to ensure security within the facility. Blackburn, an adult female was visiting her brother in the county jail facility and was searched prior to her visit. She argued that such searches violated her Fourth Amendment rights. Subsequently, the district court entered a temporary restraining order to cease such searches upon which the Sheriff permanently discontinued the search policy.

The potential for correctional staff to threaten and then actually impose restrictions on mother-child visits as a way to control prisoners is reinforced by court findings that visits are a privilege, not a right. In

1968, for example, the California legislature passed the "Civil Death" doctrine, according to which prisoners were denied their civil rights during imprisonment.[66] The doctrine was repealed in 1975 and replaced by legislation entitled the "Civil Rights of Prisoners," which included the right to personal visits. However, different from the right to confidential access to an attorney, the right to own or transfer property, and the right to marry, Chapter 132 granted the Director of the Department of Corrections "greater control of prisoner activities such as visitation."[67]

In California, the argument for Chapter 132 was that shifting visitation from a right to a privilege provided the Department of Corrections a tool to teach prisoners that they were responsible for their actions and responsible for the consequences of breaking prison rules. Further, visitation as a privilege can be used as a management tool to enhance security. However, making visits with children a management tool to promote security completely ignores the needs of the children. Although some correctional institutions no doubt make efforts to use suspension of visits with children only in the most extreme cases, the overcrowding, inadequate mental health and substance abuse treatment, and a myriad of other pressures on prisons and both the staff and offenders who are locked inside of them create an environment where staff will be searching for effective controls. Suspending contact with children is likely to be one of the most controlling things that can be done to a mother. Since most women in prison have no history of violence and violence within a prison for women is rare, the necessity for such extreme control seems minimal. Punitive withdrawal of the mother's opportunity to interact with her children is a questionable practice in light of the children's needs.

THE PRISON'S RESPONSE TO MOTHERS IN PRISON

In state correctional systems, there is no uniform or adequate attention to mothers' needs and concerns, and the impact of incarceration on children is certainly not viewed as a responsibility of the correctional enterprise. The National Survey[68] revealed that many women are not screened to determine whether they have responsibilities, concerns, or pressures related to their children, particularly in large prisons. Specifically, just 40 percent of administrators in the states with 500 or more women in prison indicated that there was routine screening relevant to mothering for all women. In contrast, in the 7 states with under 100 incarcerated women, routine screening was done in all but one. Still, overall, these data indicate that many criminal justice systems have limited information on the parental circumstances and the children of incarcerated women.

Not only do many prison administrators and staff lack systematic knowledge of women prisoners' involvement with their children and immediate concerns about them, but their feelings about the need to attend to mothering and children is often overshadowed by a sense that women's needs for substance abuse and mental health programming are even greater and more immediately pressing. After all, substance abuse brings many women into the prison system, and institutions must respond to women's mental health needs, either because of the law, to maintain some level of order, or out of compassion. Unfortunately, because of unawareness or very real limitations on time and resources, attention to mothers and their children by prison administrators and staff can be very minimal. This lack of attention is inconsistent with the persistent anguish that many incarcerated mothers experience when they have difficulty finding out where their children are or how they are doing, or when they feel powerless to assist children who are experiencing school or other problems. This institutional approach is also inconsistent with widespread beliefs about the great importance of motherhood.

Administrators in one third of the innovative and promising prison-based programs for women offenders where data were collected for the National Survey said that at least one major focus of programming was parenting and mother-child relationships. However, community programs had an even greater emphasis in this area, with over half of the administrators reporting a program focus on parenting. As we will emphasize in chapter 8, the exigencies of institutional life— maintaining order, providing food and housing, responding to emergencies that arise in a group living situation—usually take precedence. There are few programs that reduce women's difficulties in meeting their children's needs. The absence of children in all but a very few settings (e.g., New York prison nurseries, weekend arrangements for children to live with mothers on weekends in Minnesota) makes it almost impossible to maintain a strong and positive relationship with children—a positive incentive for mothers to desist from criminality.

During the Conference Proceedings of the National Symposium on Women Offenders, Elaine Lord, Superintendent of the Bedford Hills Correctional Facility for women in New York, commented that initially she was not convinced that prisons should deal with issues surrounding mothers and their children. Her experience working with women prisoners, however, "led her to conclude that long-term success with mothers requires that prison systems help these families 'stop and regroup.' It is important not to look at incarcerated women as 'just mothers' . . . but these women do remain mothers in our society, even when they go to prison."[69] Thus, prison administrators need to recognize this reality and address these issues in programs for women prisoners and their children.

Staff in prisons and advocacy groups in the community have succeeded in establishing some programs for women and their children. Some programs are supported by department of corrections budgets, and some by private agencies which hire staff to come into the prison. At Bedford Hills prisoners work with community volunteers to manage and staff programs. Stand-alone or supplementary parenting programs may involve instruction for the mothers for several hours a week, or daily for a limited number of weeks; advocacy and support programs may provide counseling and understanding, along with concrete help in such areas as child custody, on an individual basis. Unfortunately, most mother-child programs are fairly rare events: a weekend visit during the summer, or a three-hour visit once a month.

One example of a time-limited program that is made available to women is *Girl Scouts Beyond Bars* (GSBB), which has been initiated and promoted as exemplary by the National Institute of Justice. It emphasizes establishing a partnership between correctional departments and a major youth service organization in an effort to address the needs of girls whose mothers are incarcerated in settings without adequate visitation programs. The Maryland Correctional Institution for Women (MCIW) was the site of the pilot program in 1992. The National Institute of Justice has assisted in establishing similar Girl Scout programs in other correctional facilities: the Jefferson Correctional Institution in Monticello, Florida; Broward Correctional Institution in Pembroke Pines, Florida; Franklin Pre-Release in Columbus, Ohio; the Ohio Reformatory for Women in Marysville; the Estrella Jail in Phoenix, Arizona; the Delaware Women's Correctional Institution; the Edna Mahan Correctional Facility for Women in New Jersey; the Kentucky Correctional Institution for Women; and the California Rehabilitation Center in Norco. Ten additional states have also demonstrated interest in establishing programs in their respective correctional facilities.[70]

The Maryland Girl Scouts program participants are daughters from ages 5 to 17 who meet their incarcerated mothers at MCIW two Saturdays a month for Girl Scout meetings in the prison gymnasium. These meetings are supervised and consist of structured play and troop projects. Activities include aerobics, a mini science fair, and arts and crafts. The meetings also include discussion of serious topics such as violence prevention, self esteem, drug abuse, dealing with family crises, anatomy and physiology of the reproduction system, and teenage pregnancy prevention. On those Saturdays that the troop does not meet at MCIW, the meetings are held at the Corpus Christi Church in Baltimore.[71]

Operational issues include criteria for women to participate. Women from any custody level, but not those with a history of child abuse or a violation of prison regulations within the last six months, can participate in the program. In addition, participants cannot violate any prison regulation while in the program. The Girl Scout volunteers must also meet certain criteria, including a criminal background check and participation in the department of corrections volunteer orientation and in-service training. Since some of the meetings are held in a correctional institution, there are additional aspects to program implementation that are not considerations when Girl Scout meetings are held outside a prison. For example, after each meeting in the prison, the mothers are strip searched for contraband.

One GSBB volunteer stated that

> If there has been little or no communication during the period of incarceration, imagine the stress both mother and daughter are likely to experience when they are suddenly expected to resume their relationship after the mother is released. . . . this program fills a tremendous need for positive communication during a period of mother-child separation.[72]

Although there is anecdotal evidence of positive effects of GSBB, given the numerous difficulties of incarcerated women and their children, it is doubtful that GSBB can have more than a limited impact; this of course does not mean that it should not be replicated and implemented, but it does mean that it should be supplemented and that there should be alternative programming available.

Prison MATCH (Mothers, Fathers and Their Children), which originated in 1978 at the Federal Correctional Institution at Pleasanton, California, is an example of a more comprehensive approach.[73] The program continued until 1988, and with federal support to provide technical assistance, the program model was widely replicated and disseminated. Due to lack of continued funding, in 1989 the Prison MATCH activities were moved from the Pleasanton facility to the San Francisco County Jail. However, it still serves as a model for programs in prisons.

The Prison MATCH model has remained relatively consistent over the years. There are four components to the program: the Children's Center for visits, social services, parenting skills education, and child development training. The Children's Center is a recreational environment including ping-pong tables, an air hockey game, music, climbing equipment, and other toys. It is located within the institution and is staffed by volunteers from various professions including social workers and early childhood educators. Prisoners and their children meet at the Children's Center for at least four hours once a week. The children are brought to the facility at 9:00 a.m. and are registered at the gate. Subsequently, the group of children are moved to the visiting area in order to be searched by the facility staff. At this point, Prison MATCH staff take the children to the Children's Center, after which parents are notified of their arrival.[74] At the Center, parents work with their children on arts and crafts projects, receive instruction when needed on parenting in a positive manner, celebrate birthdays and holidays, and pose for pictures with their children.

Essential steps to developing a parent-child program are listed in illustration 4-3. Additional requirements for successful implementation include recognizing and coordinating with any existing visiting program in the institution, obtaining needed institutional space to provide a safe environment for the visits, scheduling age-appropriate activities for the children, and providing public social service referrals and services to parents and their families.

Illustration 4-3   Steps to Developing a Parent-Child Program

Recruit community professionals with expertise in child and family services as advocates for the program.

- Establish positive communication with the facility's warden or superintendent.
- Enlist the support of one or two key correctional staff members, volunteers, and/or contract workers.
- Hold a conference with facility administrators and advocates to discuss development of the program.
- Form a task force to guide program development.
- Enlist local community leaders and public officials to serve as members of the program's governing board.
- Expect and deal carefully with correctional staff concerns about security issues.

Source: R. Weilerstein, "The Prison MATCH Program," in Katherine Gabel and Denise Johnston, eds., *Children of Incarcerated Parents* (New York: Lexington Books, 1995), p. 261–262.

Chapter 8 examines in detail whether a program that creates a niche for escape from the routines and realities of incarceration can overcome the negative ramifications of incarceration or provide support and resources for women seeking to improve their circumstances. While achievement of this feat is questionable, we can conclude that the comprehensive model provided in Prison Match and similar programs has more potential for doing this.

Nurseries in Prisons. In all but a few countries, correctional authorities allow incarcerated women to return to their homes to give birth, and then to keep their children with them in prison until they are one or two years old.[75] While women in most of the United States are not allowed to keep newborn children inside of the institution, there are some important exceptions. For example, in Shakopee Prison for women in Minnesota, one of the living facilities provides appropriate housing for mothers and their children, and children live with their mothers in a home-like atmosphere during weekends and vacation periods. The apparent feasibility of women prisoners' nurturing their children raises questions about why in most states, the mother-child relationship is routinely disrupted.

Currently in the state of New York, long-term nurseries are located at the Bedford Hills facility and the Taconic facility, which are next to each other. The mothers are able to live with their infants until they are one year old. This length of stay between mother and infant can be extended to eighteen months if it is certain that they will leave together.[76]

The average daily schedule at the Taconic nursery is presented in illustration 4-4. The nurseries try to mirror living situations outside of prisons, and thus women may take classes or participate in other programs by arranging for childcare in the nursery. Otherwise, the women remain with their babies as the primary care provider.

Katherine Gabel and Kathryn Girard conducted a descriptive study of the two long-term care nurseries in New York.[77] During their pregnancy, the prisoners received prenatal care including obstetrical exams, classes on fetal growth and development, nutrition, labor and delivery, and breast and bottle feeding. The expectant mothers were required to complete these classes before the birth of their children and the children's entry into the nursery. Also, a public health nurse provided required postpartum classes and pediatricians affiliated with

---

Illustration 4-4   Average Daily Schedule at the Taconic Nursery

6:00 A.M.	Count
7:00 A.M.	Breakfast (feeding of infants, cleaning of rooms)
8:15 A.M.	Parenting/baby care program
11:30 A.M.	Lunch
12:30 P.M.	Count
12:50 P.M.	Afternoon programs/Outdoor recreation for babies
4:00 P.M.	Count
4:30 P.M.	Dinner
5:30 P.M.	Evening programs
6:00 P.M.	Optional outdoor baby recreation during Daylight Savings Time only
10:00 P.M.	Count—all mothers in rooms with babies

Source: Katherine Gabel and Katheryn Girard, "Long-Term Care Nurseries in Prison: A Descriptive Study," in Katherine Gabel and Denise Johnston, eds., *Children of Incarcerated Parents* (New York: Lexington Books, 1995), p. 241.

a local hospital conducted clinics at the nursery every week. The babysitters, women in the general prison population who were carefully screened by the prison administration and the nursery manager, are trained and supervised by the nursery manager. However,

> [t]he nurseries and the living quarters for the mothers and babies are far from luxurious. At Bedford Hills, the women complained about the peeling paint and cockroaches. At both Bedford Hills and Taconic, the women complained about having to share rooms with other women and their babies. Differing sleep and feeding patterns, accompanied by predictable nighttime crying, can be a source of friction in cramped rooms.[78]

Despite some drawbacks due to the prison environment, the nursery area and surrounding bedrooms for the mothers and children had perhaps the most homelike appearance that is possible in a prison. Kitchens, common rooms with rugs, soft chairs and sofas, and laundry areas within the nursery provide opportunities for mothers to take care of their babies' needs and places for both mothers and babies to socialize.

Gabel and Girard identified nine types of program benefits perceived by the mothers. There were five types of benefits to the women themselves: opportunities for education, better conditions of confinement, drug education and treatment, help from other prisoners, and self respect. The woman also saw four benefits connected to their improved parenting, which resulted in good outcomes for the children: better bonding with the infant, development of parenting skills, socialization of the babies, and high-quality infant services and supplies. Some women did feel that, in addition to the overcrowding, the program had disadvantages, because high expectations and demands were placed on them, and there was some negative interaction with officers and staff.[79]

Besides the assessment of the New York nurseries, there is evidence that infant development is well supported in baby units located in prisons, and the presence of infants had a positive impact on prison life. A comparison of babies who were in the prisons with those who were not showed that the children were normal and healthy.[80] The infants benefitted not only from contact with their mothers but also with each other and other people working in the unit. The presence of the newborns seems to mute some of the harshness of prison life and to relieve the mothers of anxiety and distress.

Alternatives to Prison. We have mentioned that in a small number of states, while serving a sentence of incarceration, women who are pregnant or have newborns can live with their children in secure and supervised settings away from prison grounds. Additionally, pregnant women and those with newborns can be sentenced to a community alternative instead of a prison. An examination of policies and programs in New York State determined that even though they had a history of substance use, most mothers in prison had not been offered any alternatives to prison that might have provided drug treatment.[81] The study further found that the small number of women in alternative programs, even if the program services were very limited, responded very positively. The authors who summarized the study recommended alternative place- ment of mothers with infants and the provision of programs that pro- vided a setting for the entire family to talk about drug addiction, AIDS education, vocational training, and a follow-up program after release. The follow-up program would give women access to transitional housing, where they could live cooperatively with other recovering addicts.

Neil J. Houston House in Boston was the first community program for pregnant offenders in the United States, and it provides substance- abuse services for pregnant women incarcerated in Massachusetts. Preg- nant prisoners who are within 18 months of parole are eligible to live there. The house, where 15 mothers and their infants can live, is secured by 24-hour staff supervision and an alarm system. Additional control is provided through random urine testing. The group and individual ther- apy offered in the program are based on ideas that were summarized by Covington[82] (chapter 2), specifically that relationships are central to women and, therefore, therapy must enable women to build positive relationships. Along with therapy, the program provides parenting edu- cation, medical care from a nearby hospital, first accompanied and then independent excursions to well-baby clinics, overnight visits from older children, and assistance in securing housing before they leave. Clearly, having a program in the community, especially if it is proximate to where participants will live after completion, facilitates linking women and their children into a wide array of supportive services and opportunities.

ELEMENTS OF SUCCESSFUL MOTHER-CHILD PROGRAMS

A key feature of successful programs for women offenders and their children is that they are holistic and can be tailored to a woman's and her children's desires and circumstances. Programs typ- ically provide women with opportunities to learn and practice in areas that include interpersonal interactions, parenting, and the life skills of problem solving and budgeting. The holistic approach can extend to institutions; community or governmental agency services can visit women housed in special settings or in the general popula- tion. The staff providing mother-child programs frequently broker a variety of services, many of which the program participants can con- tinue to use after serving their sentence. For example, participants are involved in governmental and private agencies that provide spe- cialized medial services, mothers attend community college and vocational programs, and mothers and their children obtain mental health assessment and care.

Many women offenders have a full range of capacities and knowledge levels to parent successfully. Thus, it makes sense to engage these women prisoners in providing infant care in New York prison nurseries or in various roles in child visitation settings. As discussed in chapter 2, some women in prison have been poorly parented themselves, or have essentially missed a part of their childhood while they lived as runaways or were addicted to drugs. For these and other reasons, women may have difficulty in raising their children. It is common to hear staff in programs for women offenders talk about parenting the women so that they can eventually parent their children. Staff typically set clear limits, establish rewards for constructive behavior and consequences for negative behavior, and form close and nurturing relationships with their clients.

An element of mother-child programs that can empower women and give them some actual input into what happens to children is the use of prisoner committees to support and shape the experience of visits. Committees can plan activities, make decisions about program purchases, and carry out fund-raising events. At some facilities, prisoners (some of whom are not mothers) work in committees to arrange for speakers on topics related to children, design and produce posters and cards useful to the program, and publish a newsletter.

DIVERSITY IN FAMILIES AND INDIVIDUALS

Most of the research on mothers in prisons and their children summarizes the demographic characteristics of study participants, and the summary in most cases reflects the chapter 2 conclusion that a high proportion of people in contact with the justice system are nonviolent, African American, from backgrounds marked by poverty, and negatively affected by substance abuse. Within and apart from this group, there are considerable variations in families. Also, there is considerable variation in how different types of families can provide a positive setting for mothers and their children.

Clearly, most incarcerated women do not have and will not have a supportive male partner to share in the care of their children. Employment, arrangements for childcare, pooling of resources with relatives and other mothers, and managing a family in a distressed neighborhood or school system are often be part of any eventual successful family reunion when a woman is released from prison. Programs need to recognize and adapt to a variety of social, ethnic, economic, religious, and cultural differences that influence women's ideas about motherhood and family. These differences and varying circumstances also can influence the experiences of incarcerated mothers and their children. For example, a study in California revealed that compared to the relatives of black women, the relatives of white women were less likely to be a resource and to bring children for visits during incarceration.[83] Mother-child programs and policies need to be tailored so that they provide a variety of alternatives and are effective for women with differing circumstances and backgrounds.

CONCLUSION

Citing an American Correctional Association survey, Barbara Owen noted that when asked to name "the most important person in your life right now," over half of the women prisoners responded that their children were the most important person to them. Given this, Owen emphasized that the importance of mother-child relationships greatly influences the prison culture in various ways. For instance, many conversations center around children. These conversations allow the women to express the intensity and grief associated with these relationships and the hurt they have caused their children due to their incarceration.[84] Many women prisoners feel intense guilt and shame about their children as well as society's labeling them as "bad" mothers; reuniting with their children is a significant goal for these women.[85] For this to be a realistic goal, however, these women need various resources and assistance. Unfortunately, most incarcerated women have little or no contact with their children, and the children of incarcerated mothers are typically not considered a responsibility of either the criminal justice system or the social services system.[86]

In this chapter, we first examined societal conceptions of motherhood and how these notions influence perceptions of mothers in prison. Even though mothers are incarcerated, their identity as mothers is central. However, many children are negatively affected by their mothers' incarceration, and thus they are referred to by some as hidden victims of incarceration. Furthermore, the prison environment is not conducive to maintaining or establishing the mother-child bond. Even when programs exist in the prison, they often are of short duration and lack adequate facilities. Programs that get beyond the assumption that all that is needed is retraining in parenting skills, or that women's needs are limited to the parenting area, are few and far between. Just a few prisons in the U.S. allow prolonged and regular contact, or enable mothers to influence decisions about their children and custody arrangements for them.

This chapter has highlighted one serious consequence resulting from the ever-increasing preference to incarcerate female offenders. Incarceration not only affects mothers, but also their children and the mother-child relationship. A mother's anticipation of a strip search after her children leave a visit, or a child's experience of an oppressive and invasive prison setting, can create or perpetuate negative mother-child interactions. The potential abuse of the power to ban a woman from seeing her children is another concern raised by lengthy periods of incarceration as punishment.

ENDNOTES

[1] Lawrence A. Greenfeld and Tracy L. Snell, *Women Offenders: Special Report* (Washington, DC: U.S. Department of Justice, Office of Justice Programs, 1999).

[2] Christopher J. Mumola, *Incarcerated Parents and Their Children: Special Report* (Washington, DC: U.S. Department of Justice, Office of Justice Programs, 2000).

[3] Phyllis Jo Baunach, *Mothers in Prison* (New Brunswick, NJ: Transaction, 1985).

[4] Susan K. Datesman and Gloria L. Cales, "I'm Still the Same Mommy": Maintaining the Mother/Child Relationship in Prison," *Prison Journal* 63:142–154 (1983).

[5] Betsy Wearing, *The Ideology of Motherhood: A Study of Sydney Suburban Mothers* (Sydney: George Allen & Unwin, 1984), 72.

[6] Shari L. Thurer, *The Myths of Motherhood: How Culture Reinvents the Good Mother* (Boston: Houghton Mifflin Company, 1994), xv.

[7] Barbara Ehrenreich and Deirdre English, *For Her Own Good: 150 Years of the Experts' Advice to Women* (Garden City, NY: Anchor Press/Doubleday, 1978).

[8] *Ibid.*, 171.

[9] *Ibid.*, 172.

[10] Adela Beckerman, "Women in Prison: The Conflict Between Confinement and Parental Rights," *Social Justice* 18:172 (1991).

[11] Delila Amir and Orly Biniamin, "Abortion Approval as a Ritual of Symbolic Control," *Women and Criminal Justice* 3:22–23 (1991).

[12] Susan Mahan, *Unfit Mothers* (Palo Alto, CA: R & E Research Associates, 1982), 119–120.

[13] *Ibid.*, 134.

[14] Phyllis Jo Baunauch, *Mothers in Prison*, 1.

[15] Mary Martin, "Connected Mothers: A Follow-up Study of Incarcerated Women and Their Children," *Women and Criminal Justice* 8:1–23 (1997).

[16] James G. Fox, J. G. "Women in Prison—A Case Study in the Social Reality of Stress," in Hans Toch, ed., *Pains of Imprisonment* (Thousand Oaks, CA: Sage Publications, 1982), 205–220.

[17] Phyllis Jo Baunach, "You Can't Be a Mother and Be in Prison . . . Can You? Impacts of the Mother-Child Separation," in Barbara R. Price & Nancy J. Sokoloff, eds., *The Criminal Justice System and Women* (New York: Clark Boardman Company, Ltd., 1982), 155–169.

[18] Zelma W. Henriques, *Imprisoned Mothers and Their Children: A Descriptive and Analytical Study* (Lanham, MD: University Press of America, 1982).

[19] Judith M. Wismont. "The Lived Pregnancy Experience of Women in Prison," *Journal of Midwifery and Women's Health* 45:292–300 (2000).

[20] Susan M. Crimmins, Sandra C. Langley, B. Henry Brownstein, and B. J. Spunt, "Convicted Women Who Have Killed Children: A Self-Psychological Perspective, "*Journal of Interpersonal Violence* 12:49–69 (1997).

[21] Zelma W. Henriques, *Imprisoned Mothers and Their Children*.

[22] Larry LeFlore and Mary Ann Holston, "Perceived Importance of Parenting Behaviors as Reported by Inmate Mothers: An Exploratory Study," *Journal of Offender Counseling, Services, and Rehabilitation* 14:5–21 (1989).

[23] Susan Greene, Craig Haney, and Aida Hurtado, "Cycles of Pain: Risk Factors in the Lives of Incarcerated Mothers and Their Children," *The Prison Journal* 80:3–23 (2000).

[24] Susan J. Tarr and Jean L. Pyfer, "Physical and Motor Development of Neonates/ Infants Prenatally Exposed to Drugs in Utero: A Meta-Analysis," *Adapted Physical Activity Quarterly* 13:269–287 (1996).

[25] Eiden R. Das, "Maternal Substance Use and Mother-Infant Feeding Interactions," *Infant Mental Health Journal* 22:497–511 (2001).

[26] Heather C. Olson, Mary J. O'Connor, and Hiram E. Fitzgerald, "Lessons Learned from Study of the Developmental Impact of Parental Alcohol Use," *Infant Mental Health Journal* 22:271–290 (2001).

[27] Denise Hien and Toye Honeyman, "A Closer Look at the Drug Abuse-Maternal Aggression Link," *Journal of Interpersonal Violence* 15:503–522 (2000).

[28] William H. Sack, Jack Seidler, and Susan Thomas, "The Children of Imprisoned Parents: A Psychosocial Exploration," *American Journal of Orthopsychiatry,* 46:623 (1976).

[29] Phyllis Jo Baunach, *Mothers in Prison*; Creasie Finney Hairston, "Family Ties during Imprisonment: Important to Whom and for What?" *Journal of Sociology and Social Welfare* 18:87–104 (1991).

[30] Zelma W. Henriques, *Imprisoned Mothers and Their Children.*

[31] Peter Breen, "Advocacy Efforts on Behalf of the Children of Incarcerated Parents," in Katherine Gabel and Denise Johnston, eds., *Children of Incarcerated Parents* (New York: Lexington Books, 1995).

[32] Merry Morash, and Gwen Bramlet-Hecker, *An Evaluation of Michigan Council on Crime and Delinquency's Children's Visitation Program, Scott Correctional Facility, Plymouth, Michigan* (East Lansing: Michigan State University, 1997).

[33] Gwen Bramlet-Hecker, Merry Morash, and E. Arnovitz. *Community Services Available to Children With Mothers in Prison: A Needs Assessment and Recommendations for Programming* (East Lansing: Michigan State University, 1997).

[34] William H. Sack, Jack Seidler, and Susan Thomas, "The Children of Imprisoned Parents: A Psychosocial Exploration."

[35] Merry Morash and Gwen Bramlet-Hecker, *An Evaluation of Michigan Council on Crime and Delinquency's Children's Visitation Program, Scott Correctional Facility, Plymouth, Michigan.*

[36] Ariela Lowenstein, "Temporary Single Parenthood—The Case of Prisoners' Families," *Family Relations* 35:79–85 (1986).

[37] Cristina Jose-Kampfner, "Michigan Program Makes Children's Visits Meaningful," *Corrections Today* 53:132–134 (1991).

[38] Denise Johnston, *Children of Prisoners' Children* (Pasadena, CA: Center for Children of Incarcerated Parents, 1992); Denise Johnston, *Caregivers of Prisoners' Children* (Pasadena, CA: Center for Children of Incarcerated Parents, 1993).

[39] Susan Greene, Craig Haney, and Aida Hurtado, "Cycles of Pain: Risk Factors in the Lives of Incarcerated Mothers and Their Children."

[40] Barbara Bloom and David Steinhart, *Why Punish the Children? A Reappraisal of the Children of Incarcerated Mothers in America* (San Francisco: National Council on Crime and Delinquency, 1993), 25.

[41] Marilyn C. Moses, *Keeping Incarcerated Mothers and Their Daughters Together: Girl Scouts beyond Bars, National Institute of Justice Program Focus* (Washington, DC: National Institute of Justice, 1995), 3.

[42] Barbara Bloom and David Steinhart, *Why Punish the Children?*, 27.

[43] Joanne Belknap, *The Invisible Woman: Gender, Crime, and Justice*, 2nd ed., (Belmont, CA: Wadsworth Publishing Company, 2001), 107.

[44] Barbara Bloom and David Steinhart, *Why Punish the Children?*, 27.

[45] Phyllis Jo Baunauch, *Mothers in Prison.*

[46] Judith Clark, "The Impact of the Prison Environment on Mothers," *The Prison Journal* 75:306–329 (1995).

5 ||||| Incarcerated Women and the Courts

Prisoner litigation increased rapidly in the 1960s and in subsequent decades after the U.S. Supreme Court began to permit convicted offenders to file lawsuits under federal civil rights statutes. This litigation produced court decisions that defined the rights of prisoners. Moreover, civil rights lawsuits by prisoners provided the basis for alleging violations of various rights, including the Eighth Amendment right to equal protection of the law and the right to be free from "cruel and unusual punishment." During the 1970s, after the Supreme Court began to interpret the Equal Protection Clause against governmental discrimination based on gender, the opportunity arose for women prisoners to file equal protection claims.

Court decisions have required and inspired reforms and resulted in many changes in prison conditions. The relative importance of the courts as opposed to other mechanisms for producing change results largely from stigmatization and the related abhorrence that many in the public direct toward offenders. As Smith put it, "Because convicted offenders constitute a politically powerless minority spurned by American society, individual prisoners and advocates for prisoners' rights looked to the courts as the law- and policy-producing forum most accessible and receptive to claims of right."[1] Some of the reforms resulting from court interventions have been more relevant to women than to men. These reforms have focused specifically on gender inequality and situations that are unique to women or disproportionately relevant to women, for example sexual abuse of prisoners and adequacy of medical care for pregnant prisoners.

As explained in chapter 3 on sentencing, there are distinctions between equality for, justice for, and beneficial responsiveness to women. At the end of this chapter, we will return to a discussion of equality, special treatment of women, and justice as they pertain to how people and institutions treat women who are in prison. First, however, we will review the history of prisoner rights litigation. Outcomes of litigation influence the day-to-day lives, opportunities, and experiences of women in prison. Many women in prison feel that the conditions of confinement are unjust; some spend time researching the law in prison libraries or actively participating in filing a suit. All incarcerated women are touched by the process and by the results of filing suits. This chapter also will describe the gender-related litigation that has unique effects on women. This litigation tells us something about the atmosphere of prisons in which particularly egregious violations of human rights have occurred. Finally, in a departure from consideration of litigation against prisons and departments of corrections, we will examine women's experiences of (in)justice when they battle for custody of their children in local courts.

A HISTORY OF PRISONER LITIGATION

Until the 1960s, there were two barriers to prisoners' filing suits against prisons or the correctional agencies that oversee them. The first was the doctrine of sovereign immunity, which maintained that a private citizen was not permitted to sue a governmental entity or agent without its consent. Anglo-American legal tradition included the perception that the King could do no wrong. An additional reason was that public resources should not be apportioned for compensatory damages. Under this view, government agents need to be free from the threat of such litigation in order to administer their duties in a responsible and effective manner.[2]

The second barrier was the "hands-off" doctrine, which was based on several assumptions.[3] The first was that although a criminal suspect was entitled to all constitutional rights during the trial period, after conviction this entitlement was lost. A second assumption was that corrections could be expected to do whatever was best for both prisoners and the prison, and therefore courts did not need to intervene. Finally, consistent with the philosophy that prison is primarily a punishment, there was an assumption that prisoners had no rights, but could be given certain privileges, particularly if they behaved as required and conformed to prison regimes.

Exemplifying the hands-off doctrine, the ruling in *Ruffin v. Commonwealth* (1871) by the Supreme Court of Virginia was that the prisoner was "a slave, in a condition of penal servitude to the State, and subject to such laws and regulations as the State may choose to prescribe."[4] Although some people have identified particular judges who did recognize prisoners as individuals deserving of some fundamental rights,[5] most judicial decisions did not reflect this position until the Supreme Court broke from this doctrine.

Because state laws provide judges with few bases for intervention, state courts have rarely been called upon or chosen to intervene in the operations of prisons.[6] Moreover, as elected officials within many states, judges often are disinclined to make potentially controversial decisions. Over the last decades, political opponents have been successful in vilifying any efforts to emphasize the rights of prisoners, and this has had a spiraling effect. Politicians seeking election are fearful of trying to communicate the relatively complex notion that emphasizing protection of the rights of offenders ties them more closely to legitimate institutions and pursuits and therefore can lead to improved public safety.

The U.S. Supreme Court's decision in *Cooper v. Pate* (1964), which we discuss below, enabled prisoners to file lawsuits under federal civil rights statutes. That decision provided an opening for court intervention into the operations of prisons. Equal protection under the law and protection of individuals from state and local government actions that violate due process are guaranteed by the Fourteenth Amendment. The Eighth Amendment provides protection against cruel and unusual punishment. Combined with the Fourteenth Amendment, it has been the basis for considerations of conditions and actions within the prison that might be construed as cruel and unusual. Finally, the provisions of the Fourth Amendment direct the court to look to whether the person invoking its protection has a "justifiable," a "reasonable," or a "legitimate expectation of privacy claim."

The Supreme Court has granted review to only a small number of cases affecting prisoners, but the federal district courts in the South began in the 1960s, especially in Arkansas, to use their authority to intervene in prisons. Correctional institutions and departments try to avoid costly suits by conforming to decisions directed at institutions in other geographic locations. To assist prison systems in avoiding suits or successfully representing themselves in litigation, and to professionalize the field of corrections, national standards have been set and considerable public monies have been spent on meeting these standards. Prisons have become more bureaucratic, and administrators

are often professionally trained so that the organization can institu-
tionalize rules and procedures that conform to standards. All departments of corrections have legal staff who keep abreast of case law in
efforts to avoid and handle suits.

Although it has remained involved in prisoner litigation (due to
public opinion, political institutions, and interest groups), the
Supreme Court has shifted its orientation over time. In the 1960s, the
Warren Court expanded prisoners' access to the Court for violations of
constitutional rights, and various marginalized groups initiated movements and organized efforts to obtain rights previously denied to
them.[7] As James Jacobs noted, "[t]he broad legal reforms of the sixties
undermined traditional authority in mental hospitals, schools, and the
military, as well as prisons."[8] Movements like those for civil rights and
women created a sociopolitical context that stimulated the prisoners'
rights movement.[9] *Cooper v. Pate* (1964) initiated the abrogation of the
"hands-off" doctrine pertaining to cases of prisoner grievances.[10] The
Supreme Court ruled that under Title 42, United States Code, Section
1983 (42 U.S.C. 1983), a prisoner could sue a warden or other governmental official. Since that case, litigation has challenged the rules and
policies established by correctional administrators, the courts, and the
legislature; litigation also has challenged the failures of particular correctional officers and managers to follow and administer established
rules and policies.[11]

During the 1970s and 1980s, the federal courts became involved in
monitoring and supervising the implementation of their decisions. As
a result, they had considerable impact on state and federal departments of corrections and specific prisons in various states. For example, cases challenged prison practices that violated prisoners'
constitutional rights to freedom of religion and access to legal materials; federal courts ordered particular corrective actions or programs;
and the courts actively supervised the implementation of changes,
required additional changes if outcomes were not satisfactory, and lev-
ied fines for failure to institute change. The courts often would assign
a monitor to visit the prisons and observe implementation of decisions,
review official records, interview offenders, and interview staff. Moni-
tors would then report back to the judges. There was considerable criticism of the unprecedented involvement of the courts in the day-to-day
activities in prisons, but both inside and outside of prison, advocates
for women often applauded the courts' involvement. Malcolm Feeley
and Edward Rubin summarized the accomplishments of judicial policy
making in the context of prison reform (see table 5-1), noting that
"[w]hile other national institutions avoided the issue, and state institutions generally failed to act, the federal judiciary served as the dominant policy maker."[12]

**Table 5-1: Accomplishments of Judicial Policy
Making in Prison Reform**

What the Courts Accomplished

- The expansion of well-recognized constitutional rights to prisoners such as access to courts, freedom of speech, freedom of religion, and due process.
- The eradication of the South's plantation model.
- The emergence of professionalizing the field of corrections.
- The formulation of national standards for corrections.
- The overall bureaucratization of state prisons.

What the Courts Did Not Accomplish

- From the perspective of prisoners' rights activists, the courts did not develop new approaches to punish criminals.
- From the prisoners' perspective, the prisoner-clients were essentially excluded from the decision-making process, especially women who may have been overlooked due to their small numbers and nonviolent behavior.
- From the prison administrators' perspective, the courts failed to address the major issue of providing significant help with the increasing prison population.

Source: Malcolm M. Feeley and Edward L. Rubin, *Judicial Policy Making and the Modern State* (Cambridge, UK: Cambridge University Press, 1999), pp. 362–380.

In recent years, federal court involvement in prisons has decreased but certainly has not ceased. Consistent with the downward trend, the Prison Litigation Reform Act, which Congress passed in 1996, contracted prisoner's rights and prisoner access to the courts.[13] The act reduced federal judges' authority to order remedies for constitutional rights violations in prison and also made it much moɩe difficult for prisoners to sue for alleged constitutional rights violations by correctional officials. Among other things, the act required that plaintiffs use their personal resources, even if quite limited, to prepare the case. Also, prisoners with three prior lawsuits that have been dismissed as frivolous, malicious, or not stating any claim are not allowed to file another unless they appear to be in immediate danger.

Due partly to the escalating prison population and partly to new controversies on emerging trends, the federal courts are likely to remain involved in prisons, if for no other reason than to handle claims that previously granted rights are not being honored.[14] Women in prison, whose numbers are increasing, continue to be affected in very important ways by prisoner rights litigation.

WOMEN'S INVOLVEMENT IN PRISONER LITIGATION

Most prisoner litigation is filed by prisoners themselves. In a small number of cases the Department of Justice has filed against state and local correctional systems; in others lawyers have represented women in class action suits claiming harm to a group of women. Since prisoner litigation began, men have filed in a disproportionate number of prisoners' rights cases and they were the litigants in the earliest, groundbreaking cases. Because many of the court decisions are limited to conditions specific to an institution,[15] rulings did not always directly extend to women—though as we have noted, many institutions not involved in a particular suit take steps to avoid future suits and negative findings by changing the conditions of confinement.

Starting in the 1980s, women have become more active in prisoner litigation. In some states, women may be as actively engaged in legislation as are men. For example, in 1997 in Michigan, the proportion of suits filed by women was equivalent to the proportion of prisoners who were women.

Two studies have compared the litigation patterns of incarcerated women and men. Aylward and Thomas studied prisoners in two Illinois institutions: Dwight, which housed women, and Sheridan, which housed men.[16] They hypothesized that being litigious was positively associated with a prisoner's length of stay; and since the women generally served more time, they would be expected to file more cases. In addition, since Dwight had greater problems with overcrowding, disciplinary infractions, and adequate legal facilities, women would be expected to turn to the courts fairly often. However, women filed only .6 percent of all cases, many fewer than their proportion in the prison population.

Some of Aylward and Thomas's explanations for the lower rate of litigation were suggested by discussions with prisoners, others by theory. They explained that women might be apathetic and complacent, implicating women's individual deficiencies. They offered the prison context as an alternate explanation: women's possible concerns about lost privileges if they were labeled as troublemakers and the unavailability of in-house peer support groups and jailhouse lawyers could explain lower levels of litigation.[17] Finally, women's socialization to accept stereotypical gender roles might be a reason for less litigation. Unfortunately, Aylward and Thomas did not collect data that would confirm or disconfirm their speculations about the reasons for women's lower levels of litigation, and it is possible that their explanations perpetuate erroneous negative stereotypes of women in prison as passive and incapable.

Gabel did survey incarcerated women to ascertain why they rarely litigated despite problems with child custody and parity in prison programming.[18] Although women's institutions had adequate legal services and law libraries, most of the prisoners were unaware of their existence or unaware of how to seek these services. This finding supports the notion that peers and jailhouse lawyers are important to stimulate litigation. What we do not know is whether other pressing concerns take women's time away from litigation, staff sanctions disproportionately affect women and thus result in extreme concern with being labeled as a troublemaker, or some other influence(s) accounts for their not filing suits. Also, some experts have claimed that legal assistance and information about how to use libraries are available to women, particularly in recent years, so this may be less of a problem than in the past. As we have already noted, the rate of litigation may be equalizing, at least in some states.

LITIGATION BY PREGNANT PRISONERS

One in six women is pregnant at the time of commitment to prison.[19] The literature contains shocking examples of medical needs being blatantly misunderstood or ignored by prison staff.

**Illustration 5-1 Examples of Problems Experienced
by Pregnant Prisoners**

"I . . . was taken to the Hospital Services Unit at [MCI Framingham] and they said that they don't think I was in labor but they will take me to the hospital to shut me up. The ambulance arrived in ten minutes and I was handcuffed to the stretcher. I was taken to Framingham Union Hospital where they put me on an ultrasound machine. The nurse said, 'I can't get a heartbeat . . . your baby is dead. There is nothing we can do about it.' I started crying, saying just take her out; my baby still has air in her lungs; you can put her on a machine."

Twenty-three years old and fourteen weeks pregnant, Dorothy Charvis was convicted of arson and committed to the Massachusetts Institution at Framingham. The pregnancy was extremely difficult and on two previous occasions Dorothy asked nurses in the prison medical ward to send her to a hospital, and twice they refused. On May 12, 1991, Mother's Day, Dorothy requested help again at the prison more than two hours before prison officials called an ambulance to take her to Framingham Union Hospital.

Dorothy Charvis's baby died due to a placental disruption. Dorothy Charvis returned to MCI Framingham immediately after losing her baby and was given a bare mattress on the floor of a cell in the Health Services Unit designated for suicide watch.

Source: Mary Catherine McGurrin, "Pregnant Prisoners Right to Health Care," *New England Journal on Criminal and Civil Confinement* 20:163 (1993).

The extreme cases presented here were cited in a law review, and prison officials would no doubt dispute them. When documented, the narratives in such cases are shocking. Many of the court cases described below confirm medical mistreatment of women in prison and provide insight into the extremes of maltreatment.

Extreme instances of medical neglect have been the focus of litigation that has resulted in adequate medical care in some prisons. However, most pregnant prisoners still have limited access to the services they need.[20] Based on their survey in 1990, the American Correctional Association reported that 30 percent of all correctional facilities still lack the equipment and staff needed to provide the necessary health care of pregnant prisoners.[21] One reason for this continued lack of essential medical care is that policymakers fail to implement national protocols and minimum standards to ensure that medical needs are met.[22] The present constitutional criteria for pregnancy-related medical care is based on the Supreme Court case, *Estelle v. Gamble* (1976).[23]

In *Estelle v. Gamble*, the court established the "deliberate indifference" standard, which determines whether a prisoner's Eighth Amendment rights have been violated in the context of medical services and care. The cruel and unusual punishment clause of the Eighth Amendment extends beyond "physically barbarous punishments." The amendment also incorporates "broad and idealistic concepts of dignity, civilized standards, humanity, and decency." The court ruled that "deliberate indifference" to serious medical needs of prisoners constitutes both unnecessary and wanton infliction of pain. Deliberate indifference can occur by prison doctors not adequately addressing prisoners' medical needs or correctional staff intentionally denying or delaying access to medical care or intentionally interfering with prescribed treatment. The Supreme Court's decision in *Estelle* purports to guarantee that there will not be deliberate indifference to serious medical needs. The decision in no way guarantees good or even adequate medical care.

West v. Manson (1983) was one of the first lawsuits filed by pregnant prisoners,[24] who argued that they were not receiving adequate diets and prenatal education, were denied reasonable access to toilets and showers, and were shackled in leg irons late in pregnancy. The court ruled that the facility needed to improve conditions. Subsequent cases have addressed these and other concerns in federal courts. For example, cases in California have focused on adequate pre- and postnatal care, diets and exercise, insufficient protocols and procedures for pregnancy care, and unavailability of an obstetrician on the prison medical staff (*Harris v. McCarthy*, 1985; *Jones v. Dyer*, 1986; *Fuller v. Tidwell*, 1987; *Yeager v. Smith*, 1987; *Weeks v. Williams*, 1987). In addition to the lawsuits, various organizations have brought about further positive changes by establishing medical care criteria and standards for pregnant women in prison.[25]

An area of controversy is whether the refusal of correctional facilities to provide abortions falls under "deliberate indifference to medical needs." This was the issue in *Monmouth County Correctional Institutional Inmates v. Lanzaro* (1987) filed in the United States Court of Appeals for the Third Circuit.[26] The case originated as a class action by the prisoners of Monmouth County Correctional Institution (MCCI) challenging overcrowding and other conditions and practices, including the adequacy of health care services. In October, the district court mandated relief from the overcrowding and other conditions at the facility. Thereafter, the MCCI inmates sought additional preliminary injunctive relief especially in reference to the health care needs of pregnant prisoners. Subsequently, a Consent Judgment was issued with both parties agreeing to resolve "the most emergent of those issues having [an] impact on pregnant female inmates."

The issue on appeal, however, focused specifically on whether abortion services should be provided. MCCI's policy was that abortions were provided only if they were medically necessary because the mother's life was at risk. The MCCI prisoners claimed that the county's refusal to provide women with pregnancy-related medical care, including abortions, constituted "deliberate indifference" to their medical needs and therefore violated the Eighth and Fourteenth amendments.

The central issue in this case is whether a prisoner's *choice* to terminate her pregnancy is deemed relevant to the necessity for medical care. The MCCI prisoners claimed that the right to choose is a fundamental right. Citing *Roe v. Wade* (1973), the U.S. Court of Appeals argued that one needs to consider the effects of denying a prisoner the choice to terminate a pregnancy:

> The detriment that the State would impose upon the pregnant woman by denying her this choice altogether is apparent. Specific and direct harm medically diagnosable even in early pregnancy may be involved. Maternity, or additional offspring, may force upon the woman a distressful life and future.

> Psychological harm may be imminent. Mental and physical health may be taxed by child care. There is also the distress, for all concerned, associated with an unwanted child, and there is the problem of bringing a child into a family already unstable,

psychologically, and otherwise, to care for it. In other cases, . . . the additional difficulties and continuing stigma of unwed motherhood may be involved.[27]

The U.S. Court of Appeals ruled that denying pregnant prisoners the opportunity to have an abortion incorporates a loss of their fundamental rights. Furthermore, MCCI was deliberately indifferent to the female prisoners' medical needs. While it was argued that an elective, non-therapeutic abortion is not a "serious medical need," as outlined under *Estelle*, the consequences of not providing a prisoner with this procedure nonetheless constitute a "serious medical need." Denying prisoners an elective, non-therapeutic abortion can result in a woman enduring an "irreparable" condition.[28]

As with non-pregnancy related medical services, some women in contemporary prisons do experience benefits that have come through litigation or through statewide attempts to meet various standards. Many systems routinely arrange for abortions on demand, and indeed there has been criticism that some women are pressured to have an abortion without being offered any viable alternatives. Also, there are standards and criteria for medical care of all sorts, and states work to apply these standards in an effort to avoid costly suits. However, limited resources, difficulty in getting qualified medical personnel to work in prisons, and other forces provide counterpressures to improvements. Some women continue to struggle, and some fail, to obtain the medical care they want; certainly the choice to have an abortion is not always as available in prisons as in the community.

EQUALITY OF PROGRAMS AND SERVICES

Another crucial type of litigation filed by female prisoners revolves around issues pertaining to parity—women receiving services and programs or having an environment equal to that available in men's institutions. In the past the conditions of women's confinement were markedly poorer than for men, and some of these problems still persist. In *Glover v. Johnson* (1979), which was eventually resolved in federal district court, women incarcerated by the State of Michigan claimed that they were receiving inadequate medical services, education programs, vocational training, and law library services.[29] Prison administrators were challenged to change these conditions that were comparably less adequate than those in prisons for men. When the lawsuit was filed, the incarcerated men had access to 22 vocational training programs while the women prisoners had access to three; and job-related programs for women prepared them for characteristically low-paying and sex stereotyped work. Men also had more opportunities to pursue a college degree and to participate in apprenticeship programs, work release, and prison industries.[30] The plaintiffs argued that such inadequate services violated their constitutional rights under the Fourteenth Amendment and Title IX of the Education Amendment of 1972. The Michigan Department of Corrections argued that none of their policies violated the women's constitutional rights and that any differences in programming were likely due to "economic efficiency." Specifically, providing similar services to women prisoners was not economically feasible given the relatively smaller numbers compared to men.

The court ruled that

> [t]he women prisoners have a right to a range and quality of programming substantially equivalent to that offered the men, and the programs currently offered do not meet this standard. But additions to that program should be based on the interests and needs of the female prisoners rather than short-sighted efforts to duplicate the programs offered at male institutions. While, in many cases, equal treatment may safely be achieved by requiring identical treatment, I do not believe that, in this case, identical treatment is either wise or just.[31]

This decision emphasized that the correctional department should consider women's special interests and the realities of what jobs they could obtain. Simply providing women with the same programming opportunities as men was not sufficient. The courts specified that there should be a move away from stereotypically women's jobs such as cosmetologist.

The *Glover* case was unique in that court supervision by specialized staff hired to oversee and implement the Michigan Department of Corrections' efforts to follow the court order extended for more than ten years. During this period, considerable innovation occurred. Vocational testing and counseling established women's particular interests and abilities, and a system of helping women individually to use a variety of programs in the system was established. For example, when it was found that many women were very limited in their education, but that they were particularly interested in helping others, a program was instituted to prepare them to train seeing-eye dogs. For those with better academic potential and ability, training in the traditionally male trades, like carpentry, was introduced and adapted to be effective with women. It remains to be seen whether these innovations will remain and continue now that court oversight in the *Glover* case has ended.

In *Canterino v. Wilson* the district court found equal protection violations similar to the *Glover* case.[32] In Kentucky's only prison for women, the programs were inferior to those for men in the areas of vocational education, training, jobs, and outdoor recreation. Consistent with long-held stereotypes of appropriate work, women did not have training or experience in industrial, agricultural, or maintenance services. To obtain the most marketable skills for work in plumbing, electrical, masonry, mechanical, and carpentry jobs, women needed access to such training programs. Instead, most women were occupied with cooking and cleaning to support the prison environment.

Besides work and vocational preparation, *Canterino v. Wilson* addressed recreational opportunities. Because the institution lacked staff to provide adequate supervision, women were never allowed to recreate. In contrast, even for the highest-risk men, recreation time was provided. The court found the disparity inequitable, and the department of corrections was required to create opportunities for women to engage in recreational activity.

In *Klinger v. Nebraska Department of Correctional Services*, another case similar to *Glover v. Johnson* in its emphasis on vocational preparation, prisoners at the Nebraska Center for Women (NCW) claimed that the Nebraska Department of Corrections violated their rights as guaranteed by the equal protection clause of the Fourteenth Amendment. The plaintiffs argued that the incarcerated women were not provided with parity of treatment and that the lack of parity was due to inadequate programs concerned with employment and economic issues, educational and vocational training, the law library, medical and dental services, recreation and visitation. Initially, the district court ruled in favor of the plaintiffs.[33] The United States Court of Appeals for the Eighth Circuit, however, overturned the district court's decision, noting that

> We are asked to determine whether the district court properly applied the law in finding present and past administrators of the Nebraska Department of Correctional Services (Department) liable for violating the equal protection rights of female inmates (plaintiffs) in the Department's prison system as to the provision of prison programs and services in this class action suit. Because we hold that the plaintiffs are not similarly situated to male inmates at Nebraska State Penitentiary (NSP) for purposes of prison programs and services, we reverse the district court's order and dismiss the plaintiffs' equal protection claim.[34]

The U.S. Court of Appeals argued that the conditions for male and female prisoners in the Nebraska Department of Corrections system were different on such factors as the number of male and female prisoners in the facilities as well as the varying sentence lengths for male and female prisoners.

The Supreme Court and federal courts throughout the United States have affected incarcerated women's medical care, including care related to pregnancy, their access to various educational and job-related programming, and many other conditions of confinement. The federal courts also have been influential on women's exposure to sexual harassment and abuse by prison staff and to staff intrusions on their privacy—topics that will be covered more fully in chapter 6. For many women, litigation has become a part of the prison experience, and for all women the outcomes of litigation have affected the contemporary prison experience. Because prisons are isolated from all but the few who maintain contact because of family or employment, federal courtrooms have become the major place where criticisms of conditions are documented, examined, and addressed.

THE IMPACT OF PRISON LITIGATION ON WOMEN IN PRISON

Although it is apparent that prison litigation has provided benefits to women in prison, the extent and lasting quality of these benefits is not well documented. As mentioned previously, Feeley and Rubin outlined various accomplishments in prison reform judicial policy making such as the "transformation of . . . Southern prisons, with their plantation-style structure, into modern penal institutions with professional management, paid custodial staff, and adherence to national standards for policies and practices."[35] Outside of the South, the correctional enterprise was already becoming more professionalized, though litigation did reinforce this trend. Correctional administrators are increasingly knowledgeable about constitutional rights, and they recognize their own liability if they fail to ensure that prisoners' rights are protected. In response, they have established training and supervision programs for personnel. For instance, all Michigan correctional staff who work with women offenders must complete a curriculum that sensitizes them to court findings relevant to women and also to women's special situations and needs; similar curriculums are used in other states and institutions.

The potential for correctional staff to be held personally liable for violation of prisoner's constitutional rights may have special effects in the context of women's prisons. On the positive side, it certainly could deter staff from violating the rights of women and abusing them, for example by taking sexual liberties or sexually attacking women who are essentially powerless. However, fears of false accusations of sexual harassment and assault, though usually unfounded, can reduce staff interest in and willingness to work in women's prisons; this can reduce the pool of capable employees unless the assumption is confronted directly when recruiting and hiring staff.

CONCLUSION

An important theme exemplified by the *Glover* decision is that more replication of programs and services does not necessarily ensure that the needs of men and women have been met. The argument for equal treatment of women and men in prison cannot be adequately addressed solely by providing identical services. Speaking from her experiences as a warden of a state women's facility and later at the National Institute of Corrections, Susan Hunter explained the flaw in the argument that the exact same policies, programs, and services should exist:

> Where policies [and we would add, programs and services] differ between male and female institutions, there seems to be a general assumption that the policy in the male institution is most suitable, and therefore the women's institutions must adopt it. There seems to be a few instances of male institutions adopting policies of the female institution. Across-the-board policies are typically designed to accommodate the needs of the male institutions. Their effect on a women's prison can be difficult, devastating, and in some cases almost humorous.[36]

In this vein, the term "gender neutral" is problematic. James Fox emphasizes the importance of understanding the social realities of female prisoners.

> Equality, whether a direct result of policy changes or the outcome of court-ordered adjustments, does not necessarily mean that some will be treated more kindly. It merely translates to the *same* (or similar) treatment given to male prisoners, who have constantly struggled for more humane treatment. Hence, the central issues seem to be whether or not the elimination of sexist policies will result in greater coercive restraint or social control.[37]

The push for equality could become a strategy contributing to a backslide in the corrective reforms that court decisions have brought for women. Discontinuing rehabilitation programs to promote positive parent-child relations, educational and vocational achievement, and recovery from addiction could find favor in states dominated by legislators, an electorate, and professional administrators who favor lengthy incarceration in institutions that punish. A backslide also might occur if states shift resources from rehabilitative prison programs and community corrections to the construction of technologically sophisticated prison structures. Programs and services for women might be reduced to the inadequate levels that are being promoted in men's facilities. There have even been cases when programming needed for women has been rejected because of the cost and the trouble of providing equivalent services for men, or of demonstrating differential need.

The trend away from court supervision of its orders certainly will limit the effects of future court decisions. As Schweber and Feinman have argued, "the political reality of equality for women is that court orders and statutes are often just the beginning of the struggle." The future direction of litigation by and on behalf of incarcerated women will most likely be influenced by two social forces: (a) the increasing number of offenders being incarcerated, and (b) the increasing punitive attitudes and policies concerning offenders. Utilizing litigation as a strategy for improving prison living conditions for women has been effective, but it is fragmented and limited in its effects. A more comprehensive and all-encompassing strategy is necessary. This would involve not only changes in prison policy and procedures but also in public opinion. The current view apparently accepts the many monetary and other costs involved in holding so many women in prison.

ENDNOTES

[1] Christopher E. Smith, *Law and Contemporary Corrections* (Belmont, CA: Wadsworth, 2000), 115.

[2] John W. Palmer, *Constitutional Rights of Prisoners* (Cincinnati, OH: W.H. Anderson Company, 1973), 135.

[3] American Correctional Association, *Legal Responsibility and Authority of Correctional Officers: A Handbook on Courts, Judicial Decisions and Constitutional Requirements* (College Park, MD: American Correctional Association, 1987), 4–5.

[4] James B. Jacobs, "The Prisoners' Rights Movement and Its Impacts," in James W. Marquart and Jonathan R. Sorensen, eds., *Correctional Contexts: Contemporary and Classical Readings* (Los Angeles: Roxbury Publishing Company, 1997), 231–247.

[5] Donald H. Wallace, "Prisoners' Rights: Historical Views," in James W. Marquart and Jonathan R. Sorenson, eds., *Correctional Contexts: Contemporary and Classical Readings* (Los Angeles: Roxbury Publishing Company, 1997), 248–257.

[6] Christopher E. Smith, *Law and Contemporary Corrections*, 117–118.

[7] John A. Fliter, *Prisoners' Rights: The Supreme Court and Evolving Standards of Decency* (Westport, CT: Greenwood Press, 2001).

[8] James B. Jacobs, *Stateville: The Penitentiary in Mass Society* (Chicago: The University of Chicago Press, 1977), 105.

[9] James B. Jacobs, "The Prisoners' Rights Movement and Its Impacts," 32–233.

[10] Eric D. Poole and Mark R. Pogrebin, "Judicial Intervention and Work Alienation: A Study of Jail Guards," *The Howard Journal* 26:217–231 (1987).

[11] American Correctional Association, *Legal Responsibility and Authority of Correctional Officers*, 1.

[12] Malcolm M. Feeley and Edward L. Rubin. *Judicial Policy Making and the Modern State* (Cambridge, UK: Cambridge University Press, 1999).

[13] Christopher E. Smith, *Law and Contemporary Corrections*, 139–140; see also Ricardo Solano, "Is Congress Handcuffing Our Courts?" *Seton Hall Law Review* 28: 282–311 (1997).

[14] James W. Marquart and Jonathan R. Sorensen, *Correctional Contexts: Contemporary and Classical Readings* (Los Angeles: Roxbury Publishing Company, 1997), 230.

[15] Eileen B. Leonard, "Judicial Decisions and Prison Reform: The Impact of Litigation on Women Prisoners," *Social Problems* 31:45 (1983).

[16] Anna Aylward and Jim Thomas, "Quiescence in Women's Prisons Litigation: Some Exploratory Issues," *Justice Quarterly* 1:253–276 (1984).

[17] *Ibid.*

[18] Katherine Gabel, *Legal Issues of Female Prisoners* (Northampton, MA: Smith College for Social Work, 1982).

[19] Bureau of Justice Statistics, *Women in Prison* (Washington, DC: U.S. Department of Justice, 1994).

[20] Ellen Barry, "Legal Issues for Prisoners with Children," 159.

[21] Task Force on the Female Offender, *The Female Offender: What Does the Future Hold?* (Laurel, MD: American Correctional Association, 1990).

[22] Ellen Barry, "Legal Issues for Prisoners with Children," 158.

[23] Ellen Barry, C. Kojimoto, R. Issacs, G. Lujan, M. Kandel, et al., "Women in Prison," in C. Lefcourt, ed., *Women and the Law* (Deerfield, IL: Clark, Boardman & Callahan, 1993).

[24] Ellen Barry, "Legal Issues for Prisoners with Children," 158–160.

[25] *Ibid.*, 160.

[26] *Monmouth County Correctional Institution Prisoners v. Lanzaro* 834 F.2d 326 at 75.

[27] *Ibid.*, 77.

[28] Mary Catherine McGurrin, "Pregnant Prisoners Right to Health Care."

[29] Joycelyn M. Pollock, *Women, Prison, & Crime*, 92.

[30] *Ibid.*, 169–170.

[31] *Glover v. Johnson*, (1979), 1087.

[32] *Canterino v. Wilson*, 546 F.Supp. 174 (W.D. Ky 1982).

[33] *Klinger v. Nebraska Department of Correctional Services* 824 F.Supp. 1374 (1993).

[34] *Klinger v. Nebraska Department of Correctional Services* 31 F.3d 727 (1994), 727.

[35] Malcolm M. Feeley and Edward L. Rubin, *Judicial Policy Making and the Modern State*, 2.

[36] Susan M. Hunter, "Issues and Challenges Facing Women's Prisons in the 1980s," *The Prison Journal* 64:129–135 (1984).

[37] James G. Fox, "Women's Prison Policy, Prisoner Activism, and the Impact of the Contemporary Feminist Movement: A Case Study," *The Prison Journal* 64:15–64 (1984).

6 ||||| Staff Sexual Misconduct in Prisons for Women

Historically, incarcerated women in the United States have experienced sexual advances, coercion, and harassment by staff. These behaviors are broadly called sexual misconduct, and they include: "acts or attempts to commit such acts including but not limited to sexual assault, sexual abuse, sexual harassment, sexual contact, conduct of a sexual nature or implication, obscenity and unreasonable invasion of privacy; and conversations or correspondence which suggest a romantic or sexual relationship between a prisoner and . . . an employee, volunteer, visitor or agency representative."[1] Women in prison have had limited control over their lives and few resources to make their goals realities. They have had less power than most other women, and sexual misconduct by staff can increase these feelings of powerlessness. In addition, as discussed in chapter 2, many women in prison were victimized by sexual violence and abuse before incarceration. Any experience of sexual abuse in prison compounds the suffering.

Unfortunately, there has been little social science research on the effects of staff sexual misconduct on women. Anecdotal evidence suggests a connection to suicide. For example, three of the women involved in a lawsuit against the Michigan Department of Corrections for alleged sexual abuse by guards attempted suicide, and a Florida prisoner hanged herself from her cell door after writing to her sentencing judge and to her mother about sexual abuse by prison guards.[2]

Although it focused primarily on reports of male prisoners' sexual abuse of each other, survey research of both women and men incarcerated in Nebraska did suggest that emotional harm is a likely outcome of staff misconduct against women. This harm may extend to rape trauma syndrome and resulting loss of self-esteem and decreased ability to trust others.[3] At the very least, an atmosphere or experience marked by sexual misconduct would work against any programming designed to empower women to take control of their lives and avoid criminality after release.

Women with addictions or dependencies on drugs or alcohol and with little experience using procedures to file grievances are particularly vulnerable to coercion to have sexual relations with correctional staff. We present an excerpt from a report from Human Rights Watch (a nongovernmental agency dedicated to exposing human rights violations) that illustrates the dynamic of abuse that can occur because of incarcerated women's vulnerability in prison. In this excerpt, the complainants are referred to as Jane Doe 1, Jane Doe 2, and so on, in order to conceal their identities.

Illustration 6-1 Exploiting Female Prisoners' Vulnerabilities

[Lt. James] Philyaw also manipulated at least one prisoner's dependency on alcohol to entice her into sexual relations. Jane Doe 85 had a drinking problem prior to incarceration; she submitted to sexual relations with Philyaw because, she said, he gave her alcohol and made her believe he cared. He allegedly also suggested items such as marijuana, alcohol and cigarettes. She testified:

> I drank, and I would smoke marijuana. . . . When I got locked up I didn't know how to deal with my problems without getting high, I was real vulnerable and depressed at that time. I had not been locked up very long, and I didn't go outside much, so when he came along it was comforting to know that someone in blue could help me, so I believed him. I believed he could help me, and he gave me alcohol.

In exchange for having sexual relations with him, Philyaw provided prisoners with certain items and granted them special privileges that often violated prison policy. The first time Jane Doe 85 had sex with Philyaw, he called her into the room, locked the door and gave her a bottle of Jack Daniels which they drank, and she submitted to sexual intercourse. Jane Doe 85 told us that she and Philyaw had sexual relations on four or five occasions over a two-month period, either in a counselor's office at Colony Farm or at her work assignment. He would come to her dorm and put cigarettes in her locker or under her mattress. Philyaw promised Jane Doe 14 "that if she received any DRs [disciplinary reports] to let him know so that he could take care of them; and . . . he would write a letter in her behalf to the parole board." When a friend received a DR, Jane Doe 14 raised the issue with Philyaw and performed oral sex on him; the friend was never called on the DR. Jane Doe 15, according to the disciplinary hearing, had sexual intercourse with Philyaw seven to eleven times over a three-month period. In return, he did favors for her, such as moving prisoners at her request and permitting her to see her prison file, contrary to prison policy.

In another incident, Jane Doe 88 witnessed Philyaw having sexual intercourse with Jane Doe 111 in a secretary's office; he later approached her and "told [her] not to repeat what [she] had seen and he asked [her] was there anything he could do for [her]." Philyaw subsequently put money in her prison account. Jane Doe 88 testified that she wrote to Internal Affairs about the incident but received no response.

Philyaw often targeted prisoners who were loners or emotionally vulnerable. According to testimony at his disciplinary hearing, Philyaw called Jane Doe 13 from the prison yard to the control area and told her "he had noticed that she didn't hang around with a lot of other people and therefore felt he could trust her. . . . He told her he was attracted to her and would like to have sex with her."

Source: Human Rights Watch Women's Rights Project, *All Too Familiar: Sexual Abuse of Women in U.S. State Prisons* (New York: Human Rights Watch, 1996), pp. 139–141.

As these examples illustrate, in some correctional institutions, at certain times, staff sexual misconduct can be serious and repetitious, and it can affect multiple victims. A key issue is the degree to which it can be and has been contained and controlled by both legislation and by administrative oversight and action.

HISTORY OF STAFF SEXUAL MISCONDUCT TOWARD INCARCERATED WOMEN

In the early 1800s, women were often confined in separate wings of prisons for men.[4] The rationale was that since women made up a small proportion of the total prisoner population, it was not feasible to construct a separate prison for women. As a result, female prisoners usually endured poorer living conditions and were vulnerable to physical and sexual abuse. In the 1830s, Harriet Martineu visited the Auburn prison, which had a separate wing for female prisoners. She reported that

> [t]he arrangements for the women were extremely bad. . . . The women were all in one large room, sewing. The attempt to enforce silence was soon given up as hopeless; and the gabble of tongues among the few who were there was enough to paralyze any matron. . . . There was an engine in sight which made me doubt the evidence of my own eyes; stocks of a terrible construction; a chair, with a fastening for the head and for all the limbs. Any lunatic asylum ought to be ashamed of such an instrument. The governor liked it no better than we; but he pleaded that it was his only means of keeping his refractory female prisoners quiet while he was allowed only one room to put them all into.[5]

These conditions plus a scandal involving an Auburn female prisoner being flogged to death while she was five months pregnant resulted in New York constructing regular quarters for female prisoners.

In 1873 the Indiana Reformatory Institution for Women and Girls, the first all-female institution, was established. The Indiana Reformatory was notable not only for being a separate institution apart from a prison for men but also as the first facility to be operated by an all-woman staff.[6] Regardless of whether women were incarcerated with men communally or in separate wings, they had been supervised by male staff.[7] It was not uncommon for them to be sexually abused or forced into prostitution.[8] Reformers stressed that the sexual abuse and exploitation of female prisoners would be prevented only if there were separate institutions for women:[9]

> When women prison reformers declared that prison degraded rather than reformed women, they often spoke quite literally of sexual abuse. Hannah Chickering protested male officers' treatment of women, the [Women's Prison Association] lamented that male doorkeepers physically searched the "poorer class" of female convicts, and . . . complained that male jailers had the keys to women's quarters. In station houses and prison, Rhoda Coffin discovered, women were "huddled together like cattle in a pen," easily viewed and often assaulted by men. Josephine Shaw Lowell quoted a report about a jailer who "had wantonly assaulted and degraded numerous young women prisoners; and, when sheriff . . . had utterly brutalized three young girls."[10]

A young male prisoner revealed in his exposé on the Indiana state prison at Jeffersonville that

> [i]n this "vast bawdy house," younger female prisoners were "subjected to the worst of debasement at the hands of prison officials and guards," while the older ones were "obliged to do the work of all." When the warden "established the practice of concubinage," his deputy and other officers followed by making keys to the

women's quarters and forcing the female prisoners "to submit to their hellish outrages."[11]

Even when women joined the staff reformatories for women, officials and guards were still men, and this fact maintained the potential for abuse of prisoners.[12]

Improprieties within contemporary prisons include sexual and gender harassment, invasion of privacy in settings that include showers and toilet areas, granting of favors or privileges in exchange for sexual activity, and coercion into sexual activity. Clearly, the situation of overpowered prisoners with limited influence and resources creates a context where these abuses can occur. Challenges to historical practices have included prison reform efforts by correctional employees and by advocacy groups, related litigation to force the protection of women, compensation of women who have been subjected to staff sexual misconduct, and the efforts of professional correctional associations. A 1999 resolution of the Association of State Correctional Administrators recognized the range of improprieties and the need to eliminate them:

> NOW, THEREFORE, BE IT RESOLVED, that the Association of State Correctional Administrators strongly encourages each of its member agencies to adopt and vigorously enforce explicit policies prohibiting all forms of sexual harassment, activity, or abuse between correctional employees and offenders. These policies should: be in writing; clearly define unacceptable behavior; provide for fair and timely investigative and grievance processes; provide for criminal prosecution; and be widely communicated and emphasized to all staff through training and other appropriate methods.
>
> BE IT FURTHER RESOLVED, that the Association of Correctional Administrators supports enactment of state legislation establishing criminal penalties for sexual activity involving correctional staff and offenders and further, supports aggressive prosecution of correctional staff who violate these laws.

Thus, overt statements have emphasized that staff sexual misconduct is not tolerable and that correctional systems and institutions have a responsibility in preventing it. However, the degree to which the problem has been eradicated and the effectiveness of correctional professionals and systems in their efforts to do this are hotly debated.

CONTEMPORARY ACCOUNTS OF STAFF SEXUAL MISCONDUCT

The experiences of women in prison differ markedly over time and between locations. Certainly the presence of women staff and the restriction of men from entering areas where women are undressed or from performing pat downs and strip searches help reduce the most common form of sexual abuse in women's prisons. But just as women's experiences vary, so do the proportion of and the restrictions on men working in women's facilities. Women in one system at a particular time may be highly vulnerable to harassment, coercion, and sexual assault, and those in another may not; it is unreasonable to generalize the experiences of one group to all women in prison in all time frames. On the one hand, incarceration of a large number of women in closed institutions with staff who have considerable power over them creates a context where they are vulnerable, often leading to terrifying and scandalous conditions. On the other hand, some institutional contexts have adopted policies and procedures and selected and trained staff so that women feel safer than they did before incarceration.

Because there are many reasons for both prisoners and correctional staff not to report sexual misconduct to either researchers or to officials, reliable information is difficult to obtain. Some prisoners see themselves as consenting to sex or trading sex for favors, and therefore do not report sexual misconduct. Some prisoners benefit financially from legal findings of staff wrongdoing and file reports immediately. Many prisoners feel powerless and too intimidated to talk about their exploitation. Staff members sometimes attempt to hide incidents. Responsible personnel can be sued by other staff members who feel they have been unjustly sanctioned after an allegation of sexual misconduct.

Sexual misconduct becomes official record through a series of interactions, and the eventual label is not necessarily a valid indicator of what occurred. For example, rulings of insufficient evidence to prosecute (or to convict) do not mean the women did not suffer or feel coerced into sexual activity, or that such activity has not happened. Many legal suits end with alternative mediation, withdrawal of charges, or settlements,[13] so there are no official findings of wrongdoing. Even if there are legal findings, it is important to remember that these findings reflect a decision made according to legal rules; the court's construction of what happened may not accurately reflect a woman's actual experience.

Several differing claims have been made about sexual misconduct in contemporary women's prisons. These claims are about the acts and incidence of sexual conduct and the responses of correctional staff and administrators. Below, we contrast some claims and conclusions of social scientists, government investigators, watchdog groups, the media, and personnel employed by departments of corrections.

Research by Social Scientists

There has been a paucity of research on prison sexual coercion due to: (a) a lack of awareness of the problem, (b) misperceptions about the nature of prison sexual coercion by social scientists, and (c) discrimination against prisoner victims.[14] To illustrate this last point, Struckman-Johnson cited a poll of 400 registered voters in Massachusetts. The survey results revealed that approximately half of the respondents agreed that society as a whole accepts prison rape as a consequence offenders must endure as a result of their criminal behavior.[15] Although many people in the general public might not define prison rape as a concern, certainly most people who study prisons and the women and men who populate them don't feel this way. Most prison researchers are trying to promote better understanding and improved conditions. However, in a litigious environment, it is often not possible to obtain permission to ask questions about abuse. Just as serious, there are major concerns about harm that such research could bring to the participants, whose vulnerability might be increased by their participation or admissions.

In one anonymous survey of 1,800 men and women in a Midwestern state prison, 20 percent of the responding prisoners indicated that they had been pressured or forced at least once to have sexual contact during incarceration.[16] Prison staff were the perpetrators in 18% of the incidents. Of the women who responded to the survey, 7 percent indicated forced sexual contact by either other prisoners or by staff. The small sample of women and the related small absolute number (3) of women reporting on any incident make it very difficult to draw conclusions about the frequency or nature of sexual assault that most women in prison experience. The degree to which we can generalize about women from this study is further limited because the small facility in a largely rural state (Nebraska) is unlikely to be similar to facilities in Texas, California, or New York, for example. Additionally, just 45% of the women returned the survey, and it is unknown whether they are representative of the women in prison. Women who have been subject to sexual misconduct might either be especially fearful to turn in their surveys, or especially eager to expose the problem, or might vary in these responses.

Another study was conducted in Hawaii between 1982 and 1994.[17] The researcher, A. L. Baro, was a participant observer for 6 years, conducted interviews, and examined government documents and media reports. She found that initially victims of sexual abuse and exploitation were moved to alternative housing arrangements, but no action was taken against staff. Only when people and groups outside the prison applied pressure were formal investigations conducted and actions taken against staff. Baro concluded that incarcerated women are highly vulnerable and that any rumors or reports of staff sexual misconduct should be taken seriously and investigated.

Investigations and Studies by Government Agencies

In 1996, the National Institute of Corrections, a division of the federal Justice Department, conducted a mail survey focusing specifically on sexual misconduct involving correctional staff. The survey instrument was mailed to both state and federal agencies responsible for the administration of adult prisons. The study revealed that during the previous five years, concern about sexual misconduct involving correctional personnel was spurred by: (a) increased litigation related to sexual misconduct, and (b) legislatures passing laws addressing sexual misconduct by correctional staff.[18]

The NIC study also examined the correctional agencies' actions toward personnel and prisoners allegedly involved in some type of sexual misconduct. Actions taken depended on whether the allegations were substantiated, false, or unsubstantiated (see table 6-1). The NIC emphasized that agencies should take a more "proactive stance" toward sexual misconduct, such as monitoring the incidences of sexual misconduct as well as continued training and discussions with both corrections staff and prisoners.[19]

In 1998 and 1999, the General Accounting Office (GAO)[20] conducted a study at the request of The Honorable Eleanor Holmes Norton, a member of the U.S. House of Representatives, who had asked:

- What are the applicable laws, policies, and procedures for addressing such [sexual misconduct] in women's prisons?
- What are the number, nature, and outcome of allegations that have been made in recent years?

GAO staff collected information on the three largest correctional systems for women offenders: the Federal Bureau of Prisons (BOP), the California Department of Corrections, and the Texas Department of Criminal Justice. These three systems collectively held over one-third of incarcerated women. The District of Columbia, where 320 women were incarcerated, was also included in the study. Between 1995 and 1998, the women in the four jurisdictions made 506 allegations of staff sexual misconduct; 92 (18%) were sustained.[21]

Of course not all incidents are reported, and not all actual incidents result in cases for which charges are sustained. In addition, data on all allegations were not available from Texas and the BOP. Therefore, one would have to conclude that the actual number of incidents of sexual misconduct was higher than documented in official records. In most cases, sustained allegations resulted in the staff member's resignation or termination. Only the BOP reported any criminal prosecutions with convictions under criminal misconduct laws.

In all four jurisdictions, another gap in available data was the lack of records or comprehensive information regarding the incidents. Offi-

Table 6-1   Actions Taken toward Staff and Prisoners Involved in Alleged Sexual Misconduct

	Substantiated Allegations	False Allegations	Unsubstantiated Allegations
Staff	The majority of agencies indicated that they dismiss staff involved in sexual misconduct incidents. However, agencies indicated a range of possible actions, including oral reprimands and staff resignation as an alternative to termination. A significant number of agencies responded that they would "take appropriate disciplinary action."	Agencies generally take no action toward staff when allegations of misconduct have been found false. If placed on leave during the investigation, staff return to work and records are generally purged.	Most agencies take no action toward staff involved in unsubstantiated incidents, although about one-quarter indicated that they have a policy of reassigning the staff member. At least three agencies sometimes provide counseling or retraining on behavior or perceptions. A few agencies maintain files of such cases for a period of time.
Prisoners	Nearly all agencies would discipline prisoners involved in sexual misconduct. A few indicated that the prisoner would be transferred.	Although about one-quarter of respondents indicated that no action is taken toward prisoners involved in false allegations of sexual misconduct, most DOCs discipline prisoners who have made a false report of sexual misconduct.	No action is generally taken toward prisoners involved in unsubstantiated incidents. Ten agencies indicated the possibility of reassignment or transfer of prisoners involved.

Source: National Institute of Corrections, *Sexual Misconduct in Prisons: Law, Agency Response, and Prevention* (Longmont, CO: U.S. Department of Justice, NIC Information Center, 1999), p. 7.

cials in the jurisdictions indicated, however, that most incidents involved verbal harassment, improper visual surveillance, improper touching, and/or consensual sex—sexual assault was rare.[22]

In addition to examining official records in four jurisdictions, the GAO staff reported on the external pressure for change that had occurred because of damage suits related to sexual conduct. At least

23 departments of corrections had faced individual damage or class action suits related to staff sexual misconduct. Additionally, during the 1990s the Justice Department filed civil lawsuits alleging systemic sexual misconduct by male correctional staff in women's prisons in Arizona and Michigan. In 1999, the Justice Department and Arizona entered into a settlement agreement. According to the agreement, Arizona had to revise employee and prisoner training, strengthen the methods of investigation, and require that male officers announce their presence when they entered an area where women might be undressed, unless there was a reasonable basis to expect illegal behavior. Also in 1999, Michigan and the Department of Justice entered into an agreement with provisions that were similar to those for Arizona.

The GAO staff found that there had been considerable effort to provide training relevant to staff sexual misconduct. The National Institute of Corrections has trained correctional leaders so that they can effectively influence and develop policies and has provided technical assistance to several federal prisons and to many state departments of corrections. Various pressures have promoted change, yet there are systems that have not pursued the available training.

Since the GAO report, Michigan and Arizona in particular have made substantial changes in tracking allegations and investigations of staff sexual misconduct.

Watchdog Groups

From March 1994 to November 1996, Human Rights Watch (HRW) investigated the sexual abuse of female prisoners at eleven state prisons in various regions of the United States.[23] Their greatest focus was on California, Georgia, Illinois, Michigan, New York, and the District of Columbia. Law students and other volunteers conducted much of the investigative interviewing. Their conclusion was that

> [t]he custodial sexual misconduct documented in this report takes many forms. We found that male correctional employees have vaginally, anally, and orally raped female prisoners and sexually assaulted and abused them. We found that in the course of committing such gross misconduct, male officers have not only used actual or threatened physical force, but have also used their near total authority to provide or deny goods and privileges to female prisoners to compel them to have sex or, in other cases, to reward them for having done so. In other cases, male officers have violated their most basic professional duty and engaged in sexual contact with female prisoners absent the use or threat of force or any material exchange. In addition to engaging in sexual relations with prisoners, male officers have used mandatory pat-frisks or room searches to grope women's breasts, buttocks, and vaginal

areas and to view them inappropriately while in a state of undress or in the housing or bathroom areas. Male correctional officers and staff have also engaged in regular verbal degradation and harassment of female prisoners, thus contributing to a custodial environment in the state prisons for women which is often highly sexualized and excessively hostile.[24]

The HRW report drew public and professional attention to the humiliation felt and expressed by incarcerated women. It gave the women some voice in the dialogue about staff sexual misconduct.

HRW remains very critical of correctional departments' lack of preventive measures for and responses to complaints of sexual misconduct. For instance, they recognized that the response of the Georgia Department of Corrections (GDC) to alleged incidents of custodial sexual misconduct have changed; specifically, the GDC designated an investigator to examine allegations, referred many cases of sexual misconduct to local prosecutors to initiate criminal proceedings, changed leadership, and adopted new standard operating procedures for investigating allegations of sexual misconduct. However, HRW further reported that complainants in suits against the state experienced retaliation by both corrections officers and other prisoners; the GDC failed to fully comply with court orders and did not adequately train corrections staff on sexual harassment and sexual abuse of female prisoners.

HRW has also criticized the New York Department of Corrections.[25] Similar to the group's conclusion about Georgia, HRW recognized that the department had initiated attempts to address the problem of custodial sexual misconduct by supporting legislative reform, making public statements, enhancing relations with nongovernmental organizations, and forming a task force to investigate these issues. However, HRW also concluded that there were remaining problems that included the denial of an effective remedy through grievance and investigative procedures, a lack of confidentiality of such procedures, and bias against prisoner testimony. In addition, HRW reported that conflicts of interest also hindered adequate remedies. Specifically, throughout the hierarchy of employees, corrections officers rarely broke a "code of silence" when their colleagues were being investigated.

Media

The media also provide information on sexual misconduct, as exemplified by one story that unfolded in the newspapers and on television. On September 12, 2000 a legislative hearing of the Senate Corrections and Penology Committee opened to investigate sexual activity among corrections staff and prisoners. The South Carolina Corrections Department Director, William "Doug" Catoe, asked the National Institute of Corrections to assist in the investigation of the state's prison system.[26] In South Carolina, sexual intercourse with an inmate is a felony punishable with a possible ten year prison sentence. Over the prior two years, various allegations against corrections staff included having sex with a prisoner, giving gifts, providing contraband, and abusing prisoners verbally or physically.

A major incident that initiated this investigation involved Susan Smith, an offender whose criminal case had been widely publicized by the media. In 1995, Susan Smith was convicted of murdering her two sons. Initially, she maintained that the boys had been abducted during a carjacking. Nine days after the incident she confessed to drowning her children. While in prison, Susan Smith alleged in a tabloid report that she had been beaten and had four sexual encounters with Lt. Houston Cagle of the South Carolina Department of Corrections. When confronted, Lt. Cagle confirmed these allegations and was immediately fired.[27] Subsequently, another corrections officer, Captain Alfred R. Rowe, Jr., was charged with having sexual intercourse with Smith.[28] Media attention was one of several forces that pushed the full investigation of sexual abuses in the South Carolina prisons and created the context in which reform could take place.

Departments of Corrections Perspectives

Correctional staff and administrators do not always dispute claims of sexual misconduct; indeed, they sometimes investigate and follow up on cases vigorously. However, in some situations, they refute the claims of watchdog groups and the media. For example, in a counterclaim to charges that male correctional staff violated policy by standing outside the door when a body search was performed on a woman, correctional officials argued that this was a necessary precaution since the prisoner was agitated. The counterclaims present an alternative view of why correctional staff have acted in ways that can trigger women's humiliation and distress.

We will use Michigan as an example of differing interpretations of behavior and procedure by correctional departments and watchdog groups or the media. In 1997, Nancy Zang, the Special Administrator for Female Offender Programs for the Michigan Department of Corrections, released a page-by-page rebuttal of a HRW Report.[29] She pointed out that the allegations of attorneys who represented the prisoners in *Neal vs. MDOC et al.* were suspect given the history of the attorneys in the very institutions they were accusing. The attorneys alleged widespread sexual assault, sexual abuse, sexual harassment, and inappropriate visual surveillance perpetrated by staff against women in prison. One of the attorneys had served as the lead attorney for another case for over a decade, and the other had kept regular office hours at one of Michigan's prisons for women while she was an employee of Prison

Legal Services. Despite their regular presence in women's prisons, neither attorney—nor any of the Prison Legal Services attorneys who had
worked for six years in the women's facilities—had ever reported concerns about the sexual abuse of prisoners to administrators at those
facilities. Zang also commented that none of the charges in *Neal vs.
MDOC et al.* were substantiated in Federal District Court and that the
Judge wrote in his opinion and order that "the DOJ failed to offer any
credible evidence of injury, irreparable or otherwise."

Zang provided alternative explanations for what HRW claimed to
be department failure to appropriately respond to reports of staff misconduct. One of the prisoners named in the *Neal* lawsuit claimed retaliation, but the disciplinary action that was taken was based on the
results of a urine test that substantiated her use of drugs. Contradicting
the claim that staff were not adequately trained to work with women in
prison, the Michigan Department of Corrections was one of the first to
require that all staff who worked in women's facilities receive special
training, and they contracted with a nationally known expert to tailor a
40-hour curriculum for use in Michigan. HRW reported that women did
not have any mechanisms for reporting sexual abuse, but prisoners did
have access through an Internet mail system to any administrator at
their facility and also to staff in the central office, and they had access to
phone contact with several individuals, including the legislative corrections ombudsperson, the state appellate defender's office, Prison Legal
Services of Michigan, and attorneys representing women in federal
suits. According to Zang, none of the individuals on this list ever
received communication about an incident of sexual abuse from women
prisoners to the Michigan Department of Corrections.

Claims and counterclaims about staff sexual misconduct in prisons
for women do not center on whether abuse has ever occurred. Rather, the
disagreements are about whether all reports of offenders are accurate,
how widespread staff sexual misconduct is, and whether all reasonable
measures for prevention and follow-up have been taken. Unfortunately,
as we have already noted, social science research has not provided much
information to address these questions, particularly as they pertain to
women. Watchdog groups, the media, women's advocates inside and outside of correctional departments, and government investigations have
raised awareness of the negative experiences and outcomes for many
women affected by misconduct and have created pressure to institute
policies and procedures to protect inmates from sexual misconduct.

INTERNATIONAL STANDARDS AND U.S. LAW

Watchdog groups in particular have emphasized that the realities
for women in U.S. prisons are at sharp odds with international human

rights standards. Also, just as has been true in other aspects of prison life (chapter 5), U.S. constitutional law has been used to push for reform in practices and policies relevant to sexual misconduct. A final protection in most states, as seen in the South Carolina example, is explicit law that criminalizes sexual contact by a member of the correctional staff with an offender in custody.

International Human Rights Standards

For over 50 years, the United States has been a leading advocate in the development of an international system of human rights protection. Under the International Covenant on Civil and Political Rights (ICCPR) and the Convention against Torture and Other Cruel, Inhuman or Degrading Treatment or Punishment (Convention against Torture), the rape of a woman prisoner by a corrections officer constitutes torture and the sexual abuse of a woman prisoner violates human dignity as well as the right to privacy. In 1992, the United States ratified ICCPR. However, it maintained the right to refrain from administering certain provisions or restricting their application. In 1994, the United States ratified the Convention against Torture. As with the ICCPR, the government made some reservations in its compliance.[30]

Human Rights Watch has argued that the "U.S. attempted to limit [its] obligations under these treaties by attaching reservations, declarations, and understandings to both. Several of these reservations, declarations, and understandings were designed to limit U.S. accountability under the treaties in ways that are extremely adverse, among other things, to the elimination of custodial sexual misconduct."[31] Amnesty International, another watchdog and advocacy group, also has maintained that the United States' reluctance to make international human rights commitments is best illustrated by its failure to ratify the Convention on the Elimination of All Forms of Discrimination against Women. One hundred and sixty-one countries have ratified this Convention. In the mid-1990s, the President, many members of Congress, and the public supported ratification, but the Senate prevented this step by never reaching agreement.[32]

Constitutional Protection

Prisoners' constitutional protection from cruel and unusual punishment has been extended in the courts to include protection from sexual misconduct by correctional staff and the right to privacy. The courts also have afforded some protection from sexual harassment.

Claims about privacy involve allegations that viewing nude prisoners of the opposite sex and cross-gender searches are a violation. The right to privacy issue was basic to *Forts v. Ward* (471 F. Supp. 1095 [S.D.N.Y. 1978]), a case in which women imprisoned in New York claimed that having male officers in the housing unit violated their rights. The court ruled in favor of the women. However, since that time cases have been decided not only on the basis of intrusions into the rights of offenders but also based on claims by female correctional employees that gender-based circumscription of their duties denied them equal opportunity for job experience and related advancement.[33] There are, however, limits to what would be allowable in terms of cross-gender searches and visual observation. In 1986, a federal case established that body cavity searches of female prisoners conducted by police officers in the presence of male officers clearly were in violation of the Fourth-Amendment right to be free from unreasonable searches.[34] In general, federal court cases have stressed that cross-gender viewing of a nude prisoner or body cavity searches of offenders is a violation of constitutional rights primarily when it occurs on a regular basis and in situations that are not severe emergencies, but it is allowable if necessary to address security concerns.[35]

In contrast, cases involving non-invasive pat searches of men by women have generally been found permissible under the law.[36] In *Jordan v. Gardner* (986 Fed. 2nd 1521), the U.S. Court of Appeals prohibited random searches of clothed women. These searches had involved male officers totally flattening the breasts of women being searched, inflicting pain and suffering on women, many of whom had been sexually victimized before incarceration. Male staff had been conducting the searches because of prior female staff grievances that they had their break periods routinely interrupted so that they could search women. The decision was that this conduct was offensive in the extreme and that the correctional staff had totally disregarded the reasonable reactions of the women being searched.

A particularly dramatic sexual abuse case occurred in Georgia, where 14 former Department of Corrections employees (10 men, including the deputy warden, and 4 women) were indicted on sexual abuse charges—specifically rape, sexual assault, and sodomy. Women had even been abused in the warden's home. The case was not settled for 8 years. It finally ended in 1992 and was a major impetus to reform in Georgia and also in some other states.

Sexual Misconduct Legislation

Individuals and groups aware of sexual misconduct in women's prisons have emphasized the need to criminalize sexual activity, including consensual activity, between staff, contractors and volunteers, and incarcerated individuals. Many states have had such legal prohibitions for some time; others have instituted them more recently. A recent review found that sexual abuse of prisoners by correctional employees was a felony in 33 states, a misdemeanor in 9 states, and either a misdemeanor or a felony in 5 states, depending on the nature of the offense and circumstances.[37] There were no laws in four states. Of course, laws against sexual assault would apply within the prison, but the more common forms of abuse—consensual involvement (though there may be coercion and favors involved) and pat downs or physical examinations motivated by desire for sexual gratification— are unique to the institutional setting. In addition to criminal law, incarcerated women can file civil actions for intentional infliction of emotional distress, negligence, and assault and/or battery.

Some states have criminal laws that apply broadly to individuals in all types of custodial institutions (for example, hospitals and juvenile detention centers); others have laws that are specific to prisons and jails. Generally, sexual penetration or intercourse and sexual contact (that is, contact for the purpose of sexual gratification) are deemed illegal and penalties are attached. Penalties vary tremendously. In Washington, D.C., engaging in a sex act with an offender can carry a penalty of up to ten years, and any sexual contact can result in a sentence of up to 5 years. In Georgia, if a staff member commits a sexual assault with an offender, the penalty is not less than one or more than three years incarceration. The legislation in many states specifies that the consent of the prisoner is not a defense for the correctional employee. In a few states, offenders who consent to sexual contact or penetration with an employee can also be convicted of an offense.

The legislation in a small number of states specifically directs correctional institutions how to respond to or to prevent sexual activity between employees and prisoners. For example, in Florida the law stipulates that employees must report knowledge of such acts and that the correctional officer training program must include materials specifically designed to explain the parameters of the laws regarding sexual contact and to teach sexual assault identification and prevention methods and techniques.[38]

Constitutional Law

The Eighth Amendment prohibits both the federal and state governments from inflicting "cruel and unusual" punishment. In *Jordan v. Gardner*, the female prisoners argued that the "pat-down" searches conducted by corrections staff involved motions such as "rubbing," "squeezing," and "kneading."[39] Although the psychologists on staff warned that these cross-gender searchers could cause severe emotional distress (i.e., psychological harm) among some prisoners, the warden instituted this procedure on 5 July 1989. The actions, according to the female prisoners, violated their eighth-amendment protection against cruel and unusual punishment. The U.S. Court of Appeals for the Ninth Circuit agreed and ruled that

the record more than adequately supports the district court's finding of psychological harm, and the harm is sufficient to meet the
constitutional minima. Furthermore, the infliction of this pain is
"unnecessary and wanton" under the applicable legal standards.[40]

Two additional cases in the District of Columbia also ruled that sexual
contact between corrections staff and prisoners is an eighth-amendment violation.[41]

The Fourth Amendment ensures an individual's right to privacy:
"the right of the people to be secure in their persons . . . against unreasonable searches and seizures, shall not be violated." The Supreme Court
has not firmly outlined the extent of a prisoner's right to privacy, especially in reference to bodily privacy (e.g., pat frisks and strip searches).
The lower federal courts, however, have recognized the prisoners' limited
right to bodily privacy in rulings that restrict cross-gender frisks,[42] prohibit cross-gender strip searches,[43] and limit cross-gender viewing when
prisoners are taking showers or engaging in other personal activities.[44]

RECOMMENDED CHANGES IN
CORRECTIONAL POLICIES AND PROCEDURES

HRW has recommended several needs that states and the federal
prison system can consider in strengthening the protection of women
in prison from sexual misconduct (see illustration 6-2).

**Illustration 6-2   Issues for Consideration by
                    All State Governments**

- the need to prohibit expressly sexual misconduct in custody in
  both the administrative codes for departments of corrections
  and, where appropriate, in criminal law, in fulfillment of
  international human rights prohibitions on cruel, inhuman,
  or degrading treatment and punishment;

- the need, in every state, to set forth and enforce policies that
  secure privacy protections and protections against verbal degradation that are consistent with U.S. obligations under international human rights law, such as policies that limit strip
  searches, pat frisks, and inappropriate visual surveillance of
  prisoners by employees of the opposite sex;

- the need for thorough training for all current and future correctional employees regarding sexual misconduct and cross-
  gender guarding issues and the implications of international
  human rights treaties and federal and state laws for the conduct of each prison system and its staff;

- the need to reward correctional employees (deputy wardens and wardens in particular) for taking clear action to prevent and punish custodial sexual misconduct and to sanction those who do not;

- the need to ensure that prisoners who are impregnated by corrections staff are not automatically subject to administrative segregation and that they receive timely and adequate medical care, including psychiatric counseling when requested;

- the need to ensure that prisoners who become pregnant as a result of custodial sexual abuse are not pressured in any way to undergo abortions;

- the need to prevent the hiring or rehiring of employees who previously have been fired or have resigned from a job as a corrections employee pursuant to allegations of sexual misconduct;

- the need to establish accessible and effective grievance and investigatory procedures consistent with the right under the International Covenant on Civil and Political Rights, the Torture Convention, and the Standard Minimum Rules to file complaints of official misconduct without fear of retribution or punishment;

- the need to guarantee that such procedures would ensure, *inter alia,* confidentiality of the complainant during the period of time in which the officer is still potentially in contact with her, ensure that her name is not made available to the general population, and impartial investigations are conducted by persons other than the implicated officials, and include meaningful appeal mechanisms;

- the need to protect prisoners from retaliation by implicated officers;

- the need to refrain from directly or indirectly punishing prisoners who have lodged complaints about sexual misconduct and, in particular, to examine the inappropriate and *de facto* punitive use of administrative segregation to punish and/or intimidate prisoners involved in investigations of sexual misconduct;

- the need, consistent with the U.S.'s international human rights obligations, to ensure that those employees who engage in sexual abuse of prisoners under their protection are punished to fullest extent of the law;

- the need to ensure that independent monitoring groups, like many of those mentioned in this report, are able to investigate and evaluate the compliance of the state governments and the U.S. federal government with international human rights and domestic civil rights obligations; and

> • the need to establish independent review boards or the equiva-
> lent of a legislative corrections ombudsperson mandated to
> receive and investigate complaints of sexual misconduct,
> including from prisoners, and to provide information on the
> complaints received by these independent entities to the
> Department of Justice office of data collection suggested above.
>
> Source: Human Rights Watch Women's Rights Project, *All too Familiar:
> Sexual Abuse of Women in U.S. State Prisons* (New York: Human Rights
> Watch, 1996), pp. 13–15.

U.S. correctional systems have varied in their implementation of policies to address these needs. Watchdog groups, the media, and reformers within and outside of correctional departments try to make improvements within the constraints that grow out of systems that rely on relatively uneducated personnel to work with a population that is diverse, typically needy, and increasingly large in number.

CONCLUSION

The sexual abuse of women in prison has been a problem since women were first incarcerated in the United States. It was a major impetus for reformers advocating separate facilities for women. Investigative reports, court findings of wrongdoing, and claims by watchdog groups and the media agree that custodial sexual misconduct remains a problem, though there is disagreement on the extent of the problem in particular places and on the adequacy of legal protections and responses by correctional officials.

Abuse takes many forms, ranging from rape, sexual assault, criminal sexual contact, and mistreatment of prisoners impregnated by corrections staff to abusive, degrading language and privacy violations. Women in prison have reported sexual conduct involving administrators, clergy, corrections officers, medical doctors, psychologists, and teachers. It is essential to stress that even in situations when sexual relations do not involve the overt use or threat of force, the prisoner does not have an equal status in the relationship. This is especially evident when a prisoner tries to free herself from the relationship, and correctional staff exert their power to force her to remain involved. Female prisoners need to be educated about sexual abuse and the appropriate procedures for addressing a problem; corrections staff need to be properly screened and trained on such topics as the sexual harassment and abuse of women prisoners.

Experiencing sexual abuse in prison has extremely damaging effects. Over half of the women in state facilities have reported being physically or sexually abused prior to incarceration. Their history compounds the effects of sexual abuse in prison. In addition to their offender status, many women in prison are marginalized by such characteristics as education, economic status, and ethnic background. These factors increase women's vulnerability to men (and women) in powerful positions.

ENDNOTES

[1] S. W. McCampbell and E. P. Layman, *Training Curriculum for Investigating Allegations of Staff Sexual Misconduct with Inmates* (Tamarac, FL: Center for Innovative Public Policies, 2000).

[2] Cheryl Bell, Martha Coven, John P. Cronan, Christian A. Garza, Janet Guggemos, and Laura Storto, "Rape and Sexual Misconduct in the Prison System: Analyzing America's Most 'Open' Secret," *Yale Law and Policy Review* 18:208–209 (1999).

[3] Cindy Struckman-Johnson, David Struckman-Johnson, Lila Rucker, Kurt Bumby, and Stephen Donaldson, "Sexual Coercion Reported by Men and Women in Prison," *The Journal of Sex Research* 33:67–68 (1996); see also *Farmer v. Brennan*, 511 U.S. 825 (1994) (No. 92-7247); Cheryl Bell, et al., "Rape and Sexual Misconduct in the Prison System"; Human Rights Watch Women's Rights Project, *All Too Familiar: Sexual Abuse of Women in U.S. State Prisons* (New York: Human Rights Watch, 1996).

[4] Russell P. Dobash, R. Emerson Dobash, and Sue Gutteridge, *The Imprisonment of Women* (Oxford: Basil Blackwell, 1986), 9.

[5] Nicole Hahn Rafter, *Partial Justice: Women, Prisons, and Social Control*, 2nd ed. (New Brunswick, NJ: Transaction Publishers, 1990), 6.

[6] Nicole Hahn Rafter, *Partial Justice*, 29–30.

[7] Clarice Feinman, "An Historical Overview of the Treatment of Incarcerated Women: Myths and Realities of Rehabilitation," *The Prison Journal* 70:12–26 (1983); Joycelyn M. Pollock-Byrne, *Women, Prison, & Crime*, 2nd ed. (Pacific Grove, CA: Brooks/Cole Publishing Company, 2002); Linda Zupan, "Men Guarding Women: An Analysis of the Employment of Male Corrections Officers in Prisons for Women," *Journal of Criminal Justice* 20:297–309 (1992).

[8] Estelle Freedman, *Their Sister's Keepers: Women Prison Reform in America, 1830–1930* (Ann Arbor: University of Michigan Press, 1981).

[9] Linda Zupan, "Men Guarding Women," 297–298.

[10] Estelle Freedman, *Their Sisters' Keepers*, 59.

[11] *Ibid.*, 60.

[12] Nicolette Parisi, "The Female Correctional Officer: Her Progress Toward and Prospects for Equality," *The Prison Journal* 64:92–109 (1984); Nicole Rafter, *Partial Justice*.

[13] Cheryl Bell, et al., "Rape and Sexual Misconduct in the Prison System."

[14] Cindy Struckman-Johnson, David Struckman-Johnson, Lila Rucker, Kurt Bumby, and Stephen Donaldson, "Sexual Coercion Reported by Men and Women in Prison," *The Journal of Sex Research* 33:67–68 (1996).

[15] Sennott, C. M., "Poll Finds Wide Concern about Prison Rape," *The Boston Globe*, May 17, 1994, 22.

[16] Cindy Struckman-Johnson, et al., "Sexual Coercion Reported by Men and Women in Prison."

[17] A. L. Baro, "Spheres of Consent: An Analysis of the Sexual Abuse and Sexual Exploitation of Women Incarcerated in the State of Hawaii," *Women and Criminal Justice* 8:61–84 (1997).

[18] National Institute of Corrections, *Sexual Misconduct in Prisons: Law, Agency Response, and Prevention* (Longmont, CO: U.S. Department of Justice, NIC Information Center, 1999).

[19] *Ibid.*, 8.

[20] D. E. Burton, E. Erdman, et al. *Women in Prison: Issues and Challenges Confronting U.S. Correctional Systems* (Washington, DC: General Accounting Office, 1999).

[21] General Accounting Office. *Women in Prison: Sexual Misconduct by Correctional Staff.* (Washington, DC: General Accounting Office, 1999), 32.

[22] *Ibid.*

[23] Human Rights Watch Women's Rights Project, *All Too Familiar.*

[24] *Ibid.*, 1–2.

[25] *Ibid.*, 281–326.

[26] Jeffrey Collins, "Legislative Hearing Begins on Sex in S.C. Prisons," *The Associated Press State & Local Wire.* On-line. Available: http://web.lexis-nexis.com/universise... d5=d737b7219e45bf796019c02d2fac3c88 (September 12, 2000).

[27] North County Times—The Californian, "Prison Guard Fired after Admitting Sex with Susan Smith," *NCTimes Net.* On-line. Available: http://nctimes.com/news/090200/ gg.html (September 9, 2000).

[28] Jeffrey Collins, "Prisoner Sex at Governor's House Prompts Firing of Prison's Director," *The Associated Press State & Local Wire.* On-line. Available: http://web.lexis-nexis.com/universe...df=4.5a062283d3b4e0f6cfc713a4c67f526 (January 11, 2001).

[29] Nancy Zang, *Human Rights Watch Report: Page by Page Rebuttal* (Lansing: Michigan Department of Corrections, 1997).

[30] Delisa Springfield, "Sisters in Misery: Utilizing International Law to Protect United States Female Prisoners from Sexual Abuse," *Indiana International & Comparative Law Review* 10:457–486 (2000).

[31] Human Rights Watch Women's Rights Project, *All Too Familiar*, 47.

[32] Amnesty International, "'Not Part of My Sentence.' Violations of the Human Rights of Women in Custody." On-line. Available: http://web.amnesty.org/902568F7005C.. F5C2222D1AABEA8025690000692FC4?Open (1999).

[33] *Griffin v. Michigan* 654 F. Supp. 690 (1982); *Bagley v. Watson* 579 F. Sup. 1099 (1983).

[34] *Bonitz v. Fair*, 804 F.2d 164 (1st Cir. 1991).

[35] Katherine Bennett. "Constitutional Issues in Cross-Gender Searches and Visual Observation of Nude Inmates by Opposite Sex," *Officers Prison Journal* 7, 100.

[36] *Ibid.*, 102.

[37] Brenda V. Smith "State Criminal Laws Prohibiting Sexual Abuse of Prisoners by Correctional Employees," *Investigations of Staff Sexual Misconduct with Inmates* (Washington, DC: The American University, Washington College of Law, 2001).

[38] The description of legislation summarizes information provided by Brenda V. Smith, American University, Washington College of Law at the training program: Training For Investigators of Staff Sexual Misconduct, July 9–13, 2001. The program was sponsored by the National Institute of Corrections, in partnership with the American University, Washington College of Law, at the Washington College of Law, 4801 Massachusetts Ave, NW, Washington D.C. 20016-8181.

[39] *Jordan v. Gardner*, 986 F.2d 1521 (9th Cir. 1993).

[40] *Ibid.*, 1531.

[41] *Women Prisoners of the District of Columbia Department of Corrections v. District of Columbia*, 877 F.Supp. 634 (D.D.C. 1994) *reversed on other grounds*, No. 95-7041 (D.C. Cir. 1996); *Thomas v. District of Columbia*, 887 F.Supp. 1 (D.D.C. 1995).

[42] *Jordan V. Gardner*, 986 F.2d 1521 (9th Cir. 1993); *Smith v. Fairman*, 678 F.2d 52 (7th Cir. 1982), and *Madyun v. Franzen*, 704 F.2d 954 (7th Cir. 1983), *cert. denied*, 464 U.S. 996 (1983).

[43] *Hardin v. Stynchcomb*, 691 F.2d 1364 (11th Cir. 1982), *rehearing denied*, 696 F.2d 1007 (11th Cir. 1983), and *Canedy v. Boardman,* 16 F.3d 183 (7th Cir. 1994).

[44] *Cookish v. Powell*, 945 F.2d 441 (1st Cir. 1991); *Grummell v. Rushen*, 779 F.2d 491 (9th Cir. 1985); and *Miles v. Bell*, 621 F.Supp. 51 (D. Conn. 1985).

7 |||| Mental Illness, Labels, and Realities

Women in prison face two realities regarding mental illness. Some women inmates with mental illness are not appropriately identified and treated. Also a combination of circumstances common to women offenders (e.g., prolonged exposure to sexual abuse, severe domestic abuse) places them at high risk for particular disorders. Consistent with this view, several court cases (for both women and men) have established that correctional systems must appropriately respond to prisoners' mental health needs, even if those needs are not related to their criminal activity. Women (some of whose accounts are presented in this chapter) and the mental health experts who treat them describe the ways in which medication and other therapies—and an accurate diagnosis of a mental health problem—can bring tremendous relief. We will refer to this pattern of concern about appropriate diagnosis and treatment as the *mental health treatment perspective*.

On the other hand, there is a long tradition of writing and research that criticizes applying the label of mental illness (commonly described as *craziness* or *madness*) to women offenders, stereotyping them in theoretical explanations of their criminality and focusing attention away from other factors that influence them to break the law. Assuming that all or most women break the law as a result of mental illness is inaccurate and distracts attention from structural and contextual influences on women's criminality, like those discussed in chapter 2. Historically, the classification of women offenders as

141

"mad" was justification for physical interventions such as sterilization, electroshock, lobotomy, and psychotropic drug treatment.[1] In both theory and practice, when women's criminality is attributed solely to their own mental state, they are ultimately blamed for their own problems and are seen as inexplicably aberrant. Punitive and controlling approaches are therefore justified. In this line of reasoning, there is concern about the overuse of psychotropic drugs, which essentially keep women inmates calm in the face of the negative prison environment and numerous problems that they have suffered.

Although most of this chapter approaches mental illness from the *mental health treatment perspective*, it is important to recognize that attempts at mental health treatment in correctional settings can be more controlling than helping behavior. When correctional staff and policy support the use of medications, restraints, or confinement in the guise of mental health care but the primary purpose is to maintain control, these actions clearly do not fall within the *mental health treatment perspective*. We will consider this criticism of mental health care in prisons in the section about the *control perspective of mental health labeling*. However, first we focus on understanding the mental health needs of women in prison and then move to the responses to those needs.

THE MENTAL HEALTH TREATMENT PERSPECTIVE

When individuals with some knowledge of psychology talk about the mental health problems of offenders, they usually are referring to symptoms of mental disorder that are categorized by the Diagnostic and Statistical Manual (DSM-IIIR).[2] These include symptoms of post-traumatic stress disorder or alcohol and drug abuse. However, the definition is not used uniformly, and a professional assessment is not always done to determine whether women have a psychiatric disorder. In some studies that we describe below, women are classified by an imperfect measure—contact with the mental health system. This measure does not take into account the type and severity of the mental disorder and might be inaccurate because women who are members of ethnic minorities, poor, or who have limited education are less likely than others to seek or obtain mental health care, especially comprehensive care. Some practitioners and experts use the terms "mental illness" or "mental disorder" very imprecisely to sum up their subjective impressions that a person is suffering from a disorder that could be objectively confirmed. Others limit the application of these labels to people who have suffered from mental illness throughout their lives or to those with certain serious disorders.

Mental disorders include two affective (mood) problems that are found at higher rates for women in prison than for other women. These are depression and bipolar disorder. Depression is a persistent mood and can inhibit a person from working, interacting with others, or doing routine day-to-day activities. Bipolar disorder is marked by swings from a depressed state to a manic state, which is characterized by extreme excitement and agitation. When individuals are manic, they can engage in making plans and taking dramatic steps to achieve these plans, despite the unrealistic nature of what they hope to accomplish. For instance, a woman might decide to take a small sum of money and drive to Mexico to buy jewelry at a low cost and plan to sell the jewelry at a higher cost after her return, with no regard for import/export regulations, the limited amount of income she could actually earn, or the reliability of her car. In a brief period, she may create turmoil for herself and others around her by trying to drive a long distance, having problems in Mexico, and so on.

Personality disorders also are common among women offenders who have mental illness. Borderline personality disorder is characterized by a person's emotions overwhelming her thinking ability. Women with borderline personality disorder can have erratic mood swings and be very demanding and dependent on others at one moment and then very removed the next. They typically benefit from being in a structured setting where they receive support and can learn skills in thinking through increasingly more complex decisions. They often benefit from medications that reduce their mood swings.

Some women offenders are affected by anti-social personality disorder. These women have a disregard for other people's basic rights and for the rules and norms that are commonly accepted. Baugh, Bull and Cohen explained

> "Women with this disorder may repeatedly engage in illegal activity; disregard the wishes, rights, and feelings of others; are frequently manipulative, conning, and deceitful in order to gain personal profit or pleasure; demonstrate impulsivity manifested by failure to plan ahead, or by making decisions without considering the consequences; tend to be irritable and aggressive and may commit acts of physical assault."[3]

People with anti-social personality disorder have a history of conduct disorder before they become adults and do not show remorse or guilt. It is often difficult to design effective programming for them. While a great deal of structure and very clear and strong limits must be provided, there also has to be some graduated relaxation of the structure so people can make their own decisions. As we emphasize in chapter 8, there is a fine line between punishment and control.

A review of the research conducted on women offenders reveals that the most common disorders, listed in order of frequency, are: substance-abuse disorders, borderline and antisocial personality disorders, post-traumatic stress disorder, and the mood disorders of depression and bipolar disorder.[4] Jordan and her colleagues studied women felons who were entering prison in North Carolina.[5] They assessed women for eight different disorders, and 64 percent of the women met the criteria for at least one. At some time in their lives, 44.2 percent had problems with drug abuse or dependence, 38.6 percent with alcohol abuse or dependence, 28 percent with borderline personality disorder, 13 percent with major depression, 11.9 percent with antisocial personality disorder, 7.1 percent with dysthymia (mild depression), 5.8 percent with panic disorder, and 2.7 percent with generalized anxiety disorder. Jordan did not include post-traumatic stress disorder in her research, but other researchers have found that about a third of offenders suffer from this problem.[6]

There is considerable overlap between substance-abuse disorders and other mental illnesses. Dr. Joan Gillece, a member of the Maryland Correctional Administrator's Association Task Force, described this overlap:

> I went to the jails, looked at the folks there and realized . . . these are the same people I see in hospitals . . . I had the homeless, the jailed, the co-occurring disorders. Someday they might be in the jumpsuit in the jail; another day at the state hospital; another day in the homeless shelter . . . I realized I [was] not serving distinctive populations. Because there was not holistic, comprehensive care, [the same people] were rotating from system to system.[7]

More than men who are seriously addicted to alcohol or other drugs, addicted women are likely to experience severe depression and accompanying suicidal thoughts, as well as low self-esteem, loneliness, and isolation.[8] For imprisoned individuals with schizophrenia, major affective disorders or antisocial personality disorder, 90% also have a co-occurring substance disorder. Put another way, an estimated 13 percent of the prison population (including men and women) has both a *serious* mental illness and a substance-abuse disorder. Also, some people may not have a substance-abuse disorder, but they do have a combination of two other disorders.[9] It is not unusual for women in prison to have co-occurring addictive and mental disorders, or what is often referred to simply as "co-occurring disorders."

More than other criminal justice agencies, prisons are forced by circumstances to respond in some way to the mental health needs of offenders. Prisons typically hold offenders for a substantial period of time. The conditions of confinement can contribute to mental health problems and mental health care is consistent with treatment objectives; in many states case law requires adequate screening, assessment and treatment for mentally ill offenders. Most prisons that hold women will have some programming and professional staff available to provide mental health services, though there can be serious limitations in the proportion of women who receive ongoing assessment and screening and in the availability and quality of services. Also, the punitive setting of a prison blurs the lines between supportive mental health care to reduce a person's suffering and forced acceptance of mental health treatments, including drug therapies, that women experience as oppressive and punishing.

Mental Illness and Violence

Despite some sensational movies and books that suggest the contrary, the violence of very few women in prison could be explained by mental illness. First, very few women have committed a violent offense. As we emphasized in chapter 2, in some of the incidents of violence women acted against an abuser in self defense or out of desperation. Second, Teplin's research on women detained in jail showed that most arrests were for nonviolent crime. Except for schizophrenia, rates of disorders were much higher than in the general population.[10] Finally, Center summarized prior research:

> **Most** people with mental illnesses are no more likely to be violent than any other member of the community. However, **some** individuals, as a result of their mental illnesses at certain times, do present a greater risk. Researchers have found that violent behavior is directly linked to psychotic symptoms regardless of whether the individual has ever received mental health services, and that persons currently experiencing psychotic symptoms may be at increased risk of violence.[11]

As described in the next section, psychosis, the mental disorder most clearly connected to violence, is especially rare among women in prison.

The Prevalence and Types of Mental Illness of Women in Prison

A 1998 survey of inmates in state or federal correctional facilities categorized offenders as mentally ill if they met one of two criteria: either the inmates said they had a current mental or emotional condition, or they reported an overnight stay in a mental hospital or treatment program.[12] Using this standard, 23.6% of women in state prisons were categorized as mentally ill in random samples of inmates nationwide. The proportions were lower for men: 16% of men in state prisons were considered mentally ill. The breakdown by ethnicity for women in state prison populations was: 29% white, 20% black, and 22% Hispanic women with a history of mental illness.[13]

One reason for the sizeable group of mentally ill prison inmates is that many states have closed mental hospitals, and a number of former patients have been imprisoned. For example, from 1993 to 1997 the number of prisoners in Michigan increased by 11 percent, but the number of mentally ill prisoners increased by 23 percent.[14]

Not only are women more likely to meet the criteria for mental illness, but a high proportion of mentally ill women report prior physical and sexual abuse.[15] In fact, when only mentally ill inmates are considered, 78% of women report prior physical or sexual abuse.[16] This rate is much higher than the 30% of male inmates reporting abuse. When physical and sexual abuse are separated, female offenders categorized as mentally ill have more often experienced physical abuse (67.6% of women and 27.4% of men). The disparity by gender is even more pronounced for prior sexual abuse (58.9% of women and 15% of men). Although rates of abuse are lower for inmates who are not classified as mentally ill, especially for women, they are by no means trivial. Specifically, 40.2% (compared with 10.8% of men) of women in state prisons who were not categorized as mentally ill and reported that they had been physically abused, and 33.1% said they had been sexually abused (compared with 4.1% of men).[17] The rates are somewhat lower for mentally ill women and men in federal prisons, but the patterns are the same. These high rates for women in prison tend to mirror the pattern for people who are not involved in the justice system: in populations with mental illnesses, higher proportions of women than men have been victims of abuse, especially sexual abuse.[18]

When compared to men, women exposed to childhood maltreatment are abused over a longer period of time, and there is an increase in abuse for some women once they became adults.[19] A history of violent and sexual victimization can contribute to depression; in the general population, this is linked to co-occurrence of substance abuse and mental illness.[20] Childhood maltreatment more often explained depression and substance abuse for women than for men.

Many people have described drug and alcohol abuse as "self medication." Efforts to "self medicate" have been linked to a variety of mental health problems such as depression[21] and is more common for women than for men. For example, in a talk about families in which both mothers and daughters have been incarcerated, Toni Lory, an investigative reporter for *U.S. News and World Reports*, said:

> You know as well as I that one of the biggest culprits here is drugs. Especially crack because it allowed these poor, overwhelmed women a chance to escape their abused bodies and minds. In interviews I did with these women, they told me that crack allowed them to feel good, even if it was for just a few minutes. But don't underestimate the role that alcohol and marijuana play with these women. That is often how they start out, how they start medicating themselves to forget the pain of their lives.[22]

There is often a direct connection between being victimized and post-traumatic stress disorder (PTSD). Flashbacks about the trauma, nightmares, sudden crying or fear or anger, avoidance of activities or closeness to other people, and panic attacks are some of the symptoms of PTSD. Some women (who develop PTSD after victimization) attempt to "self medicate" with alcohol or illegal drugs, become involved in the justice system because of substance abuse, and either receive no treatment or are given inappropriate treatment for PTSD while incarcerated.

Susan Galbraith interviewed ten women offenders and several experts.[23] All of the women suffered from co-occurring disorders, and the experts were psychiatrists, psychologists, and others who were knowledgeable about and had talked directly with many women offenders. Galbraith confirmed that some women began using illegal drugs or abusing alcohol to ease the immediate pain of traumas of various types and/or because of misdiagnosis of neurologically based psychiatric disorders. One expert explained that much mental illness of women offenders is either undetected or incorrectly diagnosed. In the case of incorrect diagnosis, women are labeled as having behavioral disorders when they had neurological disorders that should have been treated with medication. The expert said: "So when they get a little older they self medicate in order to alleviate the stress of the symptoms they're experiencing and the self medication leads to illicit substances."[24]

An experience of trauma is not always connected to substance abuse. Even for women who both experience trauma and use drugs, the trauma does not necessarily *cause* substance abuse. Some of the women that Galbraith interviewed talked about using prior trauma to justify their use of alcohol or other drugs. Some talked about the trauma as the cause of their leaving home, resulting in exposure to people who encouraged and facilitated using drugs. Whether abusing drugs and alcohol is an immediate result of the pain of trauma or the unmet need for psychiatric treatment, there are several ways that a substantial number of women in prison have come to have co-occurring disorders.

In addition to substance abuse and mental illness, incarcerated women can have what Brown, Huba and Melchior called burdens. The accumulation of burdens can create a "level of burden."[25] These burdens include: use of particular types of drugs, HIV-positive status, psychological problems, cognitive impairment, health problems, and (for women in the community) homelessness. Brown and her colleagues found that women with the highest level of burdens were the least likely to remain involved in the earliest stages of a program to address their substance-abuse problems. Clearly, to help this population, which includes some mentally ill women, it is important to have intensive and varied services within the prison. This ideal is rarely achieved, although we will describe some programs that seek to meet a constellation of needs.

Galbraith's interviews and the other literature we reviewed make us aware that women with mental illness, including problems of addiction, vary widely from each other. Women differ in whether they take drugs and the primary types of drugs they take. They vary in the presence and the causes and history of disorders and their symptoms. They also differ in whether they have various "burdens" and in their level of social support.[26] Women offenders with mental illness and/or problems with addiction do not fit a common mold.

Mental Illness and the Prison Environment

The prison can easily recreate an environment and experiences that are similar to traumatic situations associated with multiple personality disorder, depression, substance abuse, and other mental illnesses. Pelvic examinations, particularly by insensitive doctors, confinement in small rooms, being visibly naked in front of men, and being strip or pat searched can flood women's minds with reminders and feelings associated with prior sexual and physical trauma and the resulting feelings of fear and helplessness. In addition, some women experience new traumatization when they are sexually harassed, sexually exploited, or exposed to other types of force perpetrated by other inmates or by staff.

Generally in our society, and even more in prisons, there are many misunderstandings and much ignorance about mental illness. Sometimes staff think that symptoms of mental illness (e.g., sobbing and depression, self mutilation, anxiety) are attempts to manipulate staff or more generally "the system."[27] Or, staff may be at a loss for effective responses to mental illness. Describing her experience of being stereotyped as an out-of-control person needing complete constraint and isolation, one woman offender with a mental illness said,

> Because there wasn't any in between—it was if you have those feelings [of wanting to hurt yourself] and can't control them, then let's strip search you, put you in a cell, and lock it. Or let's strip search you, put you in restraints, and nobody will come talk to you because we don't want to reward those behaviors. I'm not sure people understand that isn't just attention-getting behavior.[28]

Building on the belief that offenders are continuously conning, another woman offender with a mental illness said: "The men were more into the correctional mentality where there's no such thing as mental illness. Even though they were working on a forensic unit. It's—you're a convict and all convicts are manipulative."[29] Staff reaction to inmate behavior as manipulation is often coupled with arbitrary rules and regulations, social isolation, and the emphasis on program participation to earn "good time" or favors from staff. Severely limiting women offenders in personal decision making rather than encouraging them to take control of their lives is a characteristic of incarceration inconsistent with treatment for mental health problems, including substance-abuse treatment.[30]

THE MENTAL HEALTH LABELING AND CONTROL PERSPECTIVE

The research reported in this chapter reveals that a sizeable number of women in prison do suffer from mental illness, often in combination with addictive disorders. There is another important aspect to consider in relation to mental illness and women in prison. Historically, as explained in chapter 2, biological explanations were popular to explain women's criminality even when they had been discredited for men.[31] When the field of psychiatry became influential during the early twentieth century, women's criminality was described as a result of mental illness, and there was a switch from biological explanations to the explanation that mental disturbance or inadequacy best accounted for the criminality of all or most women. This simple explanation differs significantly from contemporary explanations that point to a combination of social and psychological factors that can contribute to women's criminality or that regard mental illness as a primary cause of criminality for only a very small number of women.

In the past there have been claims that correctional staff, often with the support of others in the general population, labeled women offenders as mentally ill in order to control them with medication, physical restraints, and/or isolation. Unrelated to their mental health or illness, their behavior is "psychiatrized."[32] Exemplifying this line of reasoning, Dobash, Dobash and Gutteridge made the case that when women inmates violate gender-role expectations by being rebellious or recalcitrant, they are labeled as "hysterical" and subsequently controlled through a mental health intervention, such as confinement in a mental health housing unit, or forced medication with psychotropic drugs.[33]

Dobash and her coauthors describe and criticize the gender-specific therapeutic correctional model. They identify and take issue with an assumption underlying the model, which is that higher proportions of female inmates are mentally unstable compared to their male counterparts. They also argue that prison officials and staff think that women inmates are particularly difficult to manage because they react to incarceration in more "extreme and neurotic" ways than do men.[34] Some theorists believe that mental illness is completely constructed and has no objective reality; that the label is a negative stigmatization placed by those in power on those with less power.

A team of researchers set out to determine whether female inmates more often received mental health placements within the prison system than male inmates because they violated gender-role norms (for example, by being aggressive) or because they had actual mental health needs.[35] They found that the difference was partly due to differing needs, but it also depended on whether women violated gender-role expectations by being aggressive or agitated. Women engaging in these behaviors were more likely to be placed in a mental health unit than men displaying similar behavior. Their male counterparts, though, were more often placed in disciplinary confinement. Also, depressed women were much more likely to receive mental health placement than depressed men.

Baskin and her colleagues concluded from their research that the prison was reinforcing stereotypic gender roles. However, they note that their conclusion is speculative. Indeed, without knowing exactly what happened to women in their mental health placements, there is no way to support the conclusion. It is possible that women placed in the unit were assessed and provided with appropriate mental health care and that the women did not perceive or experience the placement as oppression or punishment.

Regardless of whether there is an objective state of mental illness that can be established by an expert, women do experience and suffer what they call mental illness, and they do seek and find relief in treatments that include medication and therapy. This view is consistent with documentation of biological bases for many symptoms of mental illness. Some of the mental disorders may result because women experience prison more severely than men. They suffer more pain due to the separation from their children.

In an institution, there are major obstacles to offering effective mental health treatment. There is a high potential for subjecting women to control in the name of treatment in a total institution intended to punish offenders. Some prison staff may place more emphasis on controlling the behavior of incarcerated women than men.[36] There is a difference between offering mental health treatment and the capricious application of stigmatizing labels

Stigmatization

Mancuso and Miller noted that women who break the law and are alcohol and drug users are considered to be deviant in three different ways.[37] More than men, women are not expected to be heavy users or addicts of drugs or alcohol. Women are further stigmatized if they engage in prostitution as a means of making a basic living, and then again if they break the law in other ways.

Interviews that Chonco conducted in Michigan revealed that incarcerated women were unlikely to become involved voluntarily with a separate mental health unit (called a Critical Care Unit, or

CCU) within the prison. Their reluctance was based on fear or experience of being stigmatized if they asked for placement in the unit or because they felt the unit was designated for bizarre and/or dangerous and violent individuals.[38] These perceptions were consistent whether women self-reported that they suffered from mental illness or were assessed by staff to be mentally ill. Moreover, some women, including those whom staff felt needed treatment, resisted being in the CCU because they thought they would be forced to take unwanted psychotropic drugs. Their fears about being forced to accept medication were not consistent with prison policy that required inmate consent for medication and that allowed women to refuse continuation of medication at any time. However, it is possible that their fears and suspicions were more realistic in terms of actual staff behavior versus written policy.

INSTITUTIONAL RESPONSE TO THE MENTAL HEALTH NEEDS OF WOMEN IN PRISON

The mental health treatment perspective encompasses screening and assessment to identify women with mental health problems and proving specific forms of treatment in the prison setting.

Screening and Assessment

Ideally, every offender entering prison would be screened for mental illness by a trained professional. Depending on the outcome of the screening, a full assessment would then be conducted. There are a number of factors that limit effective screening for mental illness: the volume of offenders; limited staff training; the need to screen for substance abuse; the need to take offense history; and the need to assess suicide risk. Although many correctional and treatment staff are aware that they should report or follow up on evidence of hallucinations or other serious overt behaviors, some are unaware that withdrawn behavior can be a sign of serious mental illness. As we have noted, women in prison most commonly suffer from depression, and they frequently exhibit behaviors that should alert trained observers. Unfortunately, the constraints mentioned above often result in many incarcerated women with mental illness being overlooked.

Baugh and her coauthors wrote about Ruby, a young woman who began using drugs during adolescence.[39] She had been placed in several addiction treatment programs. However, when she was released from incarceration,

> Ruby's counselor at the center conducted a more in-depth evaluation and diagnosed coexisting conditions of ADHD [Attention Defi-

cit and Hyperactive Disorder] and a related depression disorder. The treatment goals expanded to include not only drug and alcohol counseling, but education about ADHD issues and help with developing coping skills. In addition, Ruby was referred for a psychiatric evaluation; the physician prescribed psychotropic treatment for ADHD and depression.[40]

Ruby's experiences illustrate that for some offenders, the failure to provide adequate diagnosis limits the success of treatments for substance abuse.

One purpose of screening is to examine motivation and readiness for treatment—to determine the fit with different types of programs.[41] People with substance-abuse problems often relapse, and a variety of alternative programs might need to be available to meet their needs after reassessments are completed. It is relatively rare for a prison setting to have alternative programs or repeated screening and assessment resources, though there are a few particularly large systems that approach this ideal. Even if there is screening, most prisons for women do not have adequate resources or expertise to provide the requisite variety and amount of assistance.

Mental Health Treatment in Prison

Policy Research Associates uncovered a number of deficiencies in mental health services for women prisoners: diagnostic instruments that ignored relevant information (e.g., history of abuse); failure to use mental health evaluations at all, particularly for illness that is serious but not disruptive (such as depression); and a tendency to re-traumatize women within the prison setting.[42]

Morash and her co-researchers found that although some correctional administrators are quite concerned that there is not adequate treatment for mental illness (other than substance-abuse programs), most administrators did not place mental health programs at the top of the list of programs needing expansion.[43] However, one out of three prison administrators recognized some commonalities in the circumstances and backgrounds of women offenders. One said, "While men suffer abuse themselves, generally they react to abuse differently. Women who are victims of abuse tend to continue on as victims of abuse. Men, on the other hand, tend to react to their own history of victimization by becoming the abuser themselves."

Despite the prevalence of mental illness among offenders, state mental health agencies are rarely involved in programming for prisoners. State mental health services provide programming in just 24 percent (12) of the states, and none in 64 percent (32).[44] In the remaining 6 states, it was not clear whether the state mental health agency served women in prison. Other problems identified in the same survey included:

- The inability in many prisons to separate women with a variety of difficulties—those with disruptive symptoms of mental illness, the aged, HIV-positive women. This results in inappropriate use of medication and/or punishment instead of needed mental health treatment.
- Inadequate number and background of staff to assist mentally ill inmates.
- Lack of coordination between mental health services with other agencies in the community or other departments within the prison.

Prisons were most successful in providing adequate programming for women with mental illness if there was a person in the state department of corrections who held a position with responsibility for lobbying both legislators and community agencies to meet a broad range of needs including the mental health needs of incarcerated women.

A survey of 11 "state of the art" mental health programs for women in prison revealed a striking lack of standardization in what people think should be done to help mentally ill offenders and in what they actually do.[45] Target populations are variously identified based on psychiatric diagnosis or on their ability to function in the general inmate population, and there is no consensus on which approach best serves the correctional institution and/or the women.

Program directors described the characteristics of particularly promising programs:

- Aftercare services are provided when women return to the general inmate population.
- Programs are for women only.
- The program addresses childhood victimization of participants.
- Programs administer drugs involuntarily.
- Self-inflicted injury is prevented through regular monitoring or restriction of personal possessions.

Involuntary administration of drugs against an inmate's will and restrictions to prevent self-injury are the gray areas where questions should be raised about whether mental health programming in a prison setting constitutes treatment or punitive control.

The obstacles to providing mental health treatment in a prison are evident in the common difficulties that plagued the programs. Correctional staff were rarely involved in the programmatic response to childhood victimization, and as noted previously, re-victimization is not unusual. Also, it is often impossible to transfer a woman outside the prison to a particular type of psychiatric facility when needed. Finally, special training is not typically provided to mental health workers lacking experience working in prisons.

Programs for Women with Co-Occurring Disorders

Galbraith's interviews with women with co-occurring disorders yielded some descriptions of effective interventions in prison. In talking about the things that had helped them,

> All of the women described experiences or relationships with individuals that helped them begin to change and recover. For many of the women a loving and knowledgeable person—often an inmate or female staff—was critical. For others, proper medication made an enormous difference.[46]

Often, incarcerated women described accurate diagnosis of a mental illness and related treatment as effective. For example, one woman (called Pat in the research) had a public defender and a psychiatrist in a maximum security federal prison who advocated for her and helped her to learn more about her family history of mental illness. Pat said,

> Through the public defender in Baltimore and the support of the forensic psychiatrist at the Lexington facility, they were able to work to have the case transferred so they could minimize the trauma of transporting me and being strip searched when I was already paranoid and fearful and anxious. And so they minimized some of the trauma by helping get the case moved. I stayed on the forensic unit for almost a year. And it was there that for the first time I was really on any kind of medications, found out about the history about my family, had any type of counseling.[47]

During a focus group that Morash and her research collaborators conducted, one woman explained that until coming into a community corrections program, her learning disability and bipolar disorder were not diagnosed, though her dependence on drugs was recognized.[48] The community corrections program staff referred her to community mental health services when they noticed her extreme mood changes, and to a learning disorder specialist when they recognized that she could read at only a beginning level. Given the lack of specialists in a prison setting and the numbers of women with one or more psychological problems, it is not surprising that this woman had not received treatment or learning assistance until she moved from prison to community programs.

Programs to help people with co-occurring disorders can be sequential, parallel, or integrated.[49] Sequential programs treat a person for one problem at a time; when the first treatment is complete, another program begins. Parallel programs treat individuals for different problems at the same time, but in different settings; for example, participating in a drug education and relapse prevention program and at the same time receiving medication from a psychiatrist. Integrated programs have staff who are trained to treat people for more than one problem, and the same program addresses multiple issues at the same time and in the same setting. Particularly for people with serious co-occurring disorders, integrated programs are the most effective.

In prison settings, women usually take part in sequential or parallel programs. Without an integrated approach, women must try to integrate programs themselves, but this is very difficult. Also, given the limited resources for programs in most prison systems, it is fairly unusual for women to be involved in a comprehensive program for co-occurring disorders for any length of time.

Examples of Programs for Women Offenders with Co-Occurring Disorders

Turning Point is a program offered at the Columbia River Correctional Institution in Oregon. Such programs are voluntary; women can choose to leave them and return to the regular prison setting. Both men and women are housed in the prison in separate areas; they leave the prison each day for work-release activities. Turning Point is housed in a wing of a 500-bed minimum security state prison and serves 50 women, each for between six and fifteen months. About 40 percent of the women in the program have only a substance-abuse problem, but the remaining 60 percent also are diagnosed with one or more of the following: post-traumatic stress disorder, depression, bipolar disorder, or psychotic disorders (a very small number).

A site visit to the program revealed several unique features that contribute to the program's effectiveness in treating incarcerated women who have co-occurring disorders.[50] The program should begin with a very strong assessment phase, during which various needs are identified. Treatment should continue for several months for women with multiple issues and problems. The program also recognizes that it is impossible to do therapy in an unsafe environment. Correctional staff receive long-term assignments to the unit so that they can work as a team with treatment staff. The varieties of programming offered include substance-abuse education, life skills education, and development of relapse and prevention strategies. Group sessions and a sense of community are very important to the therapeutic community environment. Some of the ten counselors themselves have recovered from substance abuse or other mental health problems, and women see them as viable role models for recovery. Finally, women in the program are linked to continuing aftercare services so that support continues after release.

Phoenix House of Texas operates a facility that houses 288 women.[51] All of the women have substance-abuse disorders, and approximately 55 percent have a major mental health disorder. The most common mental illnesses are depression and bipolar disorder, and smaller numbers of women suffer from psychosis or anxiety disorders. Like Turning Point, an intensive assessment diagnoses mental health and other problems.

Based on experiences of women in Turning Point and Phoenix House and those of other offenders with co-occurring disorders, it is possible to identify several features that seem to characterize effective programs.[52] All of the programs endorse the importance of a strong community atmosphere and include psycho-educational, 12-step, cognitive-behavioral, and relapse prevention strategies. Additionally, the programs consider women's relationships with men, their relationships and responsibilities for children, pregnancy, and prior history of abuse.[53] The programs are holistic, providing a range of activities and services relevant to the range of participants' needs, including current practical dilemmas as well as experiences and circumstances contributing to drug use or mental illness. Specific sequencing and combinations of program services are tailored and adjusted to women's immediate circumstances.

Role models who have successfully dealt with stigma and realities related to mental illness, substance abuse, and criminality are very important. One expert who worked with incarcerated women suffering from co-occurring disorders explained,

> I would like to see more role models in the mental health system in general. It's important for both providers and people receiving services to see change, growth, and strength which can be acknowledged through the presence of those who have "been there." A critical presence of those to whom the labels are applied in visible, responsible, decision-making positions is needed in order to combat preconceived notions of "competence," "ability," and "dangerousness" based on stereotyping and categorization.[54]

Other writers describe features that make programs for offenders with co-occurring disorders effective.[55] Because substance abuse can create symptoms that are like the symptoms of other mental illnesses, the assessment of problems must be ongoing and the prescription of appropriate medications initially tentative. Women who have an illness requiring drug therapy and who have substance-abuse problems need education about the differences between useful and harmful drugs. Staff also must be educated, or they might erroneously encourage women to avoid taking prescribed medications. Some women with co-occurring disorders might have difficulty with comprehension and focus, and thus meetings would need to be fairly brief, with content presented and repeated in a simple way. Whether these ideals can be accomplished in a prison is an issue that deserves careful examination.

Dilemmas in Providing Mental Health Care in Prisons

Critics of incarceration (as well as mandated or incarcerative mental health care) claim that when women cannot come and go from their treatments at will—and treatments are decided for them and allocated based on judgments by people with power that treatment is deserved—these treatments are not empowering. Unless the prison setting offers alternatives to that setting (as do Turning Point and Phoenix House) or as gender-responsive programming (discussed in chapter 8).

Some proponents of mental health treatment in the prison setting have emphasized the importance of correctional officers being fully trained to support the treatment approach. A director of a jail for women indicated,

> We try to reach out early [to new officers] to offer tips and clues about who the women are, why women are so interactive, and what issues they should know about. For example, if a woman is crying intensely or having nightmares, we try to help officers distinguish the proper level of involvement and what information to pass on quickly to counselors for the most effective intervention. The officers become allies on the women's team instead of buying into the problem-woman stereotype.[56]

Although there are some programs that have successfully trained correctional officers to support treatment, the demands to maintain order with limited resources, along with limitations of correctional officers' education and interests, are powerful forces counteracting efforts in this direction.

Interviews with the directors of several promising programs for women offenders with mental illness reveal some of the difficulties.

- The correctional officers are trained to respond in a particular way to problematic behavior in an institution. At a mental health program in the prison, different approaches sometimes are more appropriate. Some problematic behavior has to be overlooked in an effort to treat these people. Writing them up is not always the best answer.
- The most significant problems associated with mental health services is the lack of coordination with other agencies, whether they be state, federal or local. Mental health industry/agencies seem to be nothing more than island systems. Services and programs are very territorial, which prevents any type of easy transition for a patient that is being released back into the community.
- The management tends to view mental health as unnecessary. In fact, it's almost as though they view mental health service or treatment as an excuse for the inmates to be lazy. The overall attitude seems to push for a punitive approach in the treatment of the inmates. This is especially negative for the women offenders who are already battling with self-esteem issues and guilt.

The philosophy of punishment that pervades prisons, and the related stereotype that "problem women" seek mental health care in order to escape the punitive aspects of imprisonment, can mitigate against and counteract the delivery of mental health services. The conflicted environment is not attractive to mental health professionals. Some may hold negative stereotypes about women in prison and prefer to work with other populations. It is not surprising that the courts have been brought into the issue as suits have been filed against departments of corrections for their failure to meet the needs of mentally ill inmates.

Baugh and her coauthors recommend treatment for mentally ill offenders that includes a "debriefing" period to assist women in counteracting the negative influences of incarceration and that at the same time provides counseling that relies on a voluntary cooperative relationship between counselor and client.[57] They feel that effective treatment must usually be provided after prison. As an example, they describe one client, Connie, who had five children, the last of whom died as an infant. Although Sudden Infant Death Syndrome was mentioned during the trial and Connie maintained her innocence, the prison counselor pressured her to admit her guilt, which she did before release. Only after release did she receive grief counseling to help her adjust to the reality that she had lost four children to adoption and one had died. Given the many countervailing forces against effective delivery of mental health treatment in prison, it is debatable whether a "safe space" or "therapeutic niche" can be created in prisons. Many argue that it cannot, though some programs strive to do this.

CONCLUSION

Some mental illness is caused or aggravated by the social and status factors that promote criminality, or even by the conditions of imprisonment. Some incarcerated women who suffer from mental illness find relief in treatment programs that confine them apart from the general prison population or in programs that operate at particular times and places within the institution, thereby creating a niche where supportive treatment can occur. Unfortunately, these programs usually are not continuous. Rather, they often operate as emergency care or prerelease assistance. If custodial staff are not carefully screened, selected, and trained, they can undermine the efforts of mental health professionals who try to deliver the programs. Also, there are many incongruencies between mental health care and the punitive setting of prisons. However, given the apparent relief that some women get from supportive mental health services, it is of considerable importance to invest increased creativity and resources in meeting their expressed needs.

ENDNOTES

[1] Dorothy E. Chunn and Robert Menzies, "Out of Mind, Out of Law: The Regulation of 'Criminally Insane' Women inside British Columbia's Public Mental Hospitals," *Canadian Journal of Women and the Law* 10:1–32 (1998).

[2] Psychiatric Association, *Diagnostic and Statistical Manual For Mental Disorders: Fourth Edition* (Washington, DC: American Psychiatric Association, 1994).

[3] Susan Baugh, Susan Bull, and Kathy Cohen, "Mental Health Issues, Treatment, and the Female Offender," in Ruth T. Zaplin, ed., *Female Offenders: Critical Perspectives and Effective Interventions* (Gaithersburg, MD: Aspen Publishers, 1998), 215–216.

[4] *Ibid.*, 206.

[5] B. Kathleen Jordan, John A. Fairbanks, and Juesta M. Caddell, "Prevalence of Psychiatric Disorders among Incarcerated Women, II: Convicted Felons Entering Prison," *Archives of General Psychiatry* 53:513–519 (1996).

[6] Linda A. Teplin, Karen M. Abram, and Gary M. McClelland, "Prevalence of Psychiatric Disorders among Incarcerated Women," *Archives of General Psychiatry* 53:505–512 (1996).

[7] Office of Justice Programs, *Conference Proceedings: National Symposium on Women Offenders* (Washington, DC: Office of Justice Programs, 1999).

[8] Richard F. Mancuso and Brenda A. Miller, "Crime and Punishment in the Lives of Women Alcohol and Other Drug (AOD) Users: Exploring the Gender, Lifestyle, and Legal Issues," in Claire M. Renzetti and Lynne Goodstein, eds., *Women, Crime, and Criminal Justice* (Los Angeles: Roxbury Publishing Company, 2000), 93–110.

[9] B. Kathleen Jordan, "Prevalence of Psychiatric Disorders among Incarcerated Women I. Pretrial Jail Detainees," *Archives of General Psychiatry* 53:505–512 (1996).

[10] Linda A. Teplin, Karen M. Abram, and Gary M. McClelland, "Prevalence of Psychiatric Disorders among Incarcerated Women."

[11] Center, C. M. H. S., *Double Jeopardy: Persons with Mental Illnesses in the Criminal Justice System* (Unpublished manuscript, Rockville, MD, 1995).

[12] Paula M. Ditton, *Mental Health and Treatment of Inmates and Probationers* (Washington, DC: U.S. Department of Justice, 1999).

[13] *Ibid.*

[14] M. Hornbeck, "Mentally Ill Flood Prisons," *Detroit News,* 113 (1997, December 4).

[15] Paula M. Ditton, *Mental Health and Treatment of Inmates and Probationers.*

[16] *Ibid.*

[17] *Ibid.*

[18] Elaine Carmen, Patricia P. Rieker, and Trudy Mills, "Victims of Violence and Psychiatric Illness," *American Journal of Psychiatry* 14:378–383 (1984); Andrea Jacobson and Bonnie Richardson, "Assault Experiences of 100 Psychiatric Inpatients: Evidence of the Need for Routine Inquiry," *American Journal of Psychiatry* 144:908–913 (1987).

[19] Dorothy S. McClellan, David Farabee, and Ben Crouch, "Early Victimization, Drug Use and Criminality: A Comparison of Male and Female Prisoners," *Criminal Justice and Behavior* 20:455–476 (1997).

[20] M. J. Alexander, "Women with Co-Occurring Addictive and Mental Disorders: An Emerging Profile of Vulnerability," *American Journal of Orthopsychiatry* 66:61–70 (1996).

[21] James A. Inciardi and Anne Pottieger, "Crack Cocaine Use and Street Crime," *Journal of Drug Issues* 24:273–292 (1994).

[22] Office of Justice Programs, *Conference Proceedings: National Symposium on Women Offenders* (Washington, DC: Office of Justice Programs, 1999).

[23] Susan Galbraith, *And So I Began to Listen to Their Stories . . . Working with Women in the Criminal Justice System* (Delmar, New York: GAINS, 1998).

[24] *Ibid.*

[25] Vivian Brown, George J. Huba and Lisa A. Melchior, "Level of Burden: Women with More Than One Co-Occurring Disorder," *Journal of Psychoactive Drugs* 27:339–345 (1995).

[26] Anthony F. Lehman, "Heterogeneity of Person and Place: Assessing Co-Occurring Addictive and Mental Disorders," *American Journal of Substance Abuse Treatment* 5:32–41 (1996).

[27] Susan Galbraith, *And So I Began to listen to Their Stories...Working with Women in the Criminal Justice System.*

[28] *Ibid.*, 72.

[29] *Ibid.*, 71.

[30] Susan Baugh, Susan Bull, and Kathy Cohen, "Mental Health Issues, Treatment, and the Female Offender."

[31] Lucia Zedner, "Women, Crime, and Penal Responses: A Historical Account," in Michael Tonry, ed., *Crime and Justice: A Review of Research*, Vol. 14 (Chicago: University of Chicago Press, 1991), 307–362.

[32] R. R. Ross and E. A. Fabiano, *Female Offenders: Correctional Afterthoughts* (Jefferson, NC: McFarlund 1986); Carol Smart, *Women, Crime, and Criminology* (London: Routledge and Kegan Paul, 1976).

[33] Russell P. Dobash, R. Emerson Dobash, and Sue Gutteridge, *The Imprisonment of Women* (New York: Basil Blackwell, 1986).

[34] *Ibid.*

[35] Deborah R. Baskin, Ira Sommers, Richard Tessler, and Henry J. Steadman, "Role Incongruence and Gender Variation in the Provision of Prison Mental Health Services," *Journal of Health and Social Behavior* 30:305–314 (1996).

[36] Joanne Belknap, *The Invisible Woman* (Belmont, MA: Wadsworth Publishing Company, 1996).

[37] Richard F. Mancuso and Brenda A. Miller, "Crime and Punishment in the Lives of Women Alcohol and Other Drug (AOD) Users."

[38] Nobuhle N. Chonco, "The Mentally Ill Female Inmate: Do Labels Matter Behind Bars?" Unpublished Dissertation, Michigan State University, East Lansing, 1991.

[39] Susan Baugh, Susan Bull, and Kathy Cohen, "Mental Health Issues, Treatment, and the Female Offender."

[40] *Ibid.*, 212–213.

[41] Roger H. Peters and Holly Hills, *Intervention Strategies for Offenders with Co-Occurring Disorders: What Works?* (Delmar, NY: The National GAINS Center for People with Co-Occurring Disorders in the Justice System, 1997).

[42] Research Associates, *The Mental Health Services Needs of Women in the Criminal Justice System.* (Delmar, NY: The National GAINS Center for People with Co-Occurring Disorders in the Justice System, 1997).

[43] Merry Morash, Timothy Bynum and Barbara Koons, *Mental Health Supplement* (East Lansing: Michigan State University, 1996).

[44] *Ibid.*

[45] *Ibid.*

[46] Susan Galbraith, *And So I Began to Listen to Their Stories . . . Working with Women in the Criminal Justice System*, 69.

[47] *Ibid.*, 70.

[48] Merry Morash, Timothy Bynum, and Barbara Koons, *Findings from the National Study of Innovative and Promising Programs for Women Offenders* (East Lansing: Michigan State University, 1996).

[49] This discussion borrows from the website of the National GAINS Center for People with Co-Occurring Disorders in the Justice System. The address is http://www.prainc.com/gains/publicaiont/treatment.htm.

[50] Merry Morash, Timothy Bynum, and Barbara Koons, *Findings from the National Study of Innovative and Promising Programs for Women Offenders.*

[51] John F. Edens, Roger H. Peters, and Holly A. Hills, "Treating Prison Inmates with Co-Occurring Disorders."

[52] *Ibid.*

[53] Merry Morash, Timothy Bynum, and Barbara Koons, *Findings from the National Study of Innovative and Promising Programs for Women Offenders.*

[54] Susan Galbraith, *And So I Began to Listen to Their Stories . . . Working with Women in the Criminal Justice System*, 80–81.

[55] John F. Edens, Roger H. Peters, & Holly A. Hills, (1997). "Treating Prison Inmates with Co-Occurring Disorders," 84.

[56] Susan Galbraith, (1998). *And So I Began to Listen to Their Stories . . . Working with Women in the Criminal Justice System.*

[57] Susan Baugh, Susan Bull, and Kathy Cohen, "Mental Health Issues, Treatment, and the Female Offender."

8 ‖‖‖‖ Gender-Responsive Programs in Prison Settings

Given the myriad and varying challenges facing women who are motivated to stop criminal activity after release, some practitioners and theorists advocate strongly for gender-responsive programming in the prison setting. Gender-responsive programming equips women to challenge and overcome limiting and destructive stereotypes related to sex along with race, ethnicity, poverty, and age. It supports women's development of agency so they can effectively tackle problems such as abuse by an intimate partner, history of sexual abuse, and untreated mental illness. It does this by providing access to resources and opportunities, and by linking women inmates to professionals and others, including each other, so that there are various effective examples of how women negotiate and "do" gender in ways that free them from oppressive and destructive relationships.

Other activists and theorists contend that the very nature of prison contradicts efforts toward positive change, and that the focus should be on keeping and getting women out of prison. In their view, there can be no such thing as a gender-responsive program in a prison, because prison so fully undermines women's capacity to make decisions and changes in their lives. This chapter will open with a brief history that has brought us to the development of a primarily punitive and depriving prison system. Later sections more fully explore the concept of gender-responsive programming that tries to improve the lot of women inmates, and the difficulties of effective delivery in prison settings.

A BRIEF HISTORY OF PUNISHMENT AND REHABILITATION IN WOMEN'S PRISONS

Over time, ideas have changed about how women in prisons should be treated. As mentioned previously, the earliest prisons housed women and men together, and it was common for women to be subjected to sexual and other abuse by male inmates and staff. Punishment and incapacitation were the primary goals, and harsh conditions were standard. In the nineteenth century, reformers introduced the idea that prisons should rehabilitate offenders, for example by isolating them to contemplate their wrongdoing and exposing them to religious teachings. Women activists led a reform effort to establish separate prisons for women so that women staff and administrators could guide and teach offenders to lead righteous lives and assume appropriate roles, for example as servants or as wives and mothers. The reform effort usually encompassed only a small proportion of women inmates (often young white prostitutes or other morals offenders). Incarcerated African-American women and Caucasian women who departed furthest from the popular ideals of womanhood remained in harsh penitentiaries, work camps, and agricultural prisons. Also, even reformatories used dungeons for inmates considered to pose a threat to others, and many were characterized by overcrowded conditions and scandals precipitated by physically abusive staff.[1]

Although the emphasis on incarceration to protect the public and punish the offender was never completely abandoned, there was a steady increase through the 1960s in rehabilitation programs for offenders in prisons and in less restrictive settings, like halfway houses and work release centers. The increased emphasis on rehabilitation was consistent with the development of the fields of psychology, psychiatry, and social work. Many prisoners, particularly those in states where severe punishment was politically favored, still lived in harsh conditions with little or no education, preparation for work, or even basic medical care. However, in other places, substance-abuse treatment, job preparation, and education programs were established in prison, diversion, and post-release programs. The emphasis was primarily on programming for men, but some programs were replicated for women offenders or even specifically designed for them.

Even when many experts and politicians favored rehabilitation in correctional settings, three influences created special restrictions on what was available for women. First, because the ratio of female to male prisoners was very low and women's offenses were much less violent than were men's, women offenders attracted very little attention. Second, the difference in numbers raised issues of economies of scale. It is less costly per person to deliver a large range of programming to many men than to deliver a large range of programming to a small number of women. Finally, programs for women were often restricted by a narrow set of expectations related to stereotypes. Historically, even prison settings with a focus on rehabilitation emphasized "ladylike" behavior and preparation for being a wife and mother in a traditional nuclear family—despite the incongruence between such stereotypes and the realities of women's lives in abusive and unstable family or partner relationships. Similarly, despite the reality that programs concentrated on food preparation and cosmetology are unlikely to provide adequate resources for women to obtain housing outside of poorly resourced areas and to meet their own and their children's needs, most prison programs were limited to these areas.[2]

During the 1980s in the United States, politicians shifted away from supporting rehabilitation toward "getting tough on crime." Simultaneously, Robert Martinson and his coauthors concluded from a government-funded, comprehensive assessment of research that there was minimal scientific evidence of the effectiveness of correctional programs. This further fueled doubt about the value of rehabilitation and reinforced attitudes favoring punitive incarceration, with an emphasis on rigid rules and strict policies governing every aspect of the inmate's life.[3] Laws restricting judicial discretion, along with political pressures on judges to demonstrate their acceptance of punishment as the best means to protect the public, resulted in judicial decisions that swelled prison populations, including the population of women offenders. After "get tough" policies were in place, women (and men) were more likely to be sent to prison and to serve long sentences.

In the United States, there is currently much talk about identifying and meeting criminogenic needs, including those of incarcerated women. Criminogenic needs include addiction, lack of positive social support, and other factors that impede a person's moving away from criminal activity. Despite the talk, in many prisons there is little action. A study of 201 women in the Cleveland House of Corrections demonstrated the limited access women had to programming:

> Data from this study suggest that . . . a substantial number of women had problems related to sexual and physical victimization, substance abuse, mental and physical health, parenting, and social supports. Many of these women were repeat offenders recycling through the penal system numerous times. The profile of these women suggests they more closely fit the role of victim than perpetrator, with almost all being incarcerated for non-violent

offenses—offenses that in many cases were done in service of "street survival." During incarceration, few of these women's needs were addressed. They were released to return to their home environments no better off than when they had left.[4]

Several published works highlight the inadequacy of programs for incarcerated women—from medical services, education, vocational training, prison industry, law library facilities, to child care.[5] Besides the dearth of programming inside prisons, it is increasingly *un*likely that women will be involved in community programs as they transition out of prisons. As already noted, many women's prisons are far from community-based services, preventing them from learning about and gaining access to available programs before release. Also, parole-board practices and changes in law have decreased the number of women leaving prison before serving their full sentence. As a result, most women are not provided with professional services to link them to mental health treatment, substance-abuse treatment, or advocacy services. Even when women are paroled, parole officer caseloads are larger than in the past, and workers focus on supervision rather than rehabilitation, further limiting support and incentive for women to participate in community programs.[6]

Although there has been a clear overall trend away from rehabilitation and toward long, hard time, there also is a tremendous difference between states in the conditions of confinement for women. Even in the most punitive state prison systems, there are some rehabilitation programs, though they may be limited to such minimal activities as weekly 12-step substance-abuse programs led by community volunteers, or contracts with psychologists or psychiatrists external to the prison for periodic assessment, prescriptions of psychotropic drugs, or counseling. Legal cases on behalf of inmates have ensured that correctional departments make some effort to provide specified levels of medical and mental health care. One court order that had a great deal of impact on women offenders, *Glover v. Johnson*, was decided in 1979. The issue was inequity in the type of programming available to women offenders. The federal judge ruled that equal protection rights required that women prisoners have "parity of treatment," and he ordered a variety of vocational and educational programs be offered to women. In Michigan and in other states, there have been successful efforts to provide women with varied programming. For instance, Michigan developed apprenticeship programs in the building trades. Some prison wardens and other staff have welcomed the lawsuit results that require and promote programs for women. However, as the court supervision of implementation ends, as it did in 2000 for *Glover v. Johnson* in Michigan, there is a strong possibility that women's opportunities will be reduced to match reductions in men's programs under contemporary correctional policies that stress deprivation.

The emphasis on deprivation is not universal. In Minnesota, Oregon, and New York, prisons have maintained a steady emphasis on programs with a rehabilitation emphasis. However, in no state is gender-responsive programming adequate for women in prison. Most contemporary prisons are mixed facilities that combine treatment with a punitive emphasis on custody and maintenance, and the specific mix varies dramatically between state systems or even within states. As we discuss in the next section, having programs for women does not equate with gender-responsive programming that cuts at the roots of gender arrangements and differentials that promote much of women's criminality.

DESCRIPTION AND EXAMPLES OF GENDER-RESPONSIVE PROGRAMS

What unique programming could equip women to desist from criminal activity after release from prison? In some cases the needs are obvious. For example, only women need pregnancy-related services. Also, women most often are responsible for children, so they typically need resources to arrange for child-care and other necessities related to children. Programs for pregnant women and mothers can reduce the stress that could trigger relapse into drug use. Healthy, happy children are an especially positive incentive for women to desist from substance abuse and crime. Gender-responsive programs have the goal of drug-free, healthy babies born to pregnant women, and they support women's desires to see their children frequently, to reunite with them, or to arrange alternative care for them.

The essence of gender-responsive programming is not always obvious and cannot be captured by listings of broad categories of programming, such as education, vocational training, or health care. For instance, both men and women need housing after release from prison, but the shelter needs of women often are more involved and may have impacts on gender-related situations and circumstances. Sometimes women have trouble finding housing suitable for children. Many women offenders were in abusive relationships, and whether they go back to those relationships or are safe from the abuser depends on housing. Also, unsafe housing can bring back haunting memories of prior abuse and can put women at increased risk of sexual assault or other types of abuse that women experience more often than men. Effective programs within or outside of prison need to provide a safe setting, incorporate participant support networks, and provide female staff who model being a woman with agency. Reminders or repetitions of abusive relationships, along with the absence of female role models who are familiar with women's racial, ethnic, and social class experiences and context, reduce a program's relevance and effectiveness.

Stephanie Covington has argued that women have different relationship styles than men and have suffered different types and amounts of trauma (e.g., sexual exploitation and abuse). She believes that it is essential that programs respond to these differences.[7] In her view, (informed by theories of recovery from trauma), women have more need for relationships with other people and can be more strongly affected by them than are men. This can lead women into destructive relationships, for example with abusive men or pimps. It is especially important for women to enhance relationships with their children and to form positive relationships with program staff, mentors, and friends supportive of moving away from drugs. In the past, probation and parole programs have prohibited women from associating with others who are involved with the criminal justice system, and this is true in many places today. However, groups of women offenders who are helpful and caring toward each other can often form a positive and lasting support network.

According to Bloom and Covington, programs must maintain an environment free of physical, emotional, and sexual harassment.[8] To build on women's need for relationships, a nonauthoritarian group facilitator who can form a mutual exchange relationship with women is essential. Women "begin to heal" when a group facilitator is interested in understanding their experiences, listens to painful experiences, and reacts to them appropriately—but does not become overwhelmed. The facilitator needs to model how women move beyond being powerless. Finally, it is important that programs for women offenders help them recognize their own suffering and depression but also teach them methods for calming and soothing themselves. Meditation, yoga, massage, physical exercise, reading, gardening, and art are alternatives to "self medication" through substance abuse. Unfortunately, there have been no published research results on the proportion of women offenders who would benefit from the sort of programming Covington emphasizes.

At the heart of a gender-responsive program is the recognition that women exist in a social context and structure that affords access to choices and opportunities according to class, race, ethnicity, and gender. Gender-responsive programs change women and their circumstances so that they get out of destructive relationships, get access to good jobs, and can negotiate effectively for resources from welfare agencies and health care providers.

Morash and Robinson highlighted the unique and important implication of correctional programming that considers women's social location.[9] Gender-responsive programming should be relevant to incarcerated women's social location and the related opportunities (or lack of opportunities), resources, and life experiences connected to that social location. Social location is dramatically affected by gender in combination with the intertwined forces of ethnicity, race, and social class. Before, during, and after incarceration, realities of women's place in their families, communities, and workplaces include varying degrees of gender-related powerlessness and oppression. Even women with high social class or racial advantage can be sexually harassed and experience abuse by intimate partners. Gender influences the attention that teachers pay to student comments, doctor-patient interaction, and assumptions about a person's personality and abilities. These same attitudes extend to illegitimate contexts of work, including the sex trades and drug trafficking. In these situations women work under the direction of men and are at increased risk of rape, abuse, and control.

Gender-responsive programs should include women only, since mixed-gender settings tend to reproduce women's oppression and domination by men. Good programs should provide effective strategies for overcoming the limitations of gender and other statuses. They can help women inmates to support and care for each other.

Morash and Robinson identified four ways that program directors and correctional administrators conceptualize the connection of gender to correctional programs (see table 8.1). Some people in the group of correctional administrators that Morash and Robinson's studied (i.e., the group included in the National Survey) held the *gender maintenance* perspective, focusing on parenting issues to the exclusion of anything else. Especially in jails, but also in some prisons, "not much has changed since the inception of women's prisons, when administrators aimed the "social organization of prisoners into small 'family' groups," because it "has been regarded as being in the *nature* of women to need such relationships."[10] While there is no doubt that parenting programs are useful to some women and their children, they do not go far enough unless they are part of a much larger strategy for rehabilitation. A primary emphasis on parenting reflects the long-standing tradition of women's prisons to "encourage and ingrain 'appropriate' gender roles,"[11] the most acceptable roles being those of wife and mother.[12] Morash and Robinson's study showed that there is a vast difference between programming to empower women offenders by enabling them to break from traditional gender constructions and programming that practitioners or offenders find acceptable because it is consistent with traditional gender ideologies. Programs that discuss the exercise of male power through childhood sexual abuse and partner abuse break traditional gender stereotypes. Focusing on a woman's right to child custody is one example of an empowering program.

Table 8-1	**Constructions of Gender and the Nature of Correctional Programming**		
Gender Perspective	**Definition**	**Program Emphasis**	**Implications**
Gender Irrelevant	No difference between male and female inmates	Lack of gender-specific programming	Status quo; traditional female roles upheld by default; family issues ignored
Gender Maintenance	Female inmates are different; traditional gender roles should be maintained	Traditional programming that reinforces gender stereotypes—focus on parenting	Status quo; traditional female role maintained; traditional emphasis on family issues
Gender Issues	Female inmates are different; traditional gender roles are problematic	Programming to deal with emotional needs, self-esteem, abuse, victimization issues	Identify and fix women's problems; hold the individual accountable; psychological focus; therapeutic emphasis on family issues
Gender Challenge	Female inmates are different; traditional gender arrangements must be challenged; structural inequality	Non-traditional vocational pro-gramming; emphasis on relationship independence and equality, "stand alone" woman	Avoid gender stereotypes; hold the system accountable; vocational focus; family issues deemphasized

Gender-Responsive Programs in Nooks, Crannies, and Niches at the Prison

There is a tension between the ideal forms of gender-responsive programs for women offenders and key realities of prison. From their research to understand the elements of gender-responsive programs, Bloom and Covington wrote,

> Rather than attempting to cure the client of some pathology, effective programs work with clients to broaden their range of responses to various types of behavior and needs, enhancing their coping and decision making skills. These programs use an "empowerment" model of skill building to develop competencies in order to enable women to achieve independence.[13]

Empowerment is achieved by offering a range of services tailored to women's needs, and by giving women information and the opportunity to use needed services. The notion of inmates as clients who deserve empowerment and independence is at sharp odds with the reality of deprivation and control that dominate prisons. However, many prison programs borrow Seymour's idea and attempt to create alternative experiences for women in "niches" within the broader prison context.[14] Niche programs can be staffed by professionals who work for the department of corrections but are separate from custodial staff. Another alternative is staff housed in the prison but working for another organization; in some cases, custodial and treatment or educational staff work in a cooperative way to support each other's efforts. Some niche programs attempt to develop a team approach so that custodial staff collectively support empowering programs—or at least do not disable them.

Providing an example of the empowerment approach within a prison, Beth Richie described a health curriculum dealing with HIV/ AIDS for incarcerated women that promoted use of a process "designed to help individuals understand the ways that they have been made powerless in society and to support them in taking action on their own behalf. This definition implies that motivating behavior change (positive action) requires the development of a new understanding (or consciousness) about one's social and interpersonal experiences."[15] The curriculum engages women in considering their roles in sexual relationships, the influence of societal factors on the use of alcohol and other drugs, culture and gender-role behavior, and the limitations on life choices for women. A facilitator of a small group discussion of different life experiences introduces information and raises issues relevant to women's analysis of their own degree of empowerment. Although individual characteristics and circumstances are identified as a part of the causation of women's involvement in criminality and/or high-risk sexual activities, there is a shift from "individual shame, guilt and subsequent activity, to a more societal analysis of problems and then to developing empowered action plans that can lead to more effective solutions."[16]

Kendall described an empowering program of counseling in a Canadian federal prison for women. Program participants indicated considerable satisfaction with the program, which Kendall attributed to "the general philosophy and approach used by counselors, which are rooted in feminist therapy and informed by the most recent literature on trauma and recovery.[17] Consistent with the program that Richie studied, themes in feminist therapy emphasized that many women have suffered because others have enforced power and control over them and that women can resist and survive once they understand these forces. Kendall did point to difficulties at the interface of the broader prison context and the program.

> The women felt that any move they made, either inside the prison
> or upon release, was judged in relation to their status as a pris-

oner. Further, despite the almost non-existent opportunities for taking autonomous action and making real choices, women stated that correctional staff and the Parole Board expected them to make positive pro-social choices and decisions."[18]

Although the women were satisfied with the attempt at feminist therapy within the prison, they struggled to make sense of the contradictions imposed by the larger incarcerative environment.

The Bedford Hills prison in New York has created particularly bold empowering programming. There are multiple aspects to the institution-wide approach there. Because the facility holds several offenders with a life or lengthy sentence, these women essentially developed careers in providing services to other offenders. In group discussions with Morash in the mid-1990s, prisoners described several successful efforts to develop programs and ongoing implementation. In reaction to growing inmate fears about HIV and AIDS, they had a dialogue with the warden and participated in meetings with other inmates. The outcome was an inmate-run HIV/AIDS education program that was delivered to all inmates coming into the facility. Since all female inmates in the state were sent to Bedford Hills for assessment and classification, the program had broad impact. Even some staff members obtained needed information. With the support and leadership of a nun working in the prison, women were also active in making quilts to remember inmate's children who had died form AIDS, assisting women in recording children's stories to send to their children, and providing basic necessities (clothing, blankets) to caregivers for infants who had been born to inmates in the prison. A key element making it possible for women to have agency and make decisions (though always with the constraints of authority within the prison setting) was warden Elaine Lord's vision, leadership, and management style. A network of volunteers, with at least one volunteer linked to the inmate staff responsible for each program, made implementation feasible. The volunteers obtained and brought in resources, including both information and material goods—for instance, educational materials and useful items like tape recorders. Community members were allowed to come into the prison and interact with inmates and with staff much more frequently than in many prisons.

The National Survey uncovered a small number of examples of successful approaches or innovations in the classification or assessment of women in prison. These "niche-creating" strategies tailor needed and wanted programming for particular women.[19] An administrator in one state reported having developed an individualized rehabilitation program for women. It entailed biannual meetings between women and their case managers, the head of the education department, and others involved in the rehabilitation process. At each meeting, a woman's current progress in terms of test results, program participation and other factors were reviewed; a new plan for further work was then developed. According to reports, the most beneficial aspects of this system were inmates' involvement in developing their own treatment plan and the positive nature of the interaction between inmates and staff.

In a few states, special "gender-sensitive" procedures provided effective improvements. Initial assessments were conducted at two reception centers and proceeded at a relatively relaxed pace, gathering a considerable amount of qualitative information. The use of computers reduced duplication of basic identifying data, allowed an instant preliminary needs assessment, and provided a specialized assessment of drug-abuse needs. Moreover, there were biannual reevaluations aimed at reducing custody levels and re-examining programming needs. There also was a comprehensive screening process for educational needs for women under 21. To tie the state's allocation of resources for programs to women's actual circumstances and characteristics, information compiled at each reception center was forwarded to the state legislature to assist in determining future program needs.

Some prisons have tried to maintain a fairly open atmosphere within which women can be engaged, at least at some points during the day, as clients of therapeutic community programs, in educational programs, or in other supportive services. In one Oregon prison, women who did not want to participate in a therapeutic community for drug treatment (which was isolated from the rest of the institution in a separate wing of the building) were able to remain in a general population and to seek and receive other drug treatment programs, one of which was tailored to the needs and preferences of African-American women. Integration of assessment with program placement, ongoing inmate-staff discussion of immediate program needs, and a choice between programs maximize the match of women's particular characteristics and circumstances to their daily activities. However, prison settings with these characteristics are not common and depend heavily on the political context in the state as well as resources that allow hiring professional staff, making space for programs available, and covering other program-related costs.

Establishing Gender-Responsive Programming at the Prison

Usually staff within prisons initiate gender-responsive procedures and programs, but advocates in the community also play a role in providing pressure, ideas, and resources. A good example of an outside group that was able to create gender-responsive prison programming is Justice for Women, a non-profit organization, which delivered programs at the Framingham, Massachusetts Reformatory for Women. For instance, they had an HIV/AIDS education program. The program ensured a private and secure niche for a non-punitive program. The physical setting and inmates' relationships with staff were character- istic of a welcoming counseling service rather than of a depriving prison environment. Unfortunately, the philosophy of corrections at Framingham changed to emphasize that the primary cause of women's criminality was their inability to think through their life choices clearly; Justice for Women's programs in the facility were dis- continued because of a prison administrative orientation toward dep- rivation. Correctional ideology that emphasizes punishment rather than rehabilitation (and ignores empowerment completely) concen- trates resources on confinement and severely restricts the availability of programs, especially those that respond to a variety of women's needs and their differences in culture and ethnicity.

Even in the few instances where centralized planning to address the needs of women inmates exists or there are outside advocates who work to create niches for programming that women in prison feel will help them, program effectiveness may be constrained or short lived. Schram documented that even in Bedford Hills—with its considerable gender-responsive correctional programming and special training for custodial staff working with women inmates—custodial staff were more likely to apply negative and limiting stereotypes to women offenders than program staff and inmates who delivered program- ming.[20] Also, as prison environments become more controlling, more sterile, and afford less and less privacy—architectural and manage- ment features that increasingly mark new prisons—it becomes more difficult if not impossible to create "ameliorative environments."[21]

As highlighted throughout this chapter, we are left with some good ideas and models, but the reality is that many women in prison are untouched by them. As promising as these ideas may be, they are rare exceptions. In a system that spends millions of dollars on the bricks and mortar to incarcerate a growing number of women and men, there are severe limitations on the resources available to fund innovative programs. The problem is compounded by an emphasis on punitive deprivation that has become politically popular—and which extends to reasoning like "higher education is a privilege, and thus should not be afforded to inmates."

An Alternative to Programs in Niches: The Gender-Responsive Prison

Canada has tried to establish prisons for women that are gender- responsive institutions, or "feminist prisons."[22] In 1990 the Task Force on Federally Sentenced Women (TFFSW) recommended a comprehensive strategy for the management of federally sentenced women to the Correctional Service of Canada. The Task Force put forth five guiding principles:

- Empowerment—the process through which women gain insight into their situations, identify their strengths, and are supported and challenged to take positive action to gain greater control of their lives.
- Meaningful and responsible choices—women need options that allow them to make responsible choices that relate to their needs, experiences, culture, values, spirituality, abilities and skills.
- Respect and dignity—mutual respect is needed among offenders, among staff and between the two groups.
- Supportive environment—the quality of an environment can promote physical and psychological health and personal development.
- Shared responsibility—all levels of government, corrections, volunteer organizations, businesses, private-sector services, and the community have a role to play in the development of support systems and continuity of service for federally sentenced women.[23]

As a result of the recommendations, the use of an antiquated facility with inadequate programming was dramatically reduced, and four regional facilities and an Aboriginal Healing Lodge were built. The regional facilities used a community living model where women lived in houses and were responsible for housekeeping and personal care of their belongings. Women-centered programs—such as those designed for mothers and children and survivors of abuse—were provided and community residential options were developed.

Innovative correctional programs provided through the Canadian Correctional Services for incarcerated women have attempted to apply the guiding principles described above. Earlier we mentioned Kendall's evaluation of therapeutic services incorporating feminist therapy at one Canadian facility. In another example, the Peer Support Team was developed at one of the regional centers, Grand Valley Institution for Women.[24] A curriculum was developed to train selected women to provide peer support, based on observations that imprisoned women provided each other much comfort and emotional support after a crisis (for example, a suicide attempt in their living unit). At the time of the program evaluation, about half of the 78 women living in the facility had received peer support, and they reported that it was useful to them, particularly in reducing anxiety and sadness. Women who gave support also experienced positive change, including increased self-confidence, the acquisition of conflict mediation skills, and the development of empathy for others. Program evaluators recommended that the program be further improved by having the peer counselors take brief notes about sessions and then discussing them on a regular basis with a staff member who coordinated and supervised the program; another recommendation was to increase the number of women training for peer counselor, while remaining selective about the actual counselors.

The Healing Lodge for Aboriginal women, a part of the Canadian Federal Prison system, is a particularly striking example of a correctional system's efforts to offer women a prison experience that is tailored to helping them establish themselves in a position of efficacy within their cultural context. The Healing Lodge and its programs were designed during a series of meetings of a group of Aboriginal leaders and correctional staff. Following Aboriginal practices, all decisions were made by reaching consensus. The program was designed with recognition that the women in the lodge come from, and will go back to, settings that result from a history of "government indifference, political powerlessness, inadequate land base, nonexistent economic opportunities and racial hostilities."[25] Substance abuse, which stems in part from this context, is treated through providing opportunities and guidance to reconnect and reintegrate with Aboriginal culture, for example through the participation of Elders and in various ceremonies and traditions. Preparation for assuming women's roles within the specific context of the Aboriginal community is central to the Healing Lodge. In the United States, there also are programs that are culturally sensitive in the role models that staff provide, in staff and peer communication style and language, and through attention to group-specific family types and communities and the values of these groups; however, these programs do not pervade the structure and environment of an entire prison setting. Rather, they exist within it.

THE CASE FOR MORE GENDER-RESPONSIVE PROGRAMS IN PRISONS

Beginning in the late 1980s, feminist activists have increasingly argued that incarceration for women should be severely curtailed and that programs and correctional management style should be "gender responsive," or what some have instead called "gender specific." Examples of such arguments were made at a 1999 symposium sponsored by the Office of Justice Programs in the U.S. Department of Justice:

> For too long, women have received little attention, and most concern with prison design and treatment has been based on a male model which does not work well for women.[26]

> In spite of this history of failure, we do know what works well for women; programs that take into account their different needs. Programs should be based on supporting women in relationships, providing them with good role models and mentors, helping them work through their problems with sexual abuse and trauma, pro-

viding them with the job training and education they need to find productive work, and helping them gain increased feelings of self-esteem. Equality for women does not mean sameness in programs for men and women. Instead, programs should be tailored to women's lives and reflect the cultures from which they come.[27]

The focus of reform efforts has been on increasing the variety and number of gender-responsive programs, and on making them available and adapting them through a careful process of assessing, encouraging, and referring women offenders.

The Lack of Needed Assessment and Programming

Assessment. In order to motivate women to desist from criminal activity in the future, the prison needs to provide resources pertinent to earning a living sufficient to support themselves and any dependents and to overcome problems such as addiction, untreated mental illness, or associations that contributed to criminality. We have emphasized that such programs should be based on an awareness of barriers and oppressions due to gender, race, and ethnicity and should provide models and the necessary resources for overcoming these obstacles. A careful assessment of each woman's characteristics, situation, and circumstances would be necessary so that women could be made aware of available programs and experiences within the prison setting—and of the possibility that these could produce change. Since people and their motivations change, assessment would not be a one-time activity. Also, assessed motivation and willingness to use resources would need to be followed by an appropriate opportunity to select between culturally relevant programs and experiences.

With very few exceptions, some of which we have already described, common practices for assessing women entering the prison system are contrary to the idea that prisons can and will provide programs to decrease women's criminal activity. Most attempts by prison staff to understand women focus on (1) the level of "risk" a woman poses and thus the amount of security needed to protect her from herself and to protect others around her; (2) legal requirements to screen for mental health and medical problems (in some states, legal requirements extend to vocational education); and (3) other needs that might be met through programming. Some combination of interviews, testing (for example for vocational interests and aptitude, reading level), and medical examination is usually completed soon after a woman is sentenced to prison. The setting is often in a reception center, which can be a separate facility or a section of a prison that houses all newly sentenced women.

To be effective in equipping and motivating women to reposition themselves after release and to stop criminal activity, assessment would need to be followed by programming that addresses identified needs and by "housing" (placement in a facility and within the facility) that supports this programming by ensuring that correctional staff do not allow custody concerns to undermine the program efforts. Ideally, correctional staff would act to support programs.

In the National Survey, correctional administrators in 11 states (22%) reported that classification and screening were problematic.[28] They said that classification and screening did not provide needed information, were designed for men and not adapted to women, and were not useful in matching women to programming. The placement of women was often dictated by current demands on the system. One administrator, for example, explained the impact of overcrowding: "Currently, the 53 beds intended for maximum-security women are also used for HIV-positive women, women with mental health problems, and those on disciplinary detention. . . . We must downgrade some women who should be in close confinement because of the need for beds." In just 28 states (56%), a woman's security level is matched to a specific facility when the woman is placed. In 11 states, there is only one facility. Matching of housing to security level is found in all of the 12 states with the largest female incarcerated populations (over 1,000), but occurs less consistently in the states with smaller female inmate populations.

For a number of reasons, women prisoners are likely to be "over classified." This means that they are housed in a facility or a section of a facility with higher security than is warranted for the protection of the women or others. Over classification results when there is just one prison facility for women, and the entire institution is organized and managed to accommodate women considered to pose the highest security risks. It also can occur if risk-prediction instruments, which were developed to predict risk among men, mistakenly predict that a large number of women pose a risk for harming themselves or others or escaping. Some states have moved women to facilities designed originally for men, with multiple rows of barbed wire, high walls, and guard towers; others have designed women's facilities with these features. There is little connection between the high level of security and any risk to the community; one wonders how anyone could think that living in this type of setting might reduce the risk of depression and suicide. Restrictive security measures are at sharp odds with providing an experience that empowers and enables women.

The smaller the inmate population in a state, the more likely that correctional administrators will say there is not a connection between inmates' needs for programs and their placement in institutions (see table 8-2). Except for the 12 states that have the flexibility that comes with female inmate populations of 1,000 or more (i.e., multiple and large institutions, economies of scale in program delivery), classification and assessment of women often is unrelated to the kind of place in which they are incarcerated or programs to which they are referred.

Table 8-2   Effect of Program Needs on Placement in Institutions

Size of woman inmate population	Yes	No
Under 100	37.5% (5)	62.5% (5)
100–499	33.3% (6)	66.7% (12)
500–999	50.0% (6)	50.0% (6)
1000 up	41.7% (5)	58.3% (7)

The National Survey found that thirty-nine states used the same classification and assessment instrument for both men and women, seven had adapted the men's instrument for use with women offenders, three had developed a unique classification instrument for women, and one state with a very small prison population reportedly used no instrument.[29] The three prison systems incarcerating the largest numbers of women are operated by the states of California and Texas, and by the Bureau of Federal Prisons. The Bureau of Federal Prisons did require that gender-specific needs be met. Another study, however, found that California and Texas did not require programs and services to address and consider the gender-specific needs of female offenders.[30] Instead, the focus was on standardized or equal treatment of female and male inmates. Although gender-related circumstances and experiences are usually not addressed during assessments in prisons, those related to race and ethnicity are even more ignored.

Table 8-3, adapted from the final report of the National Survey, includes information on the proportion of women screened or assessed by prison systems.[31] In some systems, there is no screening by a physician for mental health problems venereal disease. In many more states, there is no screening for circumstances that are more characteristic of women than men, specifically childhood sexual abuse, abuse by a partner, and needs related to children.

Even for the promising facilities and programs of the reformed Canadian Federal Prisons, there is concern about assessment. Hannah-Moffat points out that the forward-looking group that established procedures and practices for the prisons concluded that "assessments to gain better understanding of women's needs and experiences are more appropriate than classification."[32] However, her analysis of current management practices revealed that women's needs have been redefined as "risks," and women's refusal or inability to participate in programming to reduce these needs lessens their potential to move to lower security levels, which are marked by greater privileges and freedom. As a result, "characteristics like self-injury, history of abuse and incidences of mental health problems can be used by correctional offi-

**Table 8-3   Percent of States Screening
All Women for Specific Problems**

Specific Problems	Percent of All States Screening All Women
Medical (physician)	76%
HIV Status	42%
Venereal disease	86%
Reading and math ability	86%
Vocational choice	60%
Mental health problems	86%
Substance abuse	86%
Needs related to children	48%
Spouse abuse	52%
Childhood sexual abuse	50%

cials to justify various interventions, increase security and to hold the offender accountable for her actions and life circumstances."[33] The assumption that needs are risks, and that a woman's failure to participate in "needs-reducing" programs is itself a risk factor, resulted in the establishment of an "intensive healing program," a closed unit with increased restrictions for both high-risk (i.e., violent) and high-need women. Thus, women with mental health problems are controlled in the same way as violent women or women who pose disciplinary problems. What started as a feminist critique of the correctional system's inability to understand and meet women's needs has been transformed into a way of equating needs with risk assessment, and using this interpretation to justify tighter confinement of women offenders.

Programs. We have already noted that, overall, programming for women in prison is inadequate to position them to avoid crime after release. Mancuso and Miller observed and conducted interviews with women whose lifestyle was marked by a combination of criminal activity and substance abuse—a large proportion of the female prison population. They concluded that the women were relatively untouched by programming to address their substance abuse and dependence, the lifestyle that lead to criminal behavior, cumulative problems (e.g., poor health, homelessness) resulting from this social context, and the larger gender, class, and structural barriers that affect women's lives.[34] Lacking were health and childcare, effective substance-abuse treatment, and government resources (job training, financial support) aimed at empowerment. Just as important, Mancuso and Miller found that what programming the women had experienced failed to recognize the "resiliency that these women possess in order to survive, a resilience that may have a positive impact on the next generation."[35] The programming focused on women's deficits instead of supporting their strengths.

A study of prison-based substance-abuse treatment similarly found that staff in under half of the 53 programs surveyed claimed they were able to treat all of the women who volunteered and who were eligible for treatment.[36] The programs averaged 24 weeks long. Some lasted just five weeks. Some programs did not have separate space, and many did not include a separate sleeping unit. Thus, participants had to move between treatment-oriented programming and living units where peers and staff would contradict or undermine program objectives. Most programs offered case management, relapse prevention, HIV/AIDS education, counseling, 12-step meetings, training in personal empowerment, and groups dealing with such issues as sexual abuse or battering. Only about one out of every three had support programs for parenting. The study conclusion was that since the 1970s, there had not been adequate development of high intensity and long duration substance-abuse treatment programs that assessed and met the range of areas that are problematic for women in prison.

The National Survey revealed that from the point of view of corrections administrators, including prison wardens, programs failed to meet women's needs related to substance abuse, children, work, and mental health.[37] Wardens also said that programs to address women's prior victimization were inadequate. The directors of a set of programs that experts felt were particularly effective with women emphasized the lack of transitional programming for women leaving prison, including transitional housing, vocational training or apprenticeships in the community, and aftercare services—in addition to family-oriented and substance-abuse programming.

There is a serious lack of health and medical care for women in prison. What is available has in many cases replicated what is provided to men. For example, women offenders often do not have access to reproductive services.[38] In some prison systems, dentistry is limited to pulling teeth. A woman must be in severe mental anguish to see a counselor and there are long delays to see a physician.[39]

As we discussed in chapter 4, incarcerated women who are pregnant or who have children often do not have programs available to address special needs related to childbirth or motherhood. This problem is especially acute because many offenders possess limited knowledge about birthing, nutrition, and childcare and child development. In addition, the very restrictive environment of the prison exacerbates problems. Letters may be delayed by review and phone calls difficult or impossible to make. Women must handle custody issues and manage child care under these very difficult conditions. Custody issues can be critical and outcomes will determine how well children are cared for, whether there is anyone who is able to bring a child to the prison for visits, and how easily women can regain custody of their children upon release.

Dowden and Andrews contend that the general program elements and processes that make a program effective for women are no different than those that make a program effective for men.[40] Their meta-analysis of prior research revealed that effective correctional programs concentrate services on the highest risk cases, provide services that are matched to the learning styles of offenders in the programs, and address criminogenic needs. (Criminogenic needs are individual-level risk factors that, if eliminated or reduced, are related to lower levels of criminality.) According to Dowden and Andrews these three variables—risk, offender's learning style, and need—are not related to gender. Another variable that they hypothesized to be related to positive program outcomes was what they called *type of treatment*. The score for this variable reflected the number of the three treatment principles (risk, responsivity to offender's learning style, and need) that the program followed.

Dowden and Andrews found that programs that had positive outcomes focused on providing human services rather than primarily on sanction.[41] Assuming that these variables are not related to gender, Dowden and Andrews feel that their work provides evidence that programs do not need to be gender responsive to be effective. However, this conclusion is questionable. For example, they contend that effective programs focused on needs related to family and peers, regardless of the offender's gender. It is possible that for women the focus was on avoiding associations with men who sexually exploited them, or getting out of abusive and otherwise criminogenic relationships; but for men the focus would have been on integrating them into their families, providing incentives for assuming responsibility as fathers, and not replicating abusive behavior. These specific aspects surely are gender related. Similarly, effective job programs for women might include a unique, gender-related focus on challenging gender stereotypes about appropriate jobs, but this would not be considered in programs for men. Additionally, Dowden and Andrews themselves recognize that some of the "targets" of gender-responsive programs, for example past victimization issues, were not considered in their meta-analysis; these may be important in explaining program outcomes for women offenders. There was no examination of whether relationship-oriented treatment—tailoring treatment programs to be more responsive to the specific learning styles of women offenders—had any impact on recidivism.[42] Thus, although the article describing their meta-analysis concludes that the research does not show that gender-responsive programs are more effective than other programs for women offenders, it actually demonstrates that: programs that address general categories of needs are related to program success for both women and men; the learning approaches that work best for men also work best for women; and programs that are targeted at high-risk offenders and attend to all of the areas (risk, need, learning style) work best for women as well as men. This is very different from saying that there is no difference between the programs that are effective for women and men.

EMPOWERMENT IN PRISONS: AN OXYMORON?

The constraints of prison structure and a punitive environment place enormous barriers to empowering incarcerated women. Mary Bosworth studied women's prisons in Great Britain and concluded that incarcerated women's vulnerability was compounded by the triple practice of "infantilization, medicalization, and domesticization."[43] Authorities cast women in roles as ineffective and disempowered. Under these circumstances, the opportunity to perceive themselves and function with agency is greatly reduced. The impact on women is the opposite of the empowerment that is the goal of gender-responsive programming.

Bosworth also found that women used various means within the oppressive prison environment to exert and express themselves. Ironically, they were able to "get what they wanted" by conforming to stereotypes of femininity. The prison practices and procedures reinforced "a notion of dependency which in turn, reflects an anachronistic ideal of passive femininity."[44] Likewise, in U.S. prisons, "although education and some vocational programs seem to be fairly prevalent, more specialized or nontraditional programs are lacking. Without needed skill training, women are forced into low-wage, dead-end jobs where they can barely manage to earn a subsistence living."[45] Although Bosworth finds some hope that resistance and limited agency will prepare women to manage their lives successfully after release, the realities of limited resources are difficult to overcome.

The environment in many women's prisons is more invasive and controlling than in men's. McClellan studied prisons in Texas and found that women were more often cited for rules violations and were punished more severely, even though their infractions were less serious than men's.[46] Women were most often cited for violating posted rules, and men were most often cited for refusing to work. Violations of posted rules included such things as "drying undergarments," "excessive art work" (too many family photographs on display), "failing to eat all the food on their plates," or "talking while waiting in the pill line." McClellan's follow-up interviews to understand the greater surveillance and formal sanction of women's minor infractions revealed that the wardens basically had different management styles: in the men's prisons, the wardens encouraged informal handling of rules infractions, and in the women's facilities, the wardens encouraged formal handling of all observed infractions. The differences were rooted in cultural stereotypes:

> Staff perceive female inmates to be expressive and temperamental. Female inmates, quite understandably in most cases, perceive authority figures, hence the prison staff, to be hostile and punitive. Negative feelings toward staff lead inmates to respond emotionally to some minor event, which serves to confirm the staff in its perceptions, which results in punitive disciplinary response, which reinforces the initial stereotype.[47]

McClellan claims that the disciplinary treatment of women within prison settings rests on the notion that reform depends on submission, which is consistent with the cultural stereotype that women should be submissive.

Kruttschnitt, Gartner and Miller discovered that the fundamentally coercive character of prison resulted in tremendous similarities among women inmates in their concerns about their families and their worries about turning their lives around after release.[48] However, their prison experiences including relations with staff and other inmates were also affected by their social class backgrounds, ages, and histories of abuse. In one of the more modern prisons, women were uniformly "anomic, suspicious, and detached."[49] Some of the adaptations to prison that have previously been assumed to result from women's personal characteristics and interpersonal styles (for example, the development of strong family-like peer group ties), were not found in this prison, suggesting that the cottage style of older prison facilities, not just the nature of women, produced the difference. The move to construct women's prison facilities in the image of men's, with high-tech surveillance and both material and sensory deprivations, can apparently create the pathological interactions that have so long characterized men's institutions. The small regional women's facilities that the Canadian Federal system has established or the campus-style prisons in the U.S. (such as Shakopee in Minnesota) avoid the images of guard towers, isolation, steel and sterility. They are not the norm, however, particularly among large, new prisons that touch the lives of huge numbers of women.

Hannah-Moffat has identified four very serious limitations of even the reformed Canadian Federal prisons for women.

1. There is a tendency to treat women as though they were from a homogeneous group and to ignore differences between women who are the "keepers" and the "kept," not the least of which is freedom. For Aboriginal women, prisons cannot do anything

about poverty on reserves, abuse in foster homes, and a host of other difficulties women suffered before they came to prison.

2. It is erroneous to assume that therapeutic approaches that staff and experts consider to be helpful are not experienced as oppressive and constraining by women offenders, and programs that emphasize autonomy and choice contradict the realities of incarceration; and even if prison programming is designed for women, the basic structure and purpose of a prison do not change.

3. Despite a rhetoric of moving away from constant surveillance and punishment, the new facilities in Canada have emphasized protection of the public and discipline of inmates, as reflected by the use of fences, isolation from other prisoners, and other typical constraints available to use with incarcerated populations. The inequality in power between staff and inmate, and the potential for staff to punish inmates and invade their privacy, blocks the development of supportive relationships in any real sense.

4. Many empowerment strategies used by prison programs emphasize women's taking responsibility for their problems, but do not acknowledge wider systemic barriers.[50]

In Hannah-Moffat's view, it has simply been impossible to combine the practice of incarceration with feminist ideals of empowerment. It is not enough to insert programs focused on enabling women to make sound decisions into an existing penal structure that does not challenge the social conditions and context that promote women's criminality.

ALTERNATIVES TO PRISON

While the creation of program niches or the evolving forms of alternative prisons are conceivable as program models to provide resources, support, and information that inmates seek in their efforts to improve their lot, alternative community-based programs would avoid many of the inadequacies of prisons. Any judgment that a prison program responds to the needs of women offenders is relative to the possibility that community-based programming might be even more responsive. For many of the low-risk women offenders described in chapter 2, community alternatives are a better option for linking women to multiple programs and services than even the best institutional options.

Judges make the decision to send women to prison, and in most states parole boards govern whether they will be released before serving the full sentence. In many states, the department of corrections can place women in community settings while they are committed. Table 8-4 shows the estimated proportion of women involved in alternatives at some time during their period of commitment to the department of corrections. Work release is the alternative to women's incarceration that is used by the greatest number of states. Halfway houses, pre-release centers, and day supervision also provide alternatives for a high proportion of women in some states. The category "other" most often reflects use of a combination of alternatives, for example "combination of transitional housing, halfway housing, work release and inpatient care" or "combination of work release, pre-release, and home detention." In a few cases, "other" refers to a unique response, such as "home confinement" or "electronic detention." These other alternatives are reported for several states. Boot camps also are used by a sizeable number of states (15), but affect 5 percent or less of the women in those states.

Table 8-4   Women in Alternative Sanctions after Commitment*

alternative sanction	States Reporting %		States Reporting Numbers	
	# of states	avg. %	# of states	# of women
boot camp	15	2.2	14	43.1
day supervision	9	10.0	6	203.7
work release	23	18.4	21	138.8
pre–release ctr.	5	31.4	6	725.8
halfway house	12	10.7	11	185.8
other	19	13.1	17	128.9

*States that do not use a particular type of sanction at all are omitted from the table.

With the exception of boot camps, which affect few women and have many drawbacks,[51] there seems to be room for expanded use of alternatives. At least some states use each of the alternative sanctions for a high proportion of women, and some states use a combination of alternatives. The high variability between states suggests that there are types of alternatives that could be used more extensively than they are or could be added to the available options.

There is very limited research comparing outcomes when alternatives to prison are used. The research that is available is not specific to women. Assessments of men on work release during the last 4 to 6 months of their sentence were conducted in Washington State, which uses the program extensively for both women and men.[52] In Washington, work-release participants spend their days employed and their evenings in highly structured, secure facilities. At least for the men who were studied, work-release participants were no more likely to recidivate, and they were more able to maintain employment after release.

The Women's Prison Association (WPA) in New York City exemplifies a typical program for women about to be released or just released from prison, or at high risk for incarceration.[53] The program provides education, support, and transitional services to women who are HIV-positive and for others who are homeless or about to be released from prison. Because it is located in the community, WPA staff can draw on a network of services in other local agencies and can focus on providing services that otherwise would not be available to meet women's needs. There is emphasis on helping women build a positive support system with their peers and also with volunteers and staff. Self-empowerment and peer support are critical features, and programming builds self-reliance by building independent living skills. Transitional housing is an important, very practical offering.

Prisons are total institutions that cut offenders off from community resources. Typically they are located far from the urban communities from which most women came and to which they will return, and far from state, nonprofit, and private agencies and programs and groups that could assist women during incarceration and after. Women offenders' many needs, which change over time and often become acute at the time of release (e.g., responsibility for children, need for housing) can best be met by a network of services—either attached to one program or spread over coordinated programs. Services must be designed to change as a woman's situation changes. Some of the terms that are used to describe such networks of services include: wrap-around services, continuum of care, and holistic services. For women who have addictive behaviors or self-defeating approaches to thinking through their decisions, the complex set of services may need to include structured living situations (halfway houses) and alternative responses to "slips" (temporary return to a treatment program in an incarcerative setting, supervision in a day treatment program).

Despite the logic of housing women offenders in the community, in the United States there seems to be no move to decarcerate women or men. Meda Chesney Lind attributes the "binge in women's imprisonment" to mandatory sentencing, an emphasis on gender "equality" that promotes treating both women and men harshly, and investment in building new prisons for women without any careful assessment of cost and benefits of alternatives. Other critics have pointed to the self-promotion of the prison industry (which now includes private for-profit corporations that run the prisons) in pushing for continuous upgrading and expansion.

CONCLUSION

Regardless of how much emphasis a state's prisons have on rehabilitation, it is difficult if not impossible to make the case that prisons as a whole are gender responsive. As men's prisons have become more technologically sophisticated in methods of surveillance, any attempt to make women's prisons "equal" can only make gender-responsive programs less available. As Rafter notes, equitable treatment does not mean identical treatment, but attention to the special needs of both women and men.[54] There is a misfit between the prison environment and women's chances to increase their resources, opportunities, and capacity to make decisions—all seemingly critical for women to change their lives.

As we saw in chapter 3, criminological theories point to women offenders' social location as influential in shaping their criminality. Social location is influenced by social class, race, ethnicity, and resources. Also implicated are characteristics that women have (again, often a result of their social location) such as limited education, poor health, sole responsibility for children, and addiction. Prisons by their nature place women in an even more disadvantaged social location— first as a prisoner and then as an ex-convict. As Wacquant notes (though his emphasis is on men in prison), incarceration in the long run creates a permanently unemployable group.[55] Can women use prison niche programs to improve their situations and individual characteristics so that, if they are motivated, they are likely to avoid criminal activity? Can prisons motivate women to do this?

There have been some successful efforts to create niches or to transform institutions so that there is some responsivity to gender-related characteristics of incarcerated women. Success in this area, and continued effort, is necessary, if for no other reason than it is moral to reduce human suffering and help people to live decent lives. It is equally important to examine prison reform in relation to the larger question of imprisonment of women is increasing with no evidence of much benefit for anyone.

ENDNOTES

[1] Merry Morash, "Punishing Women Offenders," in Nicole H. Rafter, ed., *Encyclopedia of Women and Crime* (Phoenix: Oryx Press, 2000), 214–219.

[2] Pamela J. Schram, "Stereotypes about Vocational Programming for Female Inmates," *The Prison Journal* 78:244–270 (1998); Neal Shover, "Institutional Corrections: Jails and Prisons," in J. F. Sheeley, ed., *Criminology: A Contemporary Handbook* (Belmont, CA: Wadsworth, 1991).

[3] Russell P. Dobash, R. Emerson Dobash, and Sue Gutteridge, *The Imprisonment of Women* (New York: Basil Blackwell, 1986); Nicole H. Rafter, "Prisons for Women, 1790–1800," in Michael Tonry and Norval Morris, eds., *Crime and Justice* (Chicago: University of Chicago Press, 1983).

[4] Mark I. Singer, J. Bussy, L. Lunghofer, H. Johnson, M. Chapin, M., Li-Yu Song, *Women Serving Time: Final Report* (Cleveland, OH: Center for Practical Innovations, Mandel School of Applied Social Science, Case Western Reserve University, 1993).

[5] Coramae Richey Mann, *Female Crime and Delinquency* (Birmingham: University of Alabama Press, 1984); Joycelyn N. Pollock-Byrne, *Women, Prison, and Crime* (Pacific Grove: Brooks/Cole Publishing, 1990); T. A. Ryan, *Adult Female Offenders and the Institutional Programs: A State of the Art Analysis* (Washington, DC: National Institute of Corrections, 1984); Ralph Weisheit and Sue Mahan, *Women, Crime and Criminal Justice* (Cincinnati: Anderson, 1988).

[6] Joan Petersilia, *When Prisoners Return to the Community: Political, Economic, and Social Consequences* (Washington, DC: U.S. Department of Justice, 2000).

[7] Stephanie S. Covington, "Women in Prison: Approaches in the Treatment of Our Most Invisible Population," *Women in Therapy* 21:141–155 (1998).

[8] Barbara Bloom and Stephanie S. Covington, *Gender-Responsivity: An Essential Element in Women's Programming. National Symposium on Women Offenders* (Washington, DC: Office of Justice Programs, 1999).

[9] Merry Morash and Amanda L. Robinson, "Correctional Administrators' Perspectives on Gender Arrangements and Family-Related Programming for Women Offenders," *Marriage and the Family Review* 32.

[10] Russell P. Dobash, R. Emerson Dobash, and Sue Gutteridge, *The Imprisonment of Women*.

[11] Joanne Belknap, *The Invisible Woman*, 2nd ed. (Belmont, CA: Wadsworth Publishing Company, 2000).

[12] Pat Carlen, *Criminal Women: Autobiographical Accounts* (Cambridge: Polity Press, 1983); Russell Dobash, R. Emerson Dobash, Sue Gutteridge, *The Imprisonment of Women*; Clarice Feinman, "An Historical Overview of the Treatment of Incarcerated Women: Myths and Realities of Rehabilitation," *Prison Journal* 63:12–26 (1983); Estelle Freedman, "Nineteenth-Century Women's Prison Reform and Its Legacy," in D. Kelly Weisberg, ed., *Women and the Law: A Social Historical Perspective*, Vol. 1 (Cambridge, MA: Schenkman Publishing, 1982), 141–157; Nicole H. Rafter, *Partial Justice: Women in State Prisons, 1800–1935* (Boston: Northeastern University Press, 1985).

[13] Barbara Bloom and Stephanie Covington, *Gender-Responsivity*.

[14] John Seymour, "Niches in Prison," in Hans Toch, ed., *Living in Prison: The Ecology of Survival* (New York: Free Press, 1977).

[15] Beth E. Richie, *The Empowerment Program* (New York: Hunter College Center on AIDS, Drugs and Community Health, 1992).

[16] *Ibid.*

[17] Kathleen Kendall, "Creating Real Choices: A Program Evaluation of Therapeutic Services at the Prison for Women," *Forum on Corrections Research* 6:19–21 (1994).

[18] *Ibid.*

[19] Merry Morash, Timothy Bynum, and Barbara Koons, *Findings from the National Study of Innovative and Promising Programs for Women Offenders*.

[20] Pamela J. Schram, *The Link between Stereotype Attitudes and Behavioral Intentions among Female Inmates, Correctional Officers, and Program Staff*. Dissertation. (Michigan State University, East Lansing, 1996).

[21] John Seymour, *Niches in Prison: Ameliorative Environments within Maximum Security Correctional Institutions* (Albany: State University of New York, 1980).

[22] Kelly Hannah-Moffat, "Feminine Fortresses: Woman-Centered Prisons?" *The Prison Journal* 75:135–164 (1995).

[23] Nancy L. Stableforth, "Effective Corrections for Women Offenders," *The Forum* 11:3–5 (1999).

[24] Fariya Syed and Kelley Blanchette, *Results of an Evaluation of the Peer Support Program at Grand Valley Institution for Women* (Correctional Services of Canada, 2000).

[25] Corrections Services Canada, http://www.csc-scc.gc.ca/test/prgrm/fsw/fsw30/fsw30e02.shtml.

[26] National Symposium on Women Offenders, Monday, December 13, 1999. Plenary 1: Building the Case—Why Focus on Women Offenders? 9.

[27] National Symposium on Women Offenders, December 13–15, 1999. Plenary III: Effective Interventions—Looking at Gender-Responsive Programming, 25.

[28] Merry Morash, Timothy Bynum, and Barbara Koons, *Findings from the National Study of Innovative and Promising Programs for Women Offenders.*

[29] *Ibid.*

[30] U.S. General Accounting Office, *Women in Prison: Issues and Challenges Confronting U.S. Correctional Systems* (Washington, DC: U.S. General Accounting Office, 1999).

[31] Merry Morash, Timothy Bynum, and Barbara Koons, *Findings from the National Study of Innovative and Promising Programs for Women Offenders.*

[32] Kelly Hannah-Moffat, "Moral Agent or Actuarial Subject: Risk and Canadian Women's Imprisonment," *Theoretical Criminology* 3:71–94 (1999).

[33] *Ibid.*

[34] Richard F. Mancuso and Brenda A. Miller, "Crime and Punishment in the Lives of Women Alcohol and Other Drug (AOD) Users: Exploring the Gender, Lifestyle, and Legal Issues," in Clair M. Renzetti and Lynne Goodstein, eds., *Women, Crime, and Criminal Justice* (Los Angeles: Roxbury Publishing Company, 2000).

[35] *Ibid.*

[36] Joan Wellisch, Michael L. Prendergast and M. Douglas Anglin, *Drug-Abusing Women Offenders: Results of a National Survey* (Washington, DC: U.S. Department of Justice, 1994).

[37] Merry Morash, Timothy Bynum and Barbara Koons, *Findings from the National Study of Innovative and Promising Programs for Women Offenders.*

[38] Coramae Richey Mann, *Female Crime and Delinquency.*

[39] Joanne Belknap, "Access to Programs and Health Care for Incarcerated Women," *Federal Probation* 60:34–39 (1996).

[40] Craig Dowden and D. A. Andrews, "What Works For Female Offenders: A Meta-Analytical Review," *Crime and Delinquency* 45:438–452 (1999).

[41] *Ibid.*

[42] *Ibid.*

[43] Mary Bosworth, *Confining Femininity: A History of Gender, Power and Imprisonment* (New York: Fordham University, 1999).

[44] *Ibid.*

[45] Coramae Richey Mann, *Female Crime and Delinquency*; Joycelyn M. Pollock-Byrne, *Women, Prison, and Crime;* Carol Smart, *Women, Crime, and Criminology* (London: Routledge and Kegan Paul, 1976).

[46] Dorothy S. McClellan, "Disparity in the Discipline of Male and Female Inmates in Texas Prisons," *Women and Criminal Justice* 5:71–97 (1994).

[47] *Ibid.*, 89.

[48] Candace Kruttschnitt, Rosemary Gartner and Amy Miller, "Doing Her Own Time?: Women's Responses to Prison in the Context of the Old and the New Penology," *Criminology* 38:681–718 (2000).

[49] *Ibid.*

[50] Kelly Hannah-Moffat, "Feminine Fortresses."

[51] Doris L. MacKenzie, Lori Elis, Sally S. Simpson and Stacy Skroban, *Female Offenders in Boot Camp Prisons: Final Report to the National Institute of Justice, Office of Justice Programs, U.S. Department of Justice* (College Park: University of Maryland, 1994).

[52] Susan Turner and Joan Petersilia, *Work Release: Recidivism and Corrections Costs in Washington State* (Washington, DC: U.S. Department of Justice, 1996).

[53] Catherine Conly, *The Women's Prison Association: Supporting Women Offenders and Their Families* (Washington, DC: U.S. Department of Justice, 1998).

[54] Nicole H. Rafter, *Partial Justice.*

[55] Loic Wacquant, *From Welfare State to Prison State: Imprisoning the American Poor.* Available online at: http://www.globalpolicy.org/socecon/global/wacquant.htm (New York: Global Policy Forum, 1998).

9 ||||| The Force of Incarceration and Women's Response

Even though there are ongoing government-sponsored data collection efforts that survey large samples of women in the justice system and some excellent in-depth studies of selected groups of women, it is a challenge to piece together and abstract a clear picture of the various and complex lives that women have led before incarceration. It also is challenging to determine the prevalence of women's sexual abuse by correctional staff in contemporary prisons, and the effectiveness of efforts to curtail it. It is clear, however, that many women suffer devastating effects of such abuse in prison. Moreover, there is almost no information on how women in the United States experience the sentencing process that changes their status from accused to imprisoned or on whether they think the process is just. Standard research methods and procedures fall short in providing concrete evidence of some crucial aspects of prisoners' lives and prison life. Research in prison is difficult to do, because authorities fear lawsuits and are not often interested in documenting the negative conditions and resulting impact of incarceration. Our best understanding comes from piecing together investigative reports by watchdog groups and government agencies, court testimony, claims and counterclaims about specific instances of abuse, and the limited available communications (either with researchers or with other sources) from women who have been or are in prison.

Throughout this book we have tried to understand controversies surrounding incarcerated women. Are women offenders increasingly violent and vicious? Are they generally unfit to care for their children, or should they be supported in fulfilling their strong drive to do this? Is mental health treatment a guise for intrusive efforts to control women through medications, isolation or talk; or is it an unavailable treatment that could bring women relief from anxiety, depression, or confusion?

The socio-cultural context for these and other controversies is characterized by gender inequity. Stereotypes emanate from and perpetuate inequities both in the larger society and in prisons. Some people stereotype women in prison as passive, as victims, and as mothers without other potential or actual viable roles. Research often reinforces the stereotypical impression that all women in prison can be described in statistical terms of mean, modal, and average. Similarly, detailed studies of a small or unique group of women are often assumed to provide information on *all* women in prison. Images of increasingly violent and "masculine" women taking over U.S. prisons are an example of this type of stereotyping. Stereotyping denies variation and thus the humanity of women, and it facilitates their objectification. Summary statistics reduce incarcerated women to a generic set of needs, of criminal characteristics, or of demographic descriptors. They are seen as representations of types based on their gender, their race, their ethnicity, and their most recent criminal activity.

Clearer but no less troubling than stereotypic, erroneous, or clouded images of women in prison is the disjuncture of the most prevalent and common prison regimes, conditions, and available programming with any semblance of either helpful or enabling social interventions. The numbers of women who are incarcerated coupled with contemporary child custody policies mitigate against women's exercise of their hopes and desires to care for their children. Many practices of mental health treatment in prison settings insult women in contradictory ways, sometimes by withholding diagnosis and helpful treatment for mental anguish and confusion, and other times by imposing involuntary and unwanted controls in the guise of mental health care. Few, if any, of most women's hours in prison are spent in an empowering environment that responds to their needs and improves their resources and opportunities to the extent that they are in an improved state of mind and advantaged social location after release.

ENVISIONED JUSTICE AND REFORM

As a counterpoint to the bleak realities of a large number of women in prison, scholars have envisioned ideal forms of justice and related reform of the court and correctional systems, and practitioners have worked to create and deliver empowering programs in prison settings. Activists and reformers have influenced training, education, policy, court outcomes and legislation. Some incarcerated women have organized, staffed, or demanded certain types of programming, and others have participated in lawsuits against the correctional enterprise or have taken their custody cases to court. The result is some marked improvement in prison conditions in selected places at certain times and opportunities for some women offenders to either avoid incarceration or to improve their situation while incarcerated.

During the Conference Proceedings of the National Symposium on Women Offenders, Nicole Rafter summarized women's prison reform in the past, present and future.[1] She emphasized that "today we know more than ever before." Specifically, research has started to provide a new direction to understanding crime and the effects of incarceration, as well as gender-related issues. For instance, research has demonstrated:

- severe sentences for drug offenders have little effect on the drug trade and mainly affect minor offenders, especially large numbers of women;
- the new drug laws have been "racist in their effects—not intentions," with the prison population consisting primarily of "petty female drug offenders . . . who are predominantly members of racial and ethnic minorities";
- prior victimization and sexual abuse are prevalent in the backgrounds of women offenders;
- women's prisons have fewer programs for rehabilitation than men's—and women have fewer alternatives to incarceration, even though their crimes are typically less violent;
- flat/determinate sentencing not only leads to prison overcrowding but to "immense increases in the costs of imprisonment."[2]

Further, Rafter envisioned that by 2025, research-based reforms in prison policy could possibly result in

- reliance on fewer, smaller prisons that house mainly violent criminals, while people who commit property and public-order crimes, as well as battered women who "strike back," will be given probation, put in half-way houses, or assigned to treatment;
- a recognition that prisons cause crime (are "criminogenic") and that both offenders and members of the community will benefit from rehabilitative alternatives to incarceration; and
- a savings of vast sums of money which might be used for drug treatment and other resources for women at risk.[3]

There are some signs that legislators and the public that supports them are becoming disillusioned with the overuse of prisons, and might support reform efforts. Policy analysis and research are increasingly revealing the devastating effects of wholesale uses of incarceration on minority and other disadvantaged communities. Yet, this shift is far from complete and many elected and appointed officials promote a continuation of "get tough" policies.

"Paint a Picture of a Different Future," Plenary V of these same conference proceedings, presented a vision of policies and planning strategies that establish a multi-systemic approach to meet the various needs of female offenders:

> Imagine, instead, that a woman does her sentence while living in an apartment building with her children, where each has an individual service plan, and there is a drug treatment program while her children get the attention and services they need. As mother gets sober and can assume more responsibility, she participates in educational and vocational activities that prepare her for a job that makes a living wage. She works and gets employment experience. When the woman is ready, she transitions back into more independent living in the community.[4]

This multi-systematic and enabling approach is essential to support women in their efforts to desist from substance abuse and criminal activity. In contrast, fragmented approaches that rely heavily on the threat or the use of incarceration are grossly inadequate.

The realities of many women's pathways to prison and their lives in prison raise questions about whether existing laws and legal processes can be just for women. The U.S. legal system is marred by the influences of stereotypes and other misconceptions about women offenders that riddle sentencing processes and drive court battles over equality of programs and services for incarcerated women and men. The debate over the desirability of "equal treatment versus special treatment" of women in comparison to men is consistent across many of the issues pertinent to women in prison. The judicial ruling in the Glover suit (chapter 8) stressed that correctional programming that is equally responsive to women and men can and indeed should recognize differential situations, interests, and needs of women and men, and therefore is not the same as equivalent programming. This is perhaps easiest to understand in relation to medical care, which for women must consider pregnancy, abortion, and childbearing. It is harder to see a clear solution in the vocational training area. If women prefer lower paying jobs suggested by stereotypic views of women's work, should programs reinforce this interest or should they challenge stereotypes and encourage consideration of a broader and more lucrative range of choices? Which course of action best promotes justice for women? We would argue that programs should enable women to understand the negative features of a sex-stratified field of occupations and to make beneficial choices for themselves within such a system. This strategy promotes justice by empowering women to understand

and to evaluate their choices, whether they ultimately choose jobs traditionally associated with feminine roles or pursue other venues.

Carol Smart maintains that one problem associated with the "equal treatment" paradigm is that it reaffirms the centrality of men—the presumption is that the male is the norm:

> Underlying such an approach in any case is the presumption that law is fundamentally a neutral object inside a liberal regime, thus wholly misconstruing the nature of power and the power of law. Law does not stand outside gender relations and adjudicate upon them. Law is part of these relations, and is always already gendered in its principles and practices. We cannot separate out one practice—called discrimination—and ask for it to cease to be gendered as it would be a meaningless request. This is not to say we cannot object to certain principles and practices, but we need to think carefully before we continue to sustain a conceptual framework which either prioritizes men as the norm, or assumes that genderlessness (or gender blindness) is either possible or desirable.[5]

Thus, women cannot be men's "equal" since equality requires sameness—more specifically, equivalent power, resources, and circumstances. Justice rather than equality is the ideal for women.[6] The pursuit of justice requires special treatment of women to adequately address their unique situation and circumstances. Consistent with reasoning we have presented throughout this book, judicial response should evaluate women's unique situations and mandate program elements that are fair and responsive to women.[7] This would mean that women's lesser roles and influence and different motivation in criminal activities with partners and groups and their actual threat to others would be considered in establishing the degree of culpability for a crime and determining a fair sentence. After sentencing, effective correctional programming to address problems and to obviate future criminal participation should be available.

Mandatory sentencing and punitive sentencing guidelines have increased the number of women in prisons (chapter 3). Judicial reasoning that parental presence is important to children persists in our courts, but it is most often applied to the white majority. During most of their days and hours in prison, women are not in programs or settings that build their capacity to overcome the disadvantages of gender, race, ethnicity, or poverty in family systems, social groups, educational settings, or job markets (chapter 7).

In U.S. prisons, gender-responsive programs, particularly those that recognize and respond to special circumstances of women of color, are an innovation and an ideal, but not the norm. Gender-responsive programs get away from the idea of providing equivalent programming for women and men, which their advocates say ignores or distorts the social realities of female inmates if equality is based on the "sameness" standard.[8] However, gender-responsive programs cannot be the norm in contemporary prisons because the empowerment of women is severely restricted in a punitive, institutional environment where most of the staff support gender inequities in their own lives— or at least do not actively challenge them. Many women in prison adhere to gender stereotypes; through their own interactions and choices, they reproduce disadvantageous gender arrangements.[9] Limiting and negative roles associated with gender, race, ethnicity, and class are produced and magnified by the power and control arrangements in prisons and the interactions of prison staff in positions of authority who approach the offender with bias.

This is not to say that gender-responsive programs do not help women or that they should not be developed and instituted. They enable some women to improve their social and material capital after release from prison. For example, work-release programs allow women to increase knowledge, skills, and monetary savings. Empowering programs inside of prisons can stimulate interactions through which women exercise changed identities. These measures are very partial solutions to the much bigger problem of how women come to break the law and the process through which women are sentenced to prison. Litigation has tried to right the process of sentencing and the adequacy and utility of correctional programs and prison conditions; at the same time, it cannot address society-wide gender and race inequities (chapter 8). Broader social forces have contributed to oppressive prison settings that contradict the very notion of empowerment. The few achievements of empowering moments within prison are often overwhelmed by the contradictory realities of incarceration.

Consideration of the "equal" versus "special" argument exposes the limitations of reform through litigation. Whether the argument is that women are equal to men or are unique from them, men are presented as the standard for comparison.[10] Carol Smart's critique of the assumption that law is outside the social order rather than being embedded in it continues:[11]

> it is law's power to define and disqualify which should become the focus of feminist strategy rather than law reform as such. It is in its ability to redefine the truth of events that feminism offers political gains . . . . Moreover the legal forum provides an excellent place to engage this process of redefinition. At the point at which law asserts its definition, feminism can assert its alternative. Law cannot be ignored precisely because of its power to define, but feminism's strategy should be focused on this power rather than on constructing legal policies which only legitimate the legal forum and the form of law.[12]

Iris Young placed these arguments in a wider context of movements of various marginalized groups including people of color, gay men and lesbians, the elderly, and the disabled.[13] Since the 1960s, marginalized groups have reclaimed a positivity and specificity to group difference which no longer implies exclusion, opposition, or deviation from the norm. She concluded that the politics of difference do not argue that equality implies sameness; rather, the objective of equality implies the full participation and inclusion of these disadvantaged groups in all of society's institutions and social positions. Further, the objective is not to give special consideration to these groups until they achieve "normality"; rather the goal is to "de-normalize" the manner in which institutions establish and maintain their rules "by revealing the plural circumstances and needs that exist, or ought to exist, within them."[14] It may be difficult to institute this ideal vision of justice for women offenders. This vision, however, provides an alternative perspective from which to explore the current processes affecting women in the criminal justice system and how some facets of these processes need to be altered.

LIVING IN PRISON

Unjust structures of gender influence and permeate life in the punitive institution, which is marked by both brutal realities and everyday tedium. This reality stands in sharp contrast to envisioned outcomes of reform efforts and feminist notions of justice. Prison life and experience have been touched by reform efforts, including the outcomes of litigation, so there are programs aimed at empowering women, opportunities for mother-child visits in comfortable environments, efforts to curtail sexual abuse, and care or treatment for emotionally and physically distressed women. However, the institution itself is essentially punitive and oppressive, and moments of positive experience—or even humane treatment—must be found and negotiated by individual women and their advocates. The broader forces of legislative and administrative punitiveness work against the possibility of positive interactions and situations within the prison. Some correctional administrators and legislators seek to dehumanize women in prison completely. Examples include making them wear men's pants, denying them access to education, and responding to them as unworthy of any opportunities or any semblance of a peaceful environment. Alternatively, others seek to reform sentencing and the prison experience. Legislators are increasingly motivated by the financial (if not the human) cost of lengthy, supermax prison confinement. Relatives have organized against the mandatory sentencing that has put their loved ones in prison for a long time. Correctional administrators have found that more benign regimes either provide subtler but more effective sorts of control or have acted on genuine motivations to create a place within the prison that supports emotional and spiritual health and development.

Despite some small opposition to oppressive and lengthy incarceration, most of women's time in prison is far removed from any vision of reform or justice. The pathway into prison has often been through a series of system failures—abusive families, ineffective schools, dangerous neighborhoods, and limited opportunities in job markets. Entry into a prison is humiliating:

> I try and forget what it was like in prison most of the time. When I got there they stripped me down and this guard did a full body search. I was shocked, I never had anyone touch me like that, especially with other guards just standing there watching me. Then they threw me these clothes and took me to a cell. While we were walking, some girls were yelling names at me. It was the most scary thing I have ever seen.[15]

In many prisons, there is constant violence and noise, described as an "atmosphere of bedlam."

> It's always loud, with a bunch of girls screaming and yelling and fighting. It's hell. There isn't any privacy. I was so lonely and I cried, I just wanted out. I never felt so bad in my life.[16]

Involvement in litigation, complaining to staff or to watchdog groups, writing and other artistic expression, and jailhouse advocacy for oneself or others are all ways that women strive to change their situations and do their time. Friendships bring and create support in prison, sometimes by meeting emotional needs for caring and kindness that have not been met in the past—and often are not met in the prison environment.

> I had a few friends. I mean you need people to talk to or you will go crazy. It's hard to know who to trust, but there was one girl who worked in the library with me. She helped me out a lot. She was real smart and she had been in before and when I would get mad she would calm me down. We would talk and we cried together a lot, but it was cool, we helped each other out. You need someone to be your friend to help you just to make it together.[17]

The literature tends to focus on homosexuality between women who are friends in prison, but many researchers have concluded that though there are exceptions, homosexual activity in women's prisons is usually in the context of a mutual friendship rather than exploitation or force.

Women do their time in different ways. Researchers who studied women in prison during the 1950s and 1960s emphasized that women form relationships and interact in ways that reproduce both their roles in traditional families and on the streets.[18] How they do their time is their response to "demands of the institution and to conditions not of their own making."[19] Based on extensive observations of the Central California Women's Facility (CCWF) [an enormous contemporary facility holding 4,000 women], Barbara Owen concluded that "most women want to do their time, leave the prison, and return to the free world. They want to avoid the mix of risky and self-defeating behavior" which can come with drug use, fighting, or damaging relationships within the prison. Many women at CCWF formed a network of relationships that mirrored a family which could provide them support and help them avoid the negative prison influences.

Women at CCWF were not uniformly negative about the effects of prison. One said, "I probably would have been dead if I had not come to prison. I probably would have ended up dead. I was living too fast and I was too young to be living that fast."[20] Another woman said that prison was "The best thing that ever happened to me. I know I would be dead if I hadn't been sent here. It has made me stop and think about what I was doing to myself and my kids."[21]

In contrast to positive views that prison provided much-needed protection from harm's way and a fast life, other women at CCWF spoke about how bitter they were, the impossibility of rehabilitation, drug abuse and fighting in prison, and intrusive efforts to impose psychiatric treatment on them. Some found peace of mind in caring relationships with other women and by carving out a place and filling their time with a routine of activities, but others felt their very being was assaulted.

Bosworth's study of a contemporary prison for women in Great Britain showed that some women were in programs that affirmed their capabilities or that being locked up provided incentive to stop using drugs.[22] She concluded that women in prison draw on a sense of self that is grounded in their "(feminine) identities as mothers, wives, girlfriends and lovers."[23] However, women with a sense of efficacy typically struggled against interactions in the prison setting that cast them in roles "as ineffective, disempowered, feminine subjects."

While we don't want to deny the agency and self-efficacy of women in prison, it is important to understand that power is a matter of degree, not an absolute. Bosworth correctly recognized that when women in prison maintain their identities as good mothers in the face of lost custody and capacity to be with their children, they are resisting restrictive definitions of what a good mother is and negative labels of themselves as bad mothers.[24] They are holding on to some positive sense of self, which is heavily conditioned by the notion that motherhood is an important aspect of a woman's identity. Prison programs that encourage mothers to record books for their children, learn new parenting skills, or write to them reinforce this positive sense of self. Yet, at the same time, we cannot ignore the greater power of most prison systems, buttressed by forces that include child welfare legislation and sentencing practices that emphasize the importance of mother's care only for members of the majority groups. These practices combat individual resistance to denigrations of women's positive sense of themselves. Similarly, from a broader view, women's efforts to maintain meaningful relationships and to carve out a semblance of self-affirming lifestyles within prisons is resistance to a behemoth state institution that in recent history perpetrates unprecedented "intrusions into the soul."[25] Women in prison are constrained by the law and justice system's embodiment of the structures of gender and race that shape and are shaped by interactions and opportunities before and during incarceration.

Women in prison are constrained and influenced by stereotypes, misconceptions of who they are and why they are in prison, and official interventions. At the same time, they speak out about the realities of who they are and what their lives are like. In some cases, research has captured their self-revelations and their resistance. Many women in prison actively participate in raising their children and some are involved in litigation to change prison conditions and to challenge the oppressions of sexual abuse. Yet, often the prison and its correctional programs prevent or undo empowerment and reinforce women's dependency. Still, women do resist, respond to, or even change these environments.

CONCLUSION

Despite the limited research on women in prison and the barriers to their being heard and understood, it is possible to distill some sense of prison life, the forces that impinge on women in prison, and the women themselves from alternative sources of information. Women prisoners' perceptions and thoughts, as well as their circumstances and characteristics, should be considered by policymakers, criminal justice practitioners, academicians, and the public. The controversies pertinent to women in prison are nettlesome and complex. A society that prides itself on justice needs to examine the foundations of its practices—and to evaluate all available inputs—to determine future effective practices.

ENDNOTES

[1] Office of Justice Programs, *National Symposium on Women Offenders: Conference Proceedings*. (Washington, DC: Office of Justice Programs, 1999).

[2] *Ibid.*, 14.

[3] *Ibid.*, 14–15.

[4] *Ibid.*, 81.

[5] Carol Smart, *Law, Crime and Sexuality: Essays in Feminism*. (Thousand Oaks, CA: Sage Publications, 1995), 43.

[6] Elizabeth H. Wolgast, *Equality and the Rights of Women* (Ithaca, NY: Cornell University Press, 1980).

[7] Ilene H. Nagel and Barry L. Johnson, "Gender Issues and the Criminal Law: The Role of Gender in a Structured Sentencing System," *Journal of Criminal Law and Criminology* 85:181–206 (1994).

[8] Susan M. Hunter, "Issues and Challenges Facing Women's Prisons in the 1980s," *The Prison Journal, 64*:129–135 (1984); James G. Fox, "Women's Prison Policy, Prisoner Activism, and the Impact of the Contemporary Feminist Movement: A Case Study," *The Prison Journal, 64*:15–64 (1984).

[9] Pamela J. Schram, "The link between stereotype attitudes and behavioral intentions among female inmates, correctional officers and program staff." Unpublished doctoral dissertation,. (Michigan State University, East Lansing, 1996).

[10] Catherine MacKinnon, *Feminism unmodified: Discourses on life and law* (London: Harvard University Press, 1987); Sally Kenny, "Reproductive Hazards in the Workplace: The Law and Sexual Difference," *International Journal of the Sociology of Law* 14:393–414 (1986); Margaret Thornton, "Feminist Jurisprudence: Illusion or Reality?" *Australian Journal of Law and Society* 3:5029 (1986).

[11] Carol Smart, *Feminism and the Power of Law* (London: Routledge, 1989), 82–85.

[12] *Ibid.*, 164–165.

[13] Iris M. Young, "Feminist Moral, Social, and Legal Theory: Difference and Policy," *University of Cincinnati Law Review* 56:535–550.

[14] *Ibid.*, 550.

[15] Mark R. Pogrebin and Mary Dodge, "Women's Accounts of Their Prison Experiences: A Retrospective View of Their Subjective Realities," *Journal of Criminal Justice* 29:531–541 (2001), 533.

[16] *Ibid.*, 535.

[17] *Ibid.*, 536.

[18] D. Ward and G. Kassenbaum *Women's Prison: Sex and Social Structure* (Chicago, Aldine-Atherton, 1965); R. Giallombardo, *Society of Women: A Study of a Women's Prison*. (New York: John Wiley and Sons, 1966).

[19] Barbara Owen, *"In the Mix": Struggle and Survival in a Women's Prison*. (Albany: State University of New York Press, 1998).

[20] *Ibid.*

[21] *Ibid.*

[22] Mary Bosworth, "Resistance and Compliance in Women's Prisons: Towards a Critique of Legitimacy," *Critical Criminology* 7:5–19 (1996).

[23] *Ibid.*

[24] *Ibid.*, 161.

[25] Michel Foucault, *Discipline and Punishment: The Birth of the Prison* (NY: Vintage Books, 1977).

‖‖‖ Bibliography

Acoca, L., & Raeder, M. S. (1999). Severing family ties: The plight of nonviolent female offenders and their children. *Stanford Law & Policy Review, 11,* 133–144.

Agozino, B. (1997). *Black Women and the Criminal Justice System.* Aldershot, England: Ashgate Publishing Company.

Albonetti, C. A. (1997). Sentencing under the Federal Sentencing Guidelines: Effects of defendant characteristics, guilty please, and departures on sentence outcomes for drug offenses, 1991–1992. *Law & Society Review, 31,* 789–819.

Alexander, C. M. (1997). Crushing equality: Gender equal sentencing in America, *Gender & Law, 6,* 199–228.

Alexander, M. J. (1996). Women with co-occurring addictive and mental disorders: An emerging profile of vulnerability. *American Journal of Orthopsychiatry, 66,* 61–70.

Alliance of NGOs on Crime Prevention and Criminal Justice. (1987). *Children in Prison with Their Mothers.* New York: Alliance of NGOs.

American Correctional Association. (1987). *Legal Responsibility and Authority of Correctional Officers: A Handbook on Courts, Judicial Decisions and Constitutional Requirements.* College Park, MD: American Correctional Association.

Amir, D., & Biniamin, O. (1991). Abortion approval as a ritual of symbolic control. *Women and Criminal Justice, 3,* 5–25.

Amnesty International. (1999). *"Not Part of My Sentence": Violations of the Human Rights of Women in Custody.* London, England: Amnesty International Publications.

Andersen, M. L. (1988). Moving our minds: Studying women of color and reconstructing sociology. *Teaching Sociology, 16,* 123–132.

Arnold, R. (1990). Women of color: Processes of victimization and criminalization of Black women. *Social Justice, 17,* 153–156.

The Associated Press. (2000, September 26). Second prison employee charged with having sex with Susan Smith. *The Associated Press State & Local Wire*. Available on-line: http://web.lexis-nexis.com/universise...d5=45522 afaa63d3495d6aac47c3a2c3acb9.

Aylward, A., & Thomas, J. (1984). Quiescence in women's prisons litigation: Some exploratory issues. *Justice Quarterly, 1,* 253–276.

Baro, A. L. (1997). Spheres of consent: An analysis of the sexual abuse and sexual exploitation of women incarcerated in the state of Hawaii. *Women and Criminal Justice, 8,* 61–84.

Barry, E. (1995). Legal issues for prisoners with children. In K. Gabel & D. Johnston (Eds.), *Children of Incarcerated Parents*, New York: Lexington. 147–166.

Barry, E., Kojimoto, C., Issacs, R., Lujan, G., Kandel, M., et al. (1993). Women in prison. In C. Lefcourt (Ed.), *Women and the Law, 18,* 1–68. Deerfield, IL: Clark Boardman Callahan.

Baskin, D. R., & Sommers, I. B. (1998). *Casualties of Community Disorder: Women's Careers in Violent Crime*. Boulder, CO: Westview Press.

Baskin, D. R., Sommers, I. B., Tessler, R., & Steadman, H. J. (1996). Role incongruence and gender variation in the provision of prison mental health services. *Journal of Health and Social Behavior, 30,* 305–314.

Baugh, S., Bull, S., & Cohen, K. (1998). Mental health issues, treatment, and the female offender. In R. T. Zaplin (Ed.), *Female Offenders: Critical Perspectives and Effective Interventions* Gaithersburg, MD: Aspen Publishers. 205–225.

Baunach, P. J. (1982). You can't be a mother and be in prison . . . can you? Impact of the mother-child separation. In B. R. Price and N. J. Sokoloff (Eds.), *The Criminal Justice System and Women*. New York: Clark Boardman Company, Ltd. 155–169.

———. (1985). *Mothers in Prison*. New Brunswick, NJ: Transaction.

Beaman, L. G. (1998). Women's defences: Contextualizing dilemmas of difference and power, *Women and Criminal Justice, 9,* 87–115.

Beck, A. J., & Karberg, J. (2001). *Prison and Jail Inmates at Midyear 2000*. Washington, DC: Bureau of Justice Statistics.

Beckerman, A. (1991). Women in prison: The conflict between confinement and parental rights. *Social Justice, 18,* 171–183.

Belknap, J. (1995). Access to programs and health care for incarcerated women. *Federal Probation, 60,* 34–39.

———. (2001). *The Invisible Woman: Gender, Crime, and Justice* (2nd ed.). Belmont, CA: Wadsworth Publishing Company.

Bell, C., Coven, M., Cronan, J. P., Garza, C. A., Guggemos, J., & Storto, L. (1999). Rape and sexual misconduct in the prison system: Analyzing America's most "open" secret. *Yale Law and Policy Review, 18,* 195–223.

Bennett, K. (1995). Constitutional issues in cross-gender searches and visual observation of nude inmates by opposite-sex officers. *Prison Journal, 75,* 90–112.

Bershad, L. (1985). Discriminatory treatment of the female offender in the criminal justice system. *Boston College Law Review, 26,* 389–438.

Bickle, G. S., & Peterson, R. D. (1991). The impact of gender-based family roles on criminal sentencing. *Social Problems, 38,* 372–394.

Bloom, B. (1995). Public policy and the children of incarcerated parents. In K. Gabel & D. Johnston (Eds.), *Children of Incarcerated Parents*. New York: Lexington Books. 271–284.

Bloom, B., Chesney-Lind, M., & Owen, B. (1994). *Women in California Prisons: Hidden Victims of the War on Drugs*. San Francisco, CA: Center on Juvenile and Criminal Justice.

Bloom, B., & Covington, S. S. (1999). *Gender-Responsivity: An Essential Element in Women's Programming. National Symposium on Women Offenders*. Washington, DC: Office of Justice Programs.

Bloom, B., & Steinhart, D. (1993). *Why Punish the Children? A Reappraisal of the Children of Incarcerated Mothers in America*. San Francisco, CA: National Council on Crime and Delinquency.

Boston University School of Law. (1991). Medicolegal reference library: Selected recent court decisions. *American Journal of Law & Medicine, 17,* 313–314.

Bosworth, M. (1999). Confining femininity: A history of gender, power, and imprisonment. New York: Fordham University.

――――. (1996). Resistance and compliance in women's prisons: Towards a critique of legitimacy. *Critical Criminology, 7,* 5–19.

Boudouris, J. (1996). *Parents in Prison: Addressing the Needs of Families*. Lanham, MD: American Correctional Association.

Bowker, L. (1978). *Women, Crime, and the Criminal Justice System*. Lexington, MA: Lexington Books.

Bramlet-Hecker, G., & Morash, M. (1997). *Community Services Available to Children with Mothers in Prison: A Needs Assessment and Recommendations for Programming*. East Lansing: Michigan State University.

Breen, P. (1995). Advocacy efforts on behalf of the children of incarcerated parents. In K. Gabel & D. Johnston (Eds.), *Children of Incarcerated Parents*. New York: Lexington Books. 292–309.

Bresler, L., & Lewis, D. K. (1983). Black and white women prisoners—differences in family ties and their programmatic implications. *The Prison Journal, 63,* 116–123.

Browne, A. (1987). *When Battered Women Kill*. New York: The Free Press.

Brown, V., Huba, G. J., & Melchior, L. A. (1995). Level of burden: Women with more than one co-occurring disorder. *Journal of Psychoactive Drugs, 27,* 339–345.

Brownstein, H. H., Spunt, B. J., Crimmins, S., & Langley, S. (1995). Women who kill in drug market situations. *Justice Quarterly, 12,* 473–498.

Bureau of Justice Statistics. (1994). *Women in Prison*. Washington, DC: U.S. Department of Justice.

――――. (2000). *Bureau of Justice Statistics 2000: At a Glance*. Washington, DC: U.S. Department of Justice.

Burkhardt, K. (1973). *Women in Prison*. Garden City, NJ: Doubleday.

Burton, D. E., et al. (1999). *Women in Prison: Issues and Challenges Confronting U.S. Correctional Systems*. Washington, DC: Genderal Accounting Office.

Cannings, K. (1990). *Bridging the Gap: Programs and Services to Facilitate Contact between Inmate Parents and Their Children*. Ottawa: Ministry of the Solicitor General of Canada.

Carlen, P. (1982). Papa's discipline: An analysis of disciplinary modes in Scottish women's prisons. *Sociological Review, 30,* 97–124.

――――. (1983). *Criminal Women: Autobiographical Accounts*. Cambridge: Polity Press.

――――. (1987). *Women's Imprisonment: A Study in Social Control*. London: Tavistock.

Carmen, E., Rieker, P. P., & Mills, T. (1984). Victims of violence and psychiatric illness. *American Journal of Psychiatry, 14,* 378–383.

Carp, S. V., & Schade, L. S. (1993). Tailoring facility programming to suit female offenders' needs. In *Female Offenders: Meeting Needs of a Neglected Population.* Lanham, MD: American Correctional Association.

Catan, L. (1989). Development of young children in prison mother and baby units. *Research Bulletin, 26,* 9–12.

Center for Mental Health Services. (1995). *Double Jeopardy: Persons with Mental Illnesses in the Criminal Justice System.* Unpublished manuscript. Rockville, MD.

Chapman, J. (1980). *Economic Realities and Female Crime.* Lexington, MA: Lexington Books.

Chesney-Lind, M. (1989). Girls' crime and woman's place: Toward a feminist model of female delinquency. *Crime and Delinquency, 35,* 5–29.

———. (1997). *The Female Offender: Girls, Women and Crime.* Thousand Oaks, CA: Sage.

Chesney-Lind, M., & Pollock, J. (1995). Women's prisons: Equality with a vengeance. In M. V. Merlo & J. M. Pollock (Eds.), *Women, Law & Social Control.* Boston: Allyn & Bacon. 155–175.

Chesney-Lind, M., & Rodriguez, N. (1983). Women under lock and key: A view from the inside. *The Prison Journal, 63,* 47–65.

Chevalier-Barrow, M. (1992). Gender and sentencing: An investigation of prior record, current offense, family status and sociodemographic characteristics. Unpublished doctoral dissertation, Fordham University.

Chodorow, N. (1978). *The Reproduction of Mothering.* Berkeley: University of California Press.

Chonco, N. N. (1991). The mentally ill female inmate: Do labels matter behind bars? Unpublished Dissertation, Michigan State University, East Lansing.

Chunn, D. E., & Menzies, R. (1998). Out of mind, out of law: The regulation of criminally insane women inside British Columbia's public mental hospitals. *Canadian Journal of Women and the Law, 10,* 1–32.

Clark, J. (1995). The impact of the prison environment on mothers. *The Prison Journal, 75,* 306–329.

Collins, J. (2000, September 12). Legislative hearing begins on sex in S.C. prisons. *The Associated Press State & Local Wire.* Available on-line: http://web.lexis-nexis.com/universe... d5=d737b7219e45bf796019c02d2fac3c88.

———. (2001, January 11). Inmate sex at governor's house prompts firing of prison's director. *The Associated Press State & Local Wire.* Available online: http://web.lexis-nexis.com/universe... df=4.5a062283d3b4e0f6 cfc713a4c67f526.

Collins, J. M., & Collins, M. D. (1999). *Female Frauds in the Corporate Suite: Biodata and Personality Predictors.* Paper presented at the Annual Conference of the American Psychological, Boston, MA.

Collins, M. M. (1999). *Integrity in the Executive Suite: Leaders Who Lie, Cheat, and Steal.* Paper presented at the Academy of Management Annual Conference.

Conly, C. (1998). *The Women's Prison Association: Supporting Women Offenders and Their Families.* Washington, DC: U.S. Department of Justice.

Corrections Services Canada, http://www.csc-scc.gc.ca/test/prgrm/fsw/fsw30/fsw30e02.shtml.

Covington, S. S. (1998). Women in prison: Approaches in the treatment of our most invisible population. *Women in Therapy, 21,* 141–155.

Crew, B. K. (1991). Sex differences in criminal sentencing: Chivalry or patriarchy? *Justice Quarterly, 80,* 59–84.

Crimmins, S. M., Langley, S. C., Brownstein, H. B., & Spunt, B. J. (1997). Convicted women who have killed children: A self-psychological perspective. *Journal of Interpersonal Violence, 12,* 49–69.

Curran, J. (1983). Judicial discretion and defendant's sex. *Criminology, 21,* 41–58.

Daly, K. (1987). Survey Results of the Niantic Interviews: December 1983 and May 1986. Unpublished manuscript.

———. (1987). Structure and practice of familial-based justice in a criminal court. *Law and Society Review, 21,* 267–290.

———. (1989). Gender and varieties of white-collar crime. *Criminology, 27,* 769–797.

———. (1992). Women's pathways to felony court: Feminist theories of lawbreaking and problems of representation. *Southern California Review of Law and Women's Studies, 2,* 11–52.

———. (1995). Looking back, looking forward: The promise of feminist transformation. In B. Raffel Price & N. J. Sokoloff (Eds.), *The Criminal Justice System and Women: Offenders, Victims, and Workers.* 2nd ed. New York: McGraw-Hill. 444–449.

Daly, K., & Bordt, R. L. (1995). Sex effects and sentencing: An analysis of the statistical literature. *Justice Quarterly, 12,* 141–175.

Daly, K., & Chesney-Lind, M. (1988). Feminism and criminology. *Justice Quarterly, 5,* 497–535.

Daly, K., & Tonry, M. (1997). Gender, race, and sentencing. *Crime and Justice, 22,* 233–235.

Das, E. R. (2001). Maternal substance use and mother-infant feeding interactions. *Infant Mental Health Journal, 22,* 497–511.

Datesman, S. K., & Cales, G. L. (1983). I'm still the same mommy": Maintaining the mother/child relationship in prison. *Prison Journal, 63,* 142–154.

Ditton, P. M. (1999, July). *Mental Health and Treatment of Inmates and Probationers.* Washington, DC: Bureau of Justice Statistics.

Ditton, P. M., & Wilson, D. J. (1999). *Truth in Sentencing in State Prisons.* Washington DC: Bureau of Justice Statistics.

Dobash, R. P., Dobash, R. E., & Gutteridge, S. (1986). *The Imprisonment of Women.* New York: Basil Blackwell.

Dowden. C., & Andrews, D. A. (1999). What works for female offenders: A meta-analytical review. *Crime and Delinquency, 45,* 438–452.

Eaton, M. (1987). The question of bail: Magistrate's responses to applications for bail on behalf of men and women. In P. Carlen & A. Worrall (Eds.), *Gender, Crime, and Justice.* Philadelphia, PA: Open University Press. 95–107.

Edens, J. F., Peters, R. H., & Hills, H. A. (1997). Treating prison inmates with co-occurring disorders: An integrative review of existing programs. *Behavioral Sciences and the Law, 15,* 439–457.

Ehrenreich, B., & English, D. (1978). *For Her Own Good: 150 years of the Experts' Advice to Women.* Garden City, NY: Anchor Press/Doubleday.

Eichler, M. (1979). *The Double Standard: A Feminist Critique of Feminist Social Science.* New York: St. Martin's Press.

Eisenstein, Z. R. (1988). *The Female Body and the Law*. Berkeley: University of California Press.

Fagan, J. (1994). Women and drugs revisited: Female participation in the cocaine economy. *Journal of Drug Issues, 24,* 179–225.

Farrington, D. P., & Morris, A. M. (1983). Sex, sentencing and reconviction. *Journal of British Criminology, 21,* 229–249.

Feeley, M. M., & Rubin. E. L. (1999). *Judicial Policy Making and the Modern State*. Cambridge, UK: Cambridge University Press.

Feinman, C. (1979). Sex role stereotypes and justice for women. *Crime and Delinquency, 25,* 57–68.

———. (1980). *Women in the Criminal Justice System*. New York: Praeger Publishers.

———. (1983). An historical overview of the treatment of incarcerated women: Myths and realities of rehabilitation. *Prison Journal, 63,* 12–26.

———. (1992). Criminal codes, criminal justice and female offenders: New Jersey as a case study. In I. L. Moyer (Ed.), *The Changing Roles of Women in the Criminal Justice System: Offenders, Victims, and Professionals*. 2nd ed. Prospect Heights, IL: Waveland Press. 57–68.

Figueria-McDonough. (1985). Gender differences in informal processing: A look at charge bargaining and sentence reduction in Washington, DC. *Journal of Research in Crime and Delinquency, 22,* 101–133.

Fishman, L. T. (1998). Images of crime and punishment: The black bogyman and white self-righteousness. In C. R. Mann & M. Zatz (Eds.), *Images of Color, Images of Crime*. Los Angeles, CA: Roxbury Publishing Company. 109–126.

Flavin, J. M. (1995). Of punishment and parenthood: The relationship between family-based social control and sentencing. Unpublished doctoral dissertation, American University.

Fleischer, S. (1998). Termination of parental rights: An additional sentence for incarcerated parents. *Seton Hall Law Review, 29,* 312–341.

Fliter, J. A. (2001). *Prisoners' Rights: The Supreme Court and Evolving Standards of Decency*. Westport, CT: Greenwood Press.

Foucault, M. (1977). *Discipline and Punishment: The Birth of the Prison*. New York: Vintage Books.

Fox, J. D. (1982). Women in prison—a case study in the social reality of stress. In H. Toch (Ed.), *Pains of Imprisonment*. Thousand Oaks, CA: Sage Publications. 205–220.

Fox, J. G. (1984). Women's prison policy, prisoner activism, and the impact of the contemporary feminist movement: A case study. *The Prison Journal, 64,* 15–36.

Frase, R. S. (1997). Sentencing guidelines are "alive and well" in the United States. In M. Tonry and K. Hatlestad (Eds.), *Sentencing Reform in Overcrowded Times: A Comparative Perspective*. New York: Oxford University Press. 12–17.

Freedman, E. B. (1981). *Their Sister's Keepers: Women Prison Reform in America, 1930–1930*. Ann Arbor: University of Michigan Press.

———. (1982). Nineteenth-Century women's prison reform and its legacy. In D. K. Weisberg (Ed.), *Women and the Law: A Social Historical Perspective*. Vol. 1. Cambridge, MA: Schenkman Publishing. 141–157.

Gabel, K. (1982). *Legal Issues of Female Inmates*. Northampton, MA: Smith College for Social Work.

Gabel, K., & Girard, K. (1995). Long-term care nurseries in prison: A descriptive study. In K. Gabel & D. Johnston (Eds.), *Children of Incarcerated Parents*. New York: Lexington Books. 237–254.

Gabel, S., & Shindledecker, R. (1993). Characteristics of children whose parents have been incarcerated. *Hospital and Community Psychiatry, 44,* 656–660.

Galbraith, S. (1998). *And So I Began To Listen to Their Stories . . . Working with Women in the Criminal Justice System*. Delmar, New York: GAINS.

Garrett, J. S. (1999). Compliance with the constitution. In P. M. Carlson & J. S. Garrett (Eds.), *Prison and Jail Administration: Practice and Theory*. Gaithersburg, MD: Aspen Publishers. 321–326.

Geer, M. A. (2000). Human rights and wrongs in our own backyard: Incorporating international human rights protections under domestic civil rights law—A case study of women in United States prisons. *The Harvard Human Rights Journal, 13,* 73–140.

Gelsthorpe, L. (1992). Social inquiry reports: Race and gender considerations, *Research Bulletin, 32,* 17–22.

General Accounting Office. (1999). *Women in Prison: Sexual Misconduct by Correctional Staff*. Washington, DC: General Accounting Office.

General Accounting Office. (1999). *Women in Prison: Issues and Challenges Confronting U.S. Correctional Systems*. Washington, DC: General Accounting Office.

Genty, P. M. (1995). Termination of parental rights among prisoners. In K. Gabel & D. Johnston (Eds.), *Children of Incarcerated Parents*. New York: Lexington Books. 167–182.

Ghali, M., & Chesney-Lind, M. (1986). Gender bias and the criminal justice system: An empirical investigation. *Sociology and Social Research, 70,* 164–171.

Giallombardo, R. (1966). *Society of Women: A Study of a Women's Prison*. New York: John Wiley and Sons.

Gilligan, C. (1982). *In a Different Voice: Psychological Theory and Women's Development*. Cambridge, MA: Harvard University Press.

Goodstein, L. (1992). Feminist perspectives and the criminal justice curriculum. *Journal of Criminal Justice Education, 3,* 61–74.

Greene, S., Haney, C., & Hurtado, A. (2000). Cycles of pain: Risk factors in the lives of incarcerated mothers and their children. *The Prison Journal, 80,* 3–23.

Greenfeld, L. A., & Snell, T. L. (1999). *Women Offenders*. Washington DC: National Institute of Justice.

Hagan, J. (1974). Extra-legal attributes and criminal sentencing: An assessment of a sociological viewpoint. *Law and Society Review, 8,* 357–381.

Hairston, C. F. (1991). Family ties during imprisonment: Important to whom and for what? *Journal of Sociology and Social Welfare, 18,* 87–104.

Hammett, T. M., Harmon, P., & Maruschak, L. M. (1999). *1996–1997 Update: HIV/AIDS, STDs, and TB in Correctional Facilities*. Washington DC: US Department of Justice.

Hannah-Moffat, K. (1995). Feminine fortresses: Woman-centered prisons? *The Prison Journal, 75,* 135–164.

———. (1999). Moral agent or actuarial subject: Risk and Canadian women's imprisonment. *Theoretical Criminology, 3,* 71–94.

Harding, S. (ed.). (1987). *Feminism and Methodology*. Bloomington: Indiana University Press.

Harlow, C. W. (1999). *Prior Abuse Reported by Inmates and Probationers.* Washington DC: U.S. Department of Justice.

Harris, A. R. (1977). Sex and theories of deviance: Toward a functional theory of deviant type-scripts. *American Sociological Review, 42,* 3–16.

Heather, D. (2000). The influence of presentence reports on sentencing in a district court in New Zealand. *Australian and New Zealand Journal of Criminology, 33,* 91–106.

Henriques, Z. W. (1982). *Imprisoned Mothers and Their Children: A Descriptive and Analytical Study.* Lanham, MD: University Press of America.

Hewitt, J. D. (1975). A multivariate analysis of legal and extralegal factors in judicial sentencing disparity. Unpublished doctoral dissertation, Washington State University.

Hien, D., & Honeyman, T. (2000). A closer look at the drug abuse-maternal aggression link. *Journal of Interpersonal Violence, 15,* 503–522.

Holmes, S. A. (1996, December 27). With more women in prison, sexual abuse by guards becomes greater concern. *New York Times.* A18.

Hornbeck, M. (1997, December 4). Mentally ill flood prisons. *Detroit News.* 113.

Huling, T. (1991, March 4). *Breaking the Silence.* New York: Correctional Association of New York.

Human Rights Watch Women's Rights Project. (1996). *All Too Familiar: Sexual Abuse of Women in U.S. State Prisons.* New York: Human Rights Watch.

Hunter, S. M. (1984). Issues and challenges facing women's prisons in the 1980s. *The Prison Journal, 64,* 129–135.

Inciardi, J. A., & Pottieger, A. (1994). Crack cocaine use and street crime. *Journal of Drug Issues, 24,* 273–292.

Jacobs, J. B. (1977). *Stateville: The Penitentiary in Mass Society.* Chicago: The University of Chicago Press.

———. (1997). The prisoners' rights movement and its impacts. In J. W. Marquart & J. R. Sorenson (Eds.), *Correctional Contexts: Contemporary and Classical Readings.* Los Angeles: Roxbury Publishing Company. 231–247.

Jacobson, A., & Richardson, B. (1987). Assault experiences of 100 psychiatric inpatients: Evidence of the need for routine inquiry. *American Journal of Psychiatry, 144,* 908–913.

Johnston, D. (1992). *Children of prisoners' children.* Pasadena, CA: Center for Children of Incarcerated Parents.

———. (1993). *Caregivers of prisoners' children.* Pasadena, CA: Center for Children of Incarcerated Parents.

———. (1995). Effects of parental incarceration. In K. Gabel & D. Johnston (Eds.), *Children of Incarcerated Parents.* New York: Lexington Books. 59–88.

Jordan, B. K., Fairbanks, J. A., & Caddell, J. M. (1996). Prevalence of psychiatric disorders among incarcerated women, II: Convicted felons entering prison. *Archives of General Psychiatry, 53,* 513–519.

Jose-Kampfner, C. (1991). Michigan program makes children's visits meaningful. *Corrections Today, 53,* 132–134.

Kaukinen, C. E. (1995). Women lawbreakers constructed in terms of traditional definitions of feminism: The sentencing of women in conflict with the law. Unpublished master's thesis. University of Windsor, Ontario, Canada.

Keller, E. F. (1978). Gender and science. *Psychoanalysis and Contemporary Thought: A Quarterly of Integrative and Interdisciplinary Studies, 1,* 409–433.

Kendall, K. (1994). Creating real choices: A program evaluation of therapeutic services at the prison for women. *Forum on Corrections Research, 6,* 19–21.

Kenny, S. (1986). Reproductive hazards in the workplace: The law and sexual difference. *International Journal of the Sociology of Law, 14,* 393–414.

Klein, D. (1995). The etiology of female crime: A review of the literature. In B. Raffel Price & N. J. Sokoloff (Eds.), *The Criminal Justice System and Women: Offenders, Victims, Workers.* 2nd ed. New York: Clark Boardman Company, Ltd. 30–53.

Koons-Witt, B. (2000). *Gender and justice: The role of gender in sentencing decisions in the state of Minnesota, pre- and post-sentencing guidelines.* Paper presented at the annual meetings of the American Society of Criminology, San Francisco, CA.

Kramer, J. H., & Ulmer, J. T. (1996). Sentencing disparity and departures from guidelines. *Justice Quarterly, 13,* 81–105.

Krohn, M., Curry, J. P., & Nelson-Kilger, S. (1983). Is chivalry dead? An analysis of changes in police dispositions of males and females. *Criminology, 21,* 417–437.

Kruttschnitt, C. (1980). Social status and sentences of female offenders. *Law and Society Review, 15,* 247–265.

———. (1982). Respectable women and the law. *The Sociological Quarterly, 23,* 221–234.

———. (1982). Women, crime and dependency: An application of the theory of law. *Criminology, 19,* 495–513.

———. (1984). Sex and criminal court dispositions: The unresolved controversy. *Journal of Research in Crime and Delinquency, 21,* 213–232.

———. (2001). Gender and violence. In C. M. Renzetti & L. Goodstein (Eds.), *Women, Crime and Criminal Justice.* Los Angeles: Roxbury Publishing Company. 77–92.

———. (1985). Legal outcomes and legal agents: Adding another dimension to the sex-sentencing controversy. *Law and Human Behavior, 9,* 287–303.

Kruttschnitt, C., & Green, D. E. (1984). The sex-sanctioning issue: Is it history? *American Sociological Review, 49,* 541–551.

Kruttschnitt, C., Gartner, R., & Miller, A. (2000). Doing her own time: Women's responses to prison in the context of the old and the new penology. *Criminology, 38,* 681–718.

LeClair, D. D. (1990). *The incarcerated female offender victim or villain?* Boston: Research Division, Massachusetts Division of Correction.

LeFlore, L., & Holston, M. A. (1989). Perceived importance of parenting behaviors as reported by inmate mothers: An exploratory study. *Journal of Offender Counseling, Services, and Rehabilitation, 14,* 5–21.

Lehman, A. F. (1996). Heterogeneity of person and place: Assessing co-occurring addictive and mental disorders. *American Journal of Substance Abuse Treatment, 5,* 32–41.

Leonard, E. B. (1983). Judicial decisions and prison reform: The impact of litigation on women prisoners. *Social Problems, 31,* 45–58.

Lorber, J., & Farrell, S. A. (1991). Principles of gender construction. In J. Lorber & S. A. Farrell (Eds.), *The Social Construction of Gender.* Newbury Park, CA: Sage Publications. 7–11.

Lowenstein, A. (1986). Temporary single parenthood—The case of prisoners' families. *Family Relations, 37,* 79–85.

MacKenzie, D. L., Elis, L., Simpson, S. S., & Skroban, S. (1994). *Female Offenders in Boot Camp Prisons: Final Report to the National Institute of Justice, Office of Justice Programs, U.S. Department of Justice.* College Park: University of Maryland.

MacKinnon, C. (1987). *Feminism Unmodified: Discourses on Life and Law.* London: Harvard University Press.

Mahan, S. (1982). *Unfit Mothers.* Palo Alto, CA: R & E Research Associates.

Maher, L. (1992). Punishment and welfare: Crack cocaine and the regulation of mothers. *Women and Criminal Justice, 3,* 47–67.

Mancuso, R. F., & Miller, B. A. (2000). Crime and punishment in the lives of women alcohol and other drug (AOD) users: Exploring the gender, lifestyle, and legal issues. In C. M. Renzetti & L. Goodstein (Eds.), *Women, Crime, and Criminal Justice.* Los Angeles: Roxbury Publishing Company. 93–110.

Mann, C. (1984). *Female Crime and Delinquency.* Tuscaloosa: The University of Alabama Press.

Marquart, J. W., & Sorensen, J. R. (1997). *Correctional Contexts: Contemporary and Classical Readings.* Los Angeles: Roxbury Publishing Company.

Martin, M. (1997). Connected mothers: A follow-up study of incarcerated women and their children. *Women and Criminal Justice, 8,* 1–23.

McCampbell, S. W., & Layman, E. P. (2000). *Training Curriculum for Investigating Allegations of Staff Sexual Misconduct with Inmates.* Tamarac, FL: Center for Innovative Public Policies.

McClellan, D. S. (1994). Disparity in the discipline of male and female inmates in Texas prisons. *Women and Criminal Justice, 5,* 71–97.

McClellan, D. S., Farabee, D., & Crouch, B. (1997). Early victimization, drug use and criminality: A comparison of male and female prisoners. *Criminal Justice and Behavior, 20,* 455–476.

McGowan, B. G., & Blumenthal, K. L. (1978). *Why Punish the Children? A Study of Children of Women Prisoners.* Hackensack, NJ: National Council on Crime and Delinquency.

McGurrin, M. C. (1993). Pregnant inmates right to health care. *New England Journal on Criminal and Civil Confinement, 20,* 163–179.

McHugh, M. C., Koeske, R. D., & Frieze, I. H. (1986). Issues to consider in conducting nonsexist psychological research. *American Psychologist, 41,* 879–890.

McIntosh, P. (1984). Interactive phases of curricular revision. In B. Spanier, A. Bloom, & D. Boroviak (Eds.), *Toward a Balanced Curriculum.* Cambridge, MA: Schenkman. 25–34.

Miller, B. (1998). Different not more difficult: Gender-specific training helps bridge the gap. *Corrections Today, 60,* 142–144.

Miller, E. M. (1986). *Street Woman.* Philadelphia: Temple University Press.

Miller, J. (1998). Up it up: Gender and the accomplishment of street robbery. *Criminology, 36,* 37–66.

Miller, J., & Levin, P. (1998). The Caucasian evasion: Victims, exceptions, and defenders of the faith. In C. R. & M. S. Zatz (Eds.), *Images of Color, Images of Crime.* Los Angeles: Roxbury Publishing Company. 217–233.

Morash, M. (2000). Punishing women offenders. In N. H. Rafter (Ed.), *Encyclopedia of Women and Crime.* Pheonix: Oryx Press. 214–219.

Morash, M., & Bramlet-Hecker, G. (1995). *State of the State Survey: Michigan Residents Support Programs for Mothers in Prison and Their Children.*

East Lansing: Institute for Public Policy and Social Research, Michigan State University.

Morash, M., & Bramlet-Hecker, G. (1997). *An Evaluation of Michigan Council on Crime and Delinquency's Children's Visitation Program, Scott Correctional Facility, Plymouth, Michigan.* East Lansing: Michigan State University.

Morash, M., Bynum, T., & Koons, B. (1996). *Findings from the National Study of Innovative and Promising Programs for Women Offenders.* East Lansing: Michigan State University.

———. (1996). *Mental Health Supplement.* East Lansing: Michigan State University.

———. (1998). *Women Offenders: Programming Needs and Promising Approaches. National Institute of Justice Research in Brief.* Washington, DC: U.S. Department of Justice.

Morash, M., Haarr, R. N., & Rucker, L. (1994). A comparison of programming for women and men in U.S. prisons in the 1980s. *Crime and Delinquency, 40,* 197–221.

Morash, M., & Robinson, A. L. (2001). Correctional administrators' perspectives on gender arrangements and family-related programming for women offenders. *Marriage & Family Review, 32* (3–4), 83–110.

Moses, M. C. (1995). *Keeping Incarcerated Mothers and Their Daughters Together: Girl Scouts beyond Bars. National Institute of Justice Program Focus.* Washington, DC: National Institute of Justice.

Moulds, E. F. (1980). "Chivalry and paternalism: Disparities of treatment in the criminal justice system. In S. K. Datesman & F. R. Scarpitti (Eds.), *Women, Crime, and Justice.* New York: Oxford University Press. 277–299.

Moyer, I. L. (1984). Deceptions and realities of life in women's prisons. *The Prison Journal, 64,* 45–56.

Mumola, C. J. (2000). *Incarcerated Parents and Their Children: Special Report.* Washington, DC: U.S. Department of Justice, Office of Justice Programs.

Murphy, J., & Edwards, W. (1992). *In the Decade of the Child: Addicted Mothers, Imprisonment, and Alternatives.* Washington, DC: National Institute of Justice.

Mustard, D. B. (2001). Racial, ethnic, and gender disparities in sentencing: Evidence from the U.S. federal courts. *Law and Economics, 44,* 285–312.

Naffine, N. (1987). *Female Crime: The Construction of Women in Criminology.* Winchester, MA: Allen & Unwin.

Nagel, I. H., & Hagan, J. (1983). Gender and crime: Offense patterns and criminal court sanctions. In N. Morris & M. Tonry (Eds.), *Crime and Justice.* Vol. 4. Chicago: University of Chicago Press. 91–144.

Nagel, I. H., & Johnson, B. L. (1994). The role of gender in a structured sentencing system: Equal treatment, policy choices, and the sentencing of female offenders under the United States sentencing guidelines. *Journal of Criminal Law and Criminology, 85,* 181–221.

National Center on Addiction and Substance Abuse. (1998). *Behind Bars: Substance Abuse in America's Prison Population.* New York: Columbia University.

National Institute of Corrections. (1999). *Sexual Misconduct in Prisons: Law, Agency Response, and Prevention.* Longmont, CO: U.S. Department of Justice, NIC Information Center.

National Symposium on Women Offenders, Monday, December 13–15, 1999. Plenary 1: Building the Case—Why Focus on Women Offenders? 9.

National Symposium on Women Offenders, December 13–15, 1999. Plenary III: Effective Interventions—Looking at Gender Responsive Programming. 25.

Nielsen, J. M. (1990). *Feminist Research Methods: Exemplary Readings in the Social Sciences*. Boulder, CO: Westview Press.

North County Times—The Californian. (2000, September 9). Prison guard fired after admitting sex with Susan Smith. *NCTimes Net*. Available on-line: http://nctimes.com/news/090200/gg.html.

Office of Justice Programs. (1999). *Conference Proceedings: National Symposium on Women Offenders*. Washington, DC: Office of Justice Programs.

Office of Justice Programs Coordination Group on Women. (1998). *Women in Criminal Justice: A Twenty Year Update: Special Report*. Washington, DC: U.S. Department of Justice.

Olson, H. C., O'Connor, M. H., & Fitzgerald, H. E. (2001). Lessons learned from study of the developmental impact of parental alcohol use. *Infant Mental Health Journal, 22*, 271–290.

Owen, B. (1998). *"In the Mix": Struggle and Survival in a Women's Prison*. Albany: State University of New York Press.

Owen, B., & Bloom, B. (1995). Profiling women prisoners: Findings from national surveys and a California sample. *The Prison Journal, 75*, 165–185.

Palmer, J. W. (1973). *Constitutional Rights of Prisoners*. Cincinnati, OH: W. H. Anderson Company.

Parisi, N. (1984). The female correctional officer: Her progress toward and prospects for equality. *The Prison Journal, 64*, 92–109.

Peters, R. H., & Hills, H. (1997). *Intervention Strategies for Offenders with Co-Occurring Disorders: What Works?* Delmar, New York: The National Gains Center for People with Co-Occurring Disorders in the Justice System.

Petersilia, J. (2000). *When Prisoners Return to the Community: Political, Economic, and Social Consequences*. Washington, DC: U.S. Department of Justice.

Phillips, S. D., & Harm, N. (1998). Women prisoners: A contextual framework. In J. Harden & M. Hill (Eds.), *Breaking the Rules: Women in Prison and Feminist Therapy*. New York: Harwood Press. 1–9.

Pogrebin, M. R., & Dodge, M. (2001). Women's accounts of their prison experiences: A retrospective view of their subjective realities. *Journal of Criminal Justice, 29*, 531–541.

Pollak, O. (1950). *The Criminality of Women*. Philadelphia: University of Pennsylvania Press.

Pollock, J. M. (1984). Women will be women: Correctional officers' perceptions of the emotionality of women inmates. *The Prison Journal, 64*, 84–91.

———. (1999). *Criminal Women*. Cincinnati, OH: Anderson Publishing Company.

———. (2002). *Women, Prison, & Crime*. 2nd ed. Belmont, CA: Wadsworth.

Pomeroy, S. B. (1975). *Goddesses, Whores, Wives, and Slaves*. New York: Schocken Books.

Poole, E. D., & Pogrebin, M. R. (1987). Judicial intervention and work alienation: A study of jail guards. *The Howard Journal, 26*, 217–231.

President's Commission on the Status of Women. (1963). *American Women*. Executive Order No. 10,980, 3 C.F.R. 138. Washington, DC: U.S. Government Printing Office.

Psychiatric Association. (1994). *Diagnostic and Statistical Manual for Mental Disorders: Fourth Edition*. Washington, DC: American Psychiatric Association.

Raeder, M. S. (1993). Gender and sentencing: Single moms, battered women, and other sex-based anomalies in the gender-free world of the sentencing guidelines. *Pepperdine Law Review, 20,* 905–990.

Rafter, N. H. (1983). Prisons for women, 1790–1800. In M. Tonry & N. Morris (Eds.), *Crime and Justice*. Chicago: University of Chicago Press.

Rafter, N. (1990). *Partial Justice: Women, Prisons, and Social Control*. 2nd ed. New Brunswick, NJ: Transaction Publishers.

Random House College Dictionary. (1991). New York: Random.

Research Associates. (1997). *The Mental Health Services Needs of Women in the Criminal Justice System*. Delmar, New York: The National GAINS Center for People with Co-Occurring Disorders in the Justice System.

Rhode, D. L. (1989). *Justice and Gender*. Cambridge, MA: Harvard University Press.

Rhode Island Justice Alliance. (1990). *Female Offender Survey*. Rhode Island Adult Correctional Institution, Women's Division.

Richie, B. E. (1992). *The Empowerment Program*. New York: Hunter College Center on AIDS, Drugs and Community Health.

———. (1996). *Compelled to Crime: The Gender Entrapment of Battered Black Women*. New York: Routledge.

Ross, R. R., and Fabiano, E. A. (1986). *Female Offenders: Correctional Afterthoughts*. Jefferson, NC: McFarlund.

Runckel, J. O. (1997). Review of selected 1996 California legislation criminal procedure: Ending a prisoner's right to have personal visits. *University of the Pacific Law Journal, 28,* 772–777.

Ryan, T. A. (1984). *Adult Female Offenders and the Institutional Programs: A State of the Art Analysis*. Washington, DC: National Institute of Corrections.

Sack, W. H., Seidler, J., & Thomas, S. (1976). The children of imprisoned parents: A psychosocial exploration. *American Journal of Orthopsychiatry, 46,* 618–628.

Schram, P. J. (1996). The link between stereotype attitudes and behavioral intentions among female inmates, correctional officers, and program staff. Unpublished doctoral dissertation, Michigan State University, East Lansing.

Schram, P. J. (1998). Stereotypes about vocational programming for female inmates. *The Prison Journal, 78,* 244–270.

Schweber, C., & Feinman, C. (1985). The impact of legally mandated change on women prisoners. *Women & Politics, 4,* 1–10.

Sennott, C. M. (1994). Poll finds wide concern about prison rape. *The Boston Globe*. 22.

Seymour, J. (1977). Niches in prison. In H. Toch (Ed.), *Living in Prison: The Ecology of Survival*. New York: Free Press.

———. (1980). *Niches in Prison: Ameliorative Environments within Maximum-Security Correctional Institutions*. Albany: State University of New York, Albany.

Shover, N. (1991). Institutional corrections: Jails and prisons. In J. F. Sheeley (Ed.), *Criminology: A Contemporary Handbook*. Belmont, CA: Wadsworth.

Sills, D. L. (Ed.). (1968). *International Encyclopedia of the Social Sciences, Volume 11*. New York: Macmillan.

Simon, R. J., & Landis, J. (1991). *The Crimes Women Commit, the Punishments They Receive.* Lexington, MA: Lexington Books.

Singer, M. I., Bussy, J., Lunghofer, L., Johnson, H., Chapin, M., Song, L. (1993). *Women Serving Time: Final Report.* Cleveland, OH: Center for Practical Innovations, Mandel School of Applied Social Science, Case Western Reserve University.

Smart, C. (1976). *Women, Crime, and Criminology.* London: Routledge and Kegan Paul.

———. (1989). *Feminism and the Power of Law.* London: Routledge.

———. (1995). *Law, Crime and Sexuality: Essays in Feminism.* Thousand Oaks, CA: Sage Publications.

Smith, B. W. (2001). *State Criminal Laws Prohibiting Sexual Abuse of Prisoners by Correctional Employees, Investigations of Staff Sexual Misconduct with Inmates.* Washington, DC: The American University, Washington College of Law.

Smith, C. E. (2000). *Law and Contemporary Corrections.* Belmont, CA: Wadsworth.

Smith, G. (1995). Practical considerations regarding termination of incarcerated parents' rights. In K. Gabel & D. Johnston (Eds.), *Children of Incarcerated Parents.* New York: Lexington. 183–195.

Solano, R. (1997). Is congress handcuffing our courts? *Seton Hall Law Review, 28,* 282–31.

Spohn, C., & Spears, J. (1997). Gender and sentencing of drug offenders. Paper presented at the 1997 Annual Meetings of the American Society of Criminology, San Diego, CA.

Spohn, C., & Beichner, D. (2000). Is preferential treatment of female offenders a thing of the past? A multisite study of gender, race, and imprisonment. *Criminal Justice Policy Review, 11,* 149–184.

Springfield, D. (2000). Sisters in misery: Utilizing international law to protect United States female prisoners from sexual abuse. *Indiana International & Comparative Law Review, 10,* 457–486.

Stableforth, N. L. (1999). Effective corrections for women offenders. *The Forum, 11,* 3–5.

Stanley, L., & Wise, S. (1979). Feminist research, feminist consciousness, and experiences of sexism. *Women's Studies International Quarterly, 2,* 359–374.

State of Michigan. (1972). *Annual Report of the Inspectors of the State Prison of the State of Michigan.* Lansing: W. S. George & Company.

Steffensmeier, D., & Haynie, D. (2000). Structural sources of urban female violence in the United States: A macrosocial-gender-disaggregated analysis of adult and juvenile homicide offending rates. *Homicide Studies, 4,* 107–134.

Steffensmeier, D., Kramer, J., & Strife, C. (1993). Gender and imprisonment decisions. *Criminology, 31,* 411–443.

Steffensmeier, D., & Streifel, C. (1992). Time series analysis of the female percentage of arrests for property crimes, 1960–1985: A test of alternative explanations. *Justice Quarterly, 9,* 77–104.

Steffensmeier, D., Ulmer, J., & Kramer, J. (1998). The interaction of race, gender, and age in criminal sanctioning: The punishment cost of being young, black, and male. *Criminology, 36,* 763–793.

Sterk, C. E. (1999). *Fast Lives: Women Who Use Crack Cocaine.* Philadelphia: Temple University Press.

Struckman-Johnson, C., Struckman-Johnson, D., Rucker, L., Bumby, K., & Donaldson, S. (1996). Sexual coercion reported by men and women in prison. *The Journal of Sex Research, 33,* 67–76.

Syed, F., & Blanchette, K. (2000). *Results of an Evaluation of the Peer Support Program at Grand Valley Institution for Women.* Correctional Services of Canada.

Tarr, S. J., & Pyfer, J. L. (1996). Physical and motor development of neonates/infants prenatally exposed to drugs in utero: A meta-analysis. *Adapted Physical Activity Quarterly, 13,* 269–287.

Task Force on the Female Offender. (1990). *The Female Offender: What Does the Future Hold?* Laurel, MD: American Correctional Association.

Temin, C. E. (1980). Discriminatory sentencing of women offenders: The argument for ERA in a nutshell. In S. K. Datesman & F. R. Scarpitti (Eds.), *Women, Crime, and Justice,* 255–276. New York: Oxford University Press.

Teplin, L. A., Abram, K. M., & McClelland, G. M. (1996). Prevalence of psychiatric disorders among incarcerated women. *Archive of General Psychiatry, 53,* 505–512.

Thomson, R. J., & Zingraff, M. T. (1981). Detecting sentencing disparity: Some problems and evidence. *American Journal of Sociology, 86,* 869–880.

Thornton, M. (1986). Feminist jurisprudence: Illusion or reality? *Australian Journal of Law and Society, 3,* 5–29.

Thurer, S. L. (1994). *The Myths of Motherhood: How Culture Reinvents the Good Mother.* Boston: Houghton Mifflin Company.

Turner, S., & Petersillia, J. (1996). *Work Release: Recidivism and Corrections Costs in Washington State.* Washington, DC: U.S. Department of Justice.

U.S. Department of Justice. (1993). *Survey of State Prisoners.* Report No. NCJ136949. Washington, DC: Bureau of Justice Statistics.

U.S. General Accounting Office. (1999). *Women in Prison: Sexual Misconduct by Correctional Staff.* Washington, DC: United States General Accounting Office.

U.S. General Accounting Office. (1999). *Women in Prison: Issues and Challenges Confronting U.S. Correctional Systems.* Washington, DC: U.S. General Accounting Office.

Van Wormer, K., and Bartollas. (2000). *Women and the Criminal Justice System.* Boston: Allyn & Bacon.

Wacquant, L. (1998). *From Welfare State to Prison State: Imprisoning the American Poor.* New York: Global Policy Forum. Available on-line: http://www.globalpolicy.org/socecon/global/wacquant.htm.

Wallace, D. H. (1997). Prisoners' rights: Historical views. In J. W. Marquart & J. R. Sorenson (Eds.), *Correctional Contexts: Contemporary and Classical Readings.* Los Angeles: Roxbury Publishing Company. 248–257.

Wallace, H., & Wedlock, S. (1994). Federal sentencing guidelines and gender issues: Parental responsibilities, pregnancy, and domestic violence. *San Diego Justice Journal, 2,* 395–427.

Ward, D., & Kassenbaum G. (1965). *Women's Prison: Sex and Social Structure.* Chicago: Aldine-Atherton.

Wearing, B. (1984). *The Ideology of Motherhood: A Study of Sydney Suburban Mothers.* Sydney: George Allen & Unwin.

Webster's New Collegiate Dictionary. (1977). Springfield, MA: G. & C. Merriam Company.

Weilerstein, R. (1995). The prison MATCH program. In K. Gabel & D. Johnston (Eds.), *Children of Incarcerated Parents*. New York: Lexington Books. 255–264.

Weisheit, R. (1985). Trends in programs for female offenders: The use of private agencies as service providers. *International Journal of Offender Therapy and Comparative Criminology, 29,* 35–42.

Weisheit, R., & Mahan, S. (1988). *Women, Crime and Criminal Justice*. Cincinnati: Anderson.

Wellisch, J., Prendergast, M. L., & Anglin, M. D. (1994). *Drug-Abusing Women Offenders: Results of a National Survey*. Washington, DC: U.S. Department of Justice.

West, C., & Zimmerman, D. H. (1991). Doing gender. In J. Lorber & S. A. Farrell (Eds.), *The Social Construction of Gender*. Newbury Park, CA: Sage Publications.

Westkott, M. (1979). Feminist criticism of the social sciences. *Harvard Educational Review, 49,* 422–430.

Widom, C. S. (1996). Childhood sexual abuse and its criminal consequences. *Society, 33,* 47–53.

Wilkie, M. (1993). *Sentencing Women: Pre-Sentence Reports and Constructions of Female Offenders*. Nedland, WA, Australia: University of Western Australia Crime Research Center.

Williams, F. P., & McShane, M. D. (1999). *Criminological theory*. 3rd. ed. Upper Saddle River, NJ: Prentice Hall.

Williams, W. W. (1984/1985). Equality's riddle: Pregnancy and the equal treatment/special treatment debate. *New York University Review Law and Social Change, 13,* 325–80.

Wismont, J. M. (2000). The lived pregnancy experiences of women in prison. *Journal of Midwifery and Women's Health, 45,* 292–300.

Wolgast, E. H. (1980). *Equality and the Rights of Women*. Ithaca: Cornell University Press.

Young, I. M. (1987). Feminist moral, social, and legal theory: Difference and policy. *University of Cincinnati Law Review, 56,* 535–550.

Young, V. D. (1986). Gender expectation and their impact on Black female offenders and victims. *Justice Quarterly, 3,* 322–323.

Zang, N. (1997). *Human Rights Watch Report: Page by Page Rebuttal*. Lansing: Michigan Department of Corrections.

Zedner, L. (1991). Women, crime, and penal responses: A historical account. In M. Tonry (Ed.), *Crime and Justice: A Review of Research*. Vol. 14. Chicago: University of Chicago Press. 307–362.

Zingraff, M. T., & Thomson, R. J. (1984). Differential sentencing of women and men in the U.S.A. *International Journal on the Sociology of Law, 12,* 401–413.

Zupan, L. L. (1992). Men guarding women: An analysis of the employment of male corrections officers in prisons for women. *Journal of Criminal Justice, 20,* 297–309.

———. (1996). Reel women behind bars? *American Jails, 10,* 22–24.

Index

Mental illness, 13–14, 141–158.
  bipolar disorder, 143
  conditions of prison confinement
    and, 144–145
  Critical Care Unit and, 150–151
  depression, 143
  disorders of women offenders,
    143–144
  historic classification of female
    offenders as "mad," 141–142
  personality disorders and, 143
  physical interventions and, 142
  physical/sexual abuse of women
    and, 146–147
  population in prisons, 145–146
  prevalence and types of, 145–148
  prison environment and, 148–149
  screening and assessment, 151–152
  stereotyping and, 148–149
  stigmatization of, 150–151
  violence and, 145
Michigan Department of Correc-
    tions, women's facilities staff
    training of, 132
Miller, Amy, 183
Miller, Brenda A., 20, 41, 150,
    179–180
Miller, Eleanor M., 34
  study of actual experiences of
    women offenders, 31–32
Miller, Jody, 21, 43
Milwaukee, detailed, comprehensive
    case approach to female offend-
    ers in, 31–32
Minnesota, women felons in, 28–30
Mixed-gender settings, gender-
    responsive programs and, 168
*Monmouth County Correctional
    Institutional Inmates v. Lan-
    zaro,* prisoner abortions and,
    112–113
Mood disorders, 143, 144
Morash, Merry, 78, 152, 154, 167,
    168, 171
Mothers, incarcerated, 12–13, 71–100.
  Adoption and Safe Families Act
    and, 85
  commitment to parenthood of, 75
  concerns of, 75–76

differences and varying circum-
    stances of, 98–99
  mother-child programs as
    response to, 90–97
  parenting programs for, 76
  Personal Responsibility and Work
    Reconciliation Act and, 84–85
  prison culture, relationships with
    children, and, 99
  prison environment, motherhood,
    and, 80–82
  separation from children and, 71
  as single parents, 25
  sources of stress and disillusion-
    ment for, 74
  supportive services for children,
    77–78
  termination of parental rights
    and, 85–89
Mother-child programs, 90–97
  alternatives to prison, 96–97
  Girl Scouts Beyond Bars (GSBB),
    92–93
  Prison MATCH, 93–94
  prison nurseries, 94–96
  successful elements of, 97–98
  visitation, 12–13, 82–83
Motherhood
  economic marginalization, crimi-
    nality, and, 42
  idealized concept of, 8, 72–75
  mythology of, 78
  prison environment and, 80–82
  programs for women in prison,
    180–181
  sentencing outcomes and, 57, 58–59
  sentencing reform and elimina-
    tion of consideration of, 62–63
Muncy Act (Pennsylvania Act), 54
Mythology, of motherhood, 73

Nagel, Ilene H., 56, 65
National Council on Crime and
    Delinquency, curriculum to train
    correctional officers, 22
National Institute of Corrections
    (NIC)
  mail survey on sexual misconduct
    by correctional staff, 127